History of a Small Church

Liberty Free Methodist Church, Tryon, OK
1935–2022

Rev. Ron Faulk, Ph.D.

TORCH RUNNER
PUBLICATIONS

Torch Runner Publications
An Imprint of Harris House Publishing

History of a Small Church
Copyright ©2023 by Ronald H. Faulk

Published by Torch Runner Publications
An Imprint of Harris House Publishing
Colleyville, Texas, USA

ISBN: 978-1-946369-08-6
Subject heading: CHRISTIAN BOOKS & BIBLES/CHURCH HISTORY

Dedications & Acknowledgements

This history is dedicated to all who make small churches work.

I want to thank everyone who has contributed to this history, past and present. They are too numerous to list. Special thanks go to Dr. Jeff Johnson, Superintendent Emeritus of the Mid America Conference of the Free Methodist Church. Without him this never would have been written. He also read the manuscript and made suggestions. Thanks to the previous pastors of Liberty. For a complete list, see the Appendix. Thanks to the pastors who are still alive and contributed to this history: Harry Adams, Robin Grueser, and Denise Abston. Finally, great appreciation and thanks to those members of Liberty Free Methodist Church and all small churches who show up week-by-week and keep the doors open for the next generation. Pray that the next generation is as faithful as they are.

Table of Contents

Introduction

In the records of Liberty Free Methodist Church is a two-page periodical (single sheet, front and back, two columns per page) titled the "Oklahoma Conference Heritage," with "Heritage" in three-quarter inch capitals. The editor, Jim Ferguson, calls it a "conference paper." It is undated, but internal evidence indicates 1979 (on the second page, following the title "Fifty Years Ago in WMS," is a list titled "1929 Conference WMS Officers").

Mr. Ferguson, of Carmen, Oklahoma, acknowledges the conventional perception in 1979 of a "somewhat dim picture of numerous small and unsuccessful churches which are now closed" but takes encouragement at the greater truth of "men and women who dared to accept the challenge of God to take the word of God into a newly opened territory and to build the church in a new state." He goes on to say "the Lord is leading us [Free Methodists] into greater and greater adventures as we trust and follow Him. Our thoughts are turned constantly towards the future." But, he adds, "I have never been able to withstand the temptation to take a quick look over my shoulder as I try to go forward." And so, he announces the purpose of this "conference paper," which is to preserve the heritage of the Oklahoma Conference of the Free Methodist Church. Presumably this purpose is both an end-in-itself, and an encouragement to the next generations who will "accept the challenge of God to take the word of God into a newly opened territory ...."[1]

He says it is "urgent" that we tell the stories of the men and women who evangelized new territories and started new churches, because if we do not then these stories will "be lost forever." "Most of our heritage is locked away in the hearts and minds of our older members. If we are to preserve those memories, we must encourage those who hold them in trust to communicate them to

---

1. I have not found any other issues of the *Heritage*. A complete transcript of Mr. Ferguson's column may be found in the appendices. In the early 1990's the conference periodical is titled *In Touch* and published bi-monthly.

those of us who would like to know how we came to be what we are today." He writes, "this section of the (conference) paper will be published about every three months, depending on your response."

I am sympathetic with Mr. Ferguson's concerns and purposes. Yes, the Free Methodists, and other evangelicals such as the members of my own church, the Church of the Nazarene, continue to look eagerly to the future as they follow the Son of God in building the Kingdom of Heaven on earth. These small evangelical churches, despite lack of material resources (or, from a spiritual perspective, perhaps because of it) have been and continue to be one of the primary sources of home and world missions. At the same time, the legacy of the past, which is the legacy of hundreds of primarily small, and predominantly rural churches across Oklahoma and the nation, is being lost every day. It is indeed mostly "locked away in the hearts and minds of our older members," and the truth is that the great majority of these stories and histories are going to be lost to the world – as they always have been. But a few can be saved, helping us to learn something about the past, and future, of the Kingdom of Heaven on earth.

My first purpose here is to record the history of Liberty Free Methodist Church in as much detail as reasonably possible. The church is in north central Oklahoma, at the corner of Worthy and Union Roads on FR750E, Tryon, OK 74875 (four miles north of Tryon, or four miles south and three miles east of Perkins). Since the first half of its history is mostly available in Society and Board minutes and financial records (mostly handwritten, often sketchy, with many years missing) this history is somewhat technical and incomplete. I have aimed more at accuracy and detail than narrative smoothness.

My second and more general purpose assumes that Liberty is typical of its kind. Hundreds of such evangelical churches in Oklahoma, and thousands across North American, dot the landscapes (not just Free Methodist). One of their primary purposes has been and remains to fund and support world missions (as well as "home missions"). Such churches have been significantly involved in the evangelization of the world.

Most of the assemblies of new Christians around the globe today look remarkably like the beginnings of Liberty and thousands of similar churches across the U.S. They have less than fifty members, who belong to a local community, are held together by key members of a few families, have little money, an under-funded pastor, a bare bones facility, lots of faith (perhaps unevenly distributed), a good distribution of the fruits of the Spirit, are loosely connected to the greater church hierarchy, and not unusually are oppressed in one way or another by the regional powers-that-be.

That these churches look remarkably similar around the world today and since the first century is revealing. *These churches are unbreakable bridges across cultures.* They have been for two thousand years. Very remarkably, no other enduring group or institution *in all history* has ever created such fraternity and community across cultures and languages. Apparently there is no language or culture they cannot bridge. This fact is worth considering. Just such small, community focused, faith-based, family-oriented churches are the recurring norm across the two thousand years of Christianity. What began in the first few centuries has sustained itself, not only spiritually, but in similar structures, across manifold cultures, and two hundred centuries.[2] The Spirit is the unifying force across all human cultures. It is the only such unifying force. And the expression of the Spirit in the small church remains unabated. And is as active as it ever has been, regardless of the successes or failures of the culture in which the small church finds itself.

God has often used the small and humble to confound the rich and powerful, whether people or institutions. There have always been people who think the future of Christianity rests with large, wealthy churches and materially powerful institutions. If the past is a predictor of the future, this is not true. A small, poor church, led by a pastor immersed in the same struggles as the congregants, depends on a strong faith among at least a few people, who are essential for its survival, and who are recognized as such by the congregants. A rich, powerful church, led by a star pastor on a stage, does not need any persons of strong faith, and no individual is essential to its success, only money and an entertaining message and perhaps the comforts of a well-appointed hotel. There are many wonderful large churches. And it can be an exhilarating experience to worship in one place with a thousand souls. Nonetheless the foundation of the Christian church is the small church, and most Christians over the centuries were saved and spiritually formed in small churches where the pastor knew everyone's name.

---

2. A good study of the structure of the early church may be found in Rodney Stark's *The Rise of Christianity: A Sociologist Reconsiders History.* Princeton: Princeton University Press, 1996.

Religious history shows that what appears precarious from a human point of view, is often just what the Spirit sustains, and the imposing institutions and structures built by the materially wealthy and powerful, meant to endure, are just the ones that fail. I suppose history will repeat itself until the Son of God returns. Hopefully useful then, is a study of one such church, Liberty FMC, which, like its peers, has been serving the men and women of faith and their families at the most local level, however precariously, and at the same time supporting the missionaries and programs which have been evangelizing the world since the resurrection of Jesus Christ and the coming of the Holy Spirit on Pentecost. A further statement on the evangelical nature of churches like Liberty may be found in Appendix IV.

Historical Background
1889 to 1919

According to the *History of the Oklahoma Conference* (1949), the Free Methodist Church (FMC) in Oklahoma was begun by members of the Kansas Annual Conference which, in September 1889, voted to create an Oklahoma District under the Kansas Conference (Oklahoma was not a state until 1907). Ministers came to Oklahoma Territory from both the Kansas and West Kansas Conferences.[3] The appointed Chairman of the Oklahoma District was L.C. Gould, and five persons were appointed to help him. They were in Kingfisher, Oklahoma City, Guthrie, Reno City, and Lincoln Town. (Forty-six years later, in 1935, an evangelistic lay couple from Guthrie would provide the spirit for the establishment of Liberty FMC). In 1889 there were no known FMC churches or organized societies in Oklahoma Territory. These early appointees "went to organize societies with the inspiration and courage that had characterized Free Methodism from its earliest days."[4] It is not clear how much of present-day Oklahoma was in the original district.

In 1899 an Oklahoma Conference "was organized by General Superintendent B.R. Jones on October 21, at Emporia, Kansas." "The new conference consisted of seven preachers ...." "The statistical report lists 203 members, five Sunday schools, and no churches." "... the combined preacher's support from the four Oklahoma Districts the previous conference year was $597.81."[5]

Walter Nelson, the author of the *History*, goes on to write "There are no records of the activities of the conference from 1899 to 1908 other than the brief statistical report contained in the COMBINED MINUTES of the General church. The OKLAHOMA CONFERENCE RECORDS for those years have been destroyed. A.R. Martin, of Lawrence, Kansas, former member, and district

3. Wayman, Hugh. 1970. *Past Present Future/Oklahoma In Action/The Free Methodist Church*. p.1.
4. *History of the Oklahoma Conference*, p.9.
5. Ibid, p.11.

superintendent (district elder) of the Oklahoma Conference, remembers that the book containing the minutes of the conference from 1889 to 1907 was placed in the vault of the First National Bank in Guthrie, Okla. This bank later went into receivership and during the process of liquidation the OKLAHOMA CONFERENCE RECORDS were destroyed."[6]

A.R. Martin would be the Chairman of the Board for Liberty FMC 1938-39, 1943-1945, and in 1953. During these times or part of these times, Liberty apparently did not have a regular pastor, or perhaps not an ordained pastor, and/or the superintendent felt that the church needed his support and direction. Generally, in the first half of the twentieth century, the conference superintendents, and elders, who were more numerous then than in the twenty-first century, were significantly more involved in the local churches than since. In the 30's and 40's one to four official meetings a year were recorded for Liberty at which a superintendent or equivalent was usually present. Liberty records show that at least sometimes a member of the church who was in the process of formation, possibly leading to ordination, filled the pulpit. This may have often been the case when a superintendent was the chairman of the board. Records of who served as pastor for Liberty are not always complete, nor do the sources always agree with each other. This will be discussed in greater detail later (see also Appendix I, Liberty Leadership).

The *History* expresses that "There were several problems confronting the church during these years from 1909 to 1919. Among these was the problem of personnel. There were some strong men in the conference but not nearly enough to fill all the appointments. Consequently men of lesser ability and with little experience were appointed to some of the charges. (35) In addition one of the active ministers was so unwise in his business relationships that he was suspended by the conference. Although the case was handled carefully by those in authority it still hindered the work. (36)"

Another problem arose due to the competing influences of higher education schools in Campbell, Texas, and McPherson, Kansas, "for the support of the conference." Leadership was divided on the issue, until "The school problem was resolved by a resolution recognizing both schools as worthy of support and by making a schedule for each school to follow canvassing the territory." "Another problem was an adverse migration. ... due to drouths (sic),

6. Ibid, pp.11-12.

poor crops, financial pressure and desire for gain there was much restlessness among the people which led to migration to more favorable regions."[7]

The *History* states that the church in Oklahoma tried to address its membership problems in several ways. One was "with an evangelistic advance." Another was with the purchase of "a portable iron house to be used as a meeting place for evangelistic meetings." "This building commonly known in the conference as 'the sheep shed' was first erected at Newkirk. Apparently the venture was successful ...." "The "sheep shed" was then moved to El Reno but without similar success. It was later moved to Norman where it was wrecked by a tornado in the early 1930's."[8]

Nelson reports that "The membership of the conference declined to 890 in 1915 but began a gradual increase back to its second highest point of 985 in 1919." In 1919 the "conference strongholds" were in Guthrie, Oklahoma City, Cashion and Bethel, Tulsa, Enid, Prairie Queen, Oak Glade, Wisby and Geary. "Other places remained static or were in decline." Support for ministers increased from $7,873 in 1907 to $14,566 in 1919, although there was only an increase of three preachers in this time. "In 1919 there were twenty-four churches valued at $29,350 and twenty-one personages (sic) valued at $16,150."[9] There were also two "district parsonages," one at Geary and one at Guthrie.

7. Ibid, p.16.
8. Ibid, pp.16-17.
9. Ibid, p.15.

Historical Background
1920 to 1931

"The years of 1919 to 1931 reveal a steady decline in membership but a large gain in the Sunday school enrollment which by 1931 had reached a total of 1850." "The total giving rose to $31,781.66 in 1927 but settled back to $23,910.37 in 1931."

"There are several reasons contributing to the loss of this period. Crop failures occurred in the western part of the state in the early 1920's which caused considerable discouragement. Consequently a Rev. Shurts, who had previously had quite a following in that section, found it easy to persuade a number of the church members to enter into a scheme of migration to Texas. In other places the elderly pioneers in scattered localities were being removed by death and the conference lost the nuclei around which they had hoped to build churches. In addition, a migration of oil field workers caused the loss of the work at Yale and so weakened the church in Bartlesville that it was soon abandoned." Nelson had earlier noted that oil field workers had contributed significantly to the growth of the church there. The appeal of the FMC was often to working class men and women.

"These reverses were intensified by the problem of conference personnel. Some of the inexperienced ministers were unwise in the administration of their circuits and failed to make the proper impression. (44) During this period the church in some areas was known more by the things which it opposed than by the things it promoted. The negative emphasis did not make for healthful growth. There were also three unfortunate discipline cases in which preachers withdrew from the church under complaint of immoral conduct; one of them was a prominent conference leader. (45)"

"M. Wright says that a further hindrance was the reaction among Free Methodists to the Tongues movement. There was so much excessive emotionalism among this group that the Free Methodists who were always characterized by the warmth and freedom of expression of their religious feelings began to be more formal in their worship. This resulted in a loss of appeal to many people."[10]

This is an interesting observation. The problem of how to deal with "tongues" also concerned the Church of the Nazarene in Oklahoma during this time, as well as other evangelical churches. Both Free Methodists and Nazarenes generally rejected tongues as a gift of the spirit in post-apostolic times (and still do). Nonetheless, the persons who made up the congregations of both "tongues" and non-tongues churches tended to be very similar in other aspects. This remains true today. Walter Nelson recognized that churches could be both too emotional, and too emotionless. The problem is to find a proper balance. This problem remains in the twenty-first century.

"During these years there were many problems unsettled in the thinking of the conference. One concerned the number of district elders that should be elected." "Another problem was the camp meeting which had been considered an important factor in the promotion of the conference from its beginning. One of the first established customs was for the annual conference sessions to be held in connection with a camp meeting. This soon led to agitation for a permanent camp ground which resulted in the purchase of a small park in Geary, Oklahoma, in 1926. There was soon some dissatisfaction over the location of the ground and over the desirability of the park itself. A committee to secure a new location was appointed in 1928 but in 1930 the committee was discharged and steps were taken to improve the camp ground in Geary. ..... Since then the annual camp has served as a rallying point for large numbers of the members of the church."[11]

The Conference responded to these and other challenges by starting a home missions' program, adding a missionary to the Beaver district, and a conference evangelist under the direction of the Conference Board of Evangelism. Some changes in personnel were made. There were some successes, as new churches were started in Okmulgee and Clinton. And as previously noted, growth in Sunday school was pronounced, if adult growth was not. I might add, this suggests that the future of the church might have rested as much, if not more, with youth and youth-oriented programs, than with the elderly pioneers who

10. Ibid, p.17-18.
11. Ibid, p.18.

church leaders (themselves tending "elderly") hoped to make the "nuclei" of new churches.

In 1919 there were 24 churches, 21 parsonages, total giving was $26,384, with 26 active preachers, 985 members, and 1,450 enrolled in Sunday School.

In 1931 there were 25 churches, 22 parsonages, total giving was $23,930, with 25 active preachers, 802 members, and 1,850 enrolled in Sunday School. This data is from the *History of the Oklahoma Conference.*

As far as membership and buildings go, the Free Methodist Church in Oklahoma did not grow much from 1919 to 1931. The late 20's, and the 1930's, were hard times for Oklahoma, and this no doubt affected church growth.

The 1930's & the Beginning of Liberty FMC

According to the *History*, during the 1930's "the conference preachers entered into the trying years of the depression with inspiration and courage. The membership of the conference was increased to 936 by 1935. But, there was no corresponding increase in Sunday school enrollment or in the finances of the church. (53) This upward trend soon faltered and since 1935 the numerical strength of the conference has fluctuated considerably. Death and migration continued to cause losses, particularly in Beaver County where the last members disappear, according to the statistical reports. Then with the coming of the demand for war workers and the taking of the young men into the armed services there was a decided drop in Sunday school enrollment and a gradual loss in church membership. This membership loss has continued to the present, reaching a low of 812 in 1947."[12] Or as Hugh Wayman puts it, in *The Free Methodist Church/Oklahoma In Action/Past Present and Future*, "The depression of the 1930's and World War II caused many to leave the farm areas, and as a result, the church suffered havoc until it hit its low in membership in 1951" (p.2).

It was in just such trying times that Liberty FMC was established. For both the *History*, and *Oklahoma In Action*, this achievement is noteworthy. The latter states, under the heading "Efforts to Expand the Work," that "The Liberty church, south of Perkins, was started through the efforts of some laymen who went out from Guthrie to form a group in that area."[13]

Liberty Free Methodist Church was inaugurated by lay evangelists in a rural area of central Oklahoma (which had only been a state 28 years in 1935), which was relatively sparsely inhabited, mostly poor, where cash was scarce, in which neighbors depended on each other, with little crime (most of the early church

---

12. Ibid, p.19. "Present" is 1949.
13. *Oklahoma In Action*, p.2.

members did not have locks on their homes) and few professionals such as doctors, dentists and lawyers. The banks were small and sometimes unstable, and general stores the norm. Vocations at that time were primarily in farming, cattle, and the oil industry. Electricity and in-door plumbing did not generally arrive to the congregants of Liberty until after World War II.

The countryside is rolling, with grassy hills and creek bottoms covered with a remarkable variety of trees, oaks being dominant. It is generally in the "cross-timbers" region of mixed grasses and hardwoods (they had few of the red cedars that today dot the countryside). The soil tends towards red clay which, in the bottoms, makes decent crops but is decidedly inferior to the dark, loamy soils of Kansas a hundred miles north, and crop failures occurred occasionally. In 1935 the shift from farming with horses and mules to tractors was taking place. Temperatures in the summer exceed 100 degrees Fahrenheit, and in the winter occasionally drop below 0, despite which few houses were insulated. Wood stoves were the norm, and a typical house would only have one. Average rainfall is about 36 inches, with periodic droughts. Residents are sensitive to changes in rainfall because, as in much of the Old Testament, a small drop in average rainfall means crop failure and starving livestock. The "dust bowl" is not mentioned in Liberty's existing records. Nor is the wind, although this region of Oklahoma is windy all four seasons, and when the church moved in 1946 to a new building, it was located on top of a hill with an expansive view in four directions and high winds which are cold in winter and hot in summer. The church was not insulated in 1946, nor is it today, and the location must have made for cold services in the winter. Kerosene, butane, and later propane were and are regular expenses of the church. The climate is relatively challenging, and weather was certainly a common topic of conversation in 1935, as today.

The men and women of those days tended to be self-reliant in the context of a local, supporting agriculture-based community, and many people did not complete high school. The Iowa tribe is located in this region and several other tribes are within a hundred-mile range (several congregants in the twenty-first century are enrolled in the Citizen Pottawatomie Nation). The communities tended to be mixed white (majority), native-American, and black. I cannot determine if any members of Liberty in the early years were minorities. The congregation in 2020 has several persons enrolled in Native American tribes and a few Hispanics.

As previously mentioned, Liberty was formed after evangelizing by "Bro. And Sister Will Ridens" (see also below). A meeting was called August 18, 1937, "for the purpose of organizing a Free Methodist Society." Four of the five charter members were women. The pastor, G.J. Eikermann, was male, but wives typically ministered alongside their husband, and "Mrs. Lucia M. Eikermann presented her letter from Wisby society." She was one of the charter members, and was probably the pastor's wife. In the early years of Liberty it was not unusual for the roll calls to be answered by a majority of women, and the various roll calls through the years were about evenly divided between men and women, as were the elected positions. In 2021 Liberty had thirty-four elected positions which were occupied by nine women and five men. Although I have not added them up, of all the elected positions in the history of the Liberty, probably more were occupied by women than men. Of course, more men worked away from the home than women. In any case, Liberty FMC, a typical rural evangelical church of the mid-western U.S., depended on both sexes for its success and continuing existence, and as far as the genesis of Liberty goes, women were arguably as important as men, if not more so. One unknown variable is the number of persons regularly attending church who were not official members, because such non-members were mostly not recorded – they did not respond to the official "roll call." This is discussed in greater detail later.

The first numbered page of the *Account Book* is titled "The Liberty Chapel Circuit of the Free Methodist Church" and reads as follows (for a description of the *Account Book* and other reference material, see the Annotated Bibliography).

> In the spring of 1936 (crossed out and replaced by "1935") Bro. and Sister Will Ridens of Guthrie, Okla. came to the Sandyland School House to preach the old time holiness Gospel. This was the first time the Gospel had been preached here by any Free Methodist minister. Bro. & Sister K.W. Jones made it possible for Bro. Ridens' (sic) to come all summer. A few hungry souls sought the Lord and were saved.

> In Aug. 36 [the "36" is written in a darker ink and added above the line, and underlined, presumably meaning "1936"] the conference sent Bro. G.J. Eikermann to be our first pastor.

> On Aug. 18, 1937 a meeting was called at the Sandyland (Liberty) School House for the purpose of organizing a Free Methodist Society.

The meeting was called to order by G.J. Eikermann pastor in charge. The devotional exercises were omitted as the meeting followed the regular prayer meeting.

After reading the general rules of the Discipline, Floyd Rush, Flossie Rush, Beulah Thompson and Virginia Thompson were separately required to answer the seven rules for full membership. Mrs. Lucia M. Eikermann presented her letter from Wisby society.

The above named then adopted the Discipline as a whole. They were then organized into a Free Methodist Society to be known as Liberty Chapel Free Methodist Society.

Virginia Thompson was elected Secretary. By unanimous consent it was decided to have three stewards.

The following in order were elected by ballots as stewards, Floyd Rush, Beulah Thompson & Virginia Thompson. By ballot Beulah Thompson was elected Class Leader. Floyd Rush was elected as delegate to annual conf. Mrs L.M. Eikermann was elected as reserve delegate.

On motion Floyd Rush was recommended to the official board for exhorters license. On motion the meeting adjourned. / Virginia Thompson/ Sec./ G.J. Eikermann/ Chairman (pp.1-2).

Beulah was Virginia's older sister by four years. When they founded Liberty they were thirty-one and twenty-seven years of age respectively, and married to brothers Charlie and Harry. Their maiden name was Rush, and Floyd Rush was their brother. Another sister, Eda Crawford, was also a pillar of the early Liberty FMC. Plaques recognizing the contributions of Beulah, Virginia and Eda are found in the Liberty sanctuary at the present (2022). Charlie Thompson, after a conversion, will become the longest serving pastor of Liberty, and one of the most successful. But this is a decade away.

Where did the name "Liberty Chapel" come from? A clue comes from Virginia's written statement "On Aug. 18, 1937 a meeting was called at the Sandyland (Liberty) School…." In a 2022 interview with long-time church member Carol Holman, she said that Sandyland school was at first called "Liberty" school. Since the newly formed society met at the school until 1946, it was logical to name it "Liberty." At some point not too long after Liberty Church moved to its current location, or perhaps concurrent with the move, a large silver bell of about two hundred pounds was moved to the church. At one time the bell was rung as a call to services, as some of the 2022 members remember. The clapper broke, and since then the bell has remained on a stand at the front of the church (it was once stolen, that story will be told later). Carol Holman said that the bell was originally at Liberty School and was used to call the students to class. At that time few people had watches.

All of the entry quoted above appears to be one entry and is in Virginia Thompson's hand. It is probably written well after the fact (hence the corrections). She will continue making entries, off and on, into the 1970's, in her neat, slightly forward-slanting, even style, which is one of the easiest to read in the *Account Book*. Her entries as treasurer are also among the most organized and clear. She also wrote many of the entries in the *Ledger Book*. She was one of the persons who played an essential role in the success of the church for five decades and was a flexible individual who fulfilled several different roles, including playing the piano in the 1970's when no one else could (according to the memories of 2022 members of the church, some of whom knew Virginia). She memorized a few songs for the piano and that was the extent of her repertoire. The 2022 congregants describe her as very neat and proper, organized, a quiet person who tried to never hurt anyone's feelings. Virginia was married to Harry Thompson. Harry attended regularly (at least in the memories of the 2022 church members) but never became a "full member." Whereas Virginia was demure, Harry was a joker. In the 1970's he was once asked what he would do if he won the lottery. He replied that he would use it to pay bills as far as it would go. Virginia's sister, Beulah, married Harry's brother, Charley Thompson, who also attended Liberty, who became a lay leader, an exhorter, got a local license, became ordained, and pastored Liberty several times, as well as other churches in the conference. Beulah of course was one of the five charter members of Liberty along with her sister. Beulah was more outspoken than Virginia. Virginia had a daughter, Betty, who attended Liberty longer than her mother. I knew her about a year. She died in 2019. She, too, was soft-spoken, neat, kind, and detail oriented.

Charley Thompson would pastor Liberty for about fourteen years (according to my calculations), 1945-48, 1971-1979, 1980-81 and 1997. He was pastor for several of the 2022 church members, during the late 1970's and 1980. They say he was a jolly person who loved to tell real-life stories. He had "high spirits" but was "down-to-earth," a farmer who typically wore coveralls when not in church. He used to tell the congregation that he initially fought going to church. He wanted nothing to do with it. One day when he was in the field the Lord somehow so impressed him that he went to a stump and knelt and prayed. He accepted God's call then and there (although the Lord had been working on him for some time) and began going to church, and the rest is history. He eventually became ordained, pastored several churches, and became an important leader in the conference. In conversion stories, it is remarkable how often the person who resists church is the one who God calls to serve. Charley used to say that when he was troubled or needed help, he would go to that same stump to pray. The congregants remember that in those days Charley worked the ground with horses or mules (or both). I can see him, in my mind, dropping the traces and going over to the stump to pray in his old overalls as the animals stomped. Beulah, his wife, was opposite to him in temperament. She was matter of fact to the point of sometimes appearing cranky, but she was "nice," and "sweet." But everyone agrees she was "no-nonsense" and business-like.

The quotation from the minutes above states the official members of the newly formed church were required to "separately required to answer the seven rules for full membership." The *History of the Oklahoma Conference* (published 1949) lists these seven rules on pp.8-9. These rules for membership are included in Appendix II.

The *History of the Oklahoma Conference* describes the establishment of Liberty from a conference perspective.

> While the conference was debating plans for evangelism a new circuit came into being through the activity of some lay preachers. Mr. and Mrs. W. I. Ridens of Guthrie, together with a few other laymen, began holding services in the Liberty School House near Perkins, Oklahoma, and soon a few persons untied with the Free Methodist Church. The first official recognition of the new group was in the minutes of 1936. At this time the Perkins and Liberty School House Circuit appeared in the list of appointments but no preacher was appointed to the circuit. In 1939 there were ten members on the circuit with a pastor serving on the field. (p. 20).

The *Account Book* states that "In Aug. 36 the conference sent Bro. G.J. Eikermann to be our first pastor." This appears to conflict with the *History* statement that in 1936 "no preacher was appointed to the (Liberty) circuit."

However, the records I have found for the pastors of Liberty are sometimes in conflict and have gaps. Probably many of the records were constructed after the fact and according to memory, not unlike this present effort. I assume that the minutes are correct, and G.J. Eikermann was their first pastor, 1936-38. Liberty was under superintendent A.R. Martin in 1938-39; was pastored by Walter Nelson 1939-1940; and was under superintendent W.H. Maddox 1940-41.

The Sandyland School House (probably first called the "Liberty School House") was located about one mile east and one quarter mile south of the current (2022) church location at the corner of Worthy and Union Roads, about two miles east of State Highway 177, in the far north of Lincoln County, OK.

About three quarters down page two in the *Account Book*, another entry is recorded, as follows. "First official board meeting of the Free Methodist Society met at the Liberty School House. Nov. 16, 1937 at 8:30 p.m. A.R. Martin D.E. [District Elder] Presiding (1) On motion, devotional service were omitted on account of preceeding (sic). (2) Virginia Thompson was elected secretary. (3) Floyd Rush, Flossie Rush, Beulah Thompson, Mrs. Eikermann and Bro G.J. Eikermann were present (4) Reading of the minutes were omitted as the records were not here. (5) On motion Beulah Thompson was elected treasure (sic)." Item 6 reads, "On motion Floyd Rush was granted exhorter license" (pp.2-3). Items 7. through 11. are labeled "no business" and item 12 lists "$3.00 taken in as Conference claims. Pastors (sic) salary $25.40 cash $16.57 feed $8.83." Items 13 through 20 are labeled "No business" and item 21 records "On motion the meeting adjourned./ Virginia Thompson/ Sec." (p. 3).

A.R. Martin, the presiding official, is listed in the *History of the Oklahoma Conference* as District Superintendent 1937-1945 (p.31). He probably was not at Liberty most Sundays. "Bro. G.J Eikermann" probably normally filled the pulpit, while accompanied to church by his wife (Eikermann is spelled a variety of ways in the *Account Book,* as are many other names, and in general spelling is inconsistent therein).

The next recorded board meeting was January 29, 1938. A.R. Martin D.E. presided. "Pastor support for this quarter $31.99." Also noted were $3.00 for "elders claims," $1.00 for "Men and Mission," $4.00 for "debt ellimanition" (sic), then "No money in treasure" (p.3).

The next recorded board meeting was April 22, 1938. A.R. Martin, D.E. presided. A note was made that $4.00 was raised for evangelism, and $3.00 for "water system at Camp ground" (p.4). The camp ground appears periodically in the minutes and was obviously perceived to be an important asset.

Not a board meeting, but "The annual circuit and Society meeting of the Perkins and Liberty School House Circuit met at the Liberty School House July 8, 1938, 9 p.m." A reference was made to "the quarterly meeting service." At this time, and for years later, the superintendent normally met with each church on a quarterly basis. Records indicate "Flossie Rush was elected delegate to annual conference." "Floyd Rush was elected for renewel (sic) of exhortes (sic) license," etc. (p. 5).

A board meeting was held July 9, 1938, A.R. Martin presiding. "Floyd Rush, Beulah Thompson, Bro. Eikermann and Virginia Thompson answered the roll call." The secretary, Virginia Thompson, noted that the total for the pastor's supply for the year was $72.00; total for elder's support $3.00 [presumably this was for A.R. Martin]; Missions $2.30; $1.00 for "Children's Day." Also, "Time for revivial (sic) was decided sometime after first of Nov" (pp.6-7). Item IV on the agenda states "Donald Thompson was elected teller." He obviously was not on the roll and did not answer the roll call. The roll was for persons who were official members of Liberty. A roll call therefore does not necessarily, indeed probably usually does not indicate all who were present.

The next board meeting is January 10, 1939 "with Bro. A.R. Martin in charge." According to the roll, "Bro. Nelson, Floyd Rush, Flossie Rush, Charlie Thompson, Beulah Thompson, and Virginia Thompson" were present. "On motion Charley Thompson was accepted in full connection" (p.7). Charley is married to Beulah, as previously mentioned, and Charley's brother Harry is married to Virginia. The Eikermann's disappear from the minutes at this point, and it is not clear who the pastor is, if anyone.

"The official board of the Free Methodist church & Sandyland and Perkins circuit met at the Liberty School House March 18, 1939 with Bro. A.R. Martin, D.E. in charge." Six persons answered the roll call, and again no Eikermann was present. "Lillie Murray was recommended to be received in full connection." "Louse Nelson was received by letter from North Chapel, Mar. 7. 1939."

"One infant, Delores Ann Nelson was baptized (sic) Jan. 11, 1939" (pp.8-9). This is the first recorded baptism. Presumably the D.E. baptized the infant.

"The official board members of the Liberty and Perkins circuit met at the parsonage, at Perkins May 26, 1939./ The meeting was opened by singing, 'What a Friend We Have in Jesus,' and was led in prayer by Sis. Flossie Rush and Bro. A.R. Martin." Six persons answered the roll call, not including Martin. "Lillie Murray was taken in full connection April 2, 1939." "Charlie Thompson was recommended by the society to receive exhorters licenses" (p.9). "Pastoral support $21.36" and "District Elders claims $2.25." "Evangelist support $6.30." "Balance for missions $1.18." Again, the Eikermanns are not mentioned. This is the beginning of Charley Thompson's life-long service to the church, which will lead to ordination in a few years. My guess is that Charley had preached before he got his exhorter's license. And we note Liberty's consistent commitment to missions.

"The annual Society meeting of the Perkins and Liberty School House circuit met at the Liberty School House July 19, 1939 with Bro. Nelson as chairman. …. The following answered to the roll call, Lillie Murray, Flossie Rush, Floyd Rush, Charly Thompson, Beulah Thompson, Louise Nelson and Virginia Thompson." Item 4. states "Louise Nelson was elected teller." Item 7 on the agenda states, "It was decided to have 3 stewards & the following were elected, Virginia Thompson, Floyd and Flossie Rush." "9. Beulah Thompson was elected Class Leader." "10. Motion was made and seconded to elect a supt. For the young people. Charly Thompson was elected supt./ Flossie Rush was elected supt. of the childrens (sic) dept. and Virginia Thompson supt." "Virginia Thompson./ Sec." (p.10). Since Bro. Nelson is mentioned as chairman, and no superintendent is present, Bro. Walter Nelson is probably the new pastor (1939-1940). Another district superintendent, W.H. Maddox, assumes supervision of the Liberty Circuit, 1939 to 1941.[14] A.R. Martin continues as District Superintendent to 1945, and in the future will again be involved with Liberty, but for the present apparently is no longer supervising the circuit where Liberty is located.

"The official board of the Perkins and Liberty School House Circuit met at the school house, Nov. 4, 1939 for the first quarterly meeting since conf. Bro W.H. Maddox in charge." This is the first meeting at which superintendent Maddox was present. Six persons answered roll call including Bro. (presumably pastor)

14 *History of the Oklahoma Conference*, p.31.

Nelson. Item 16 states "The matter of pastor's supply deferred 17-20. No business" (p.11).

Summary of the 1930's

By the end of 1939 Liberty FMC appears to have become a stable church, although the pastors do not stay long, perhaps because the congregation is small, the pay is not enough to live on, recruiting new members in a rural area is difficult, and therefore future prospects are limited.

Beginnings are important. The future is built on the past. Liberty members consisted mostly of family members, close acquaintances, and a few transfers from other churches, who are sometimes family members. In the early years Liberty depended on the faith and day-to-day, persistent commitment of a few key persons. Looking back from the year 2022, this has been true of much of Liberty's history. Money was not essential to its beginning and was not what kept the church going. In fact, the early members probably did not have much cash. This common kind of church requires the extraordinary faith of a few people. And the continuing survival of such churches, of which there are thousands across the landscape of America, depends on a few persons of faith from the younger generation stepping into the shoes of the elders when they can no longer function effectively. Or the church will likely pass away. Unlike larger, and more affluent churches, all, or almost all, the persons in Liberty-type churches have crucial roles to play. There are few "free-riders."

From the beginning the congregants were focused on the needs of the church and its members, on their local community, and on children, as well as more generally on the sick, families with deaths, and the needy. It was committed to the needs of the greater church (especially the conference) and on evangelism, both "home missions" and "world missions." From the beginning Liberty was an evangelistic church. It was formed by evangelists. Sunday School was also important, not the least as a tool for evangelism.

The minutes of the first meeting reference "$30 taken in as Conference claims." This is more than the pastor's salary (mentioned as $25.40). In the next minutes (Jan. 29, 1938) the collection for "men & mission" is $1.60, as well as "No money in Treasure." The April 2, 1938, minutes note "money raised for evangelism $3.00" and a "class leader" was also elected. This seems to have been the beginning of Liberty's education programs. Again, "Balance in

Treasure. None." From this point forward, most of the minutes and treasurer reports mention both missions and educational and other children's activities. Through-out its history and until the present day Liberty has financially (and spiritually) supported what it terms "world missions" and "evangelism" as well as children's programs. The January 1939 minutes show "$9.45 for conference evangelist" as well as "$11.70 for evangelist offering" and "$6.49 received for revival at Perkins." The sums the church raises for missions are significant when compared to its other expenses, although from a broader socio-economic perspective the sums are small. However, the Biblical perspective is that God prefers to use the small, and in both Biblical and world history, when faith is tied to humble offerings, that is often when great things happen.

For the early years, I find no references to routine services other than Sunday morning or night. They had of course camp meetings, revivals, special meetings, baptisms, etc. In an interview May 25, 2022, Rev. Harry Adams reported that when he was pastor of Liberty 1968-69 there was not a Wednesday service, and he did not think there ever had been. In the twenty-first century, Liberty has regularly participated in bi-monthly prayer meetings (third Wednesday of the month usually) of the Tryon Church Alliance (Assembly of God, Baptist, Christian Union, and Liberty) and hosts about every fourth one. But church members report never having regular Wednesday evening services in their time, and I do not believe Liberty ever did.

Interestingly, the minutes of the church show no direct references to national or international affairs, or to state-wide affairs or events, or politics, or even the depression, or local droughts or disasters. Liberty, no doubt like most other small churches of that time, seems to have been focused on spiritual needs, and was relatively indifferent to social or political events (unlike most churches in twenty-first century). And it was obviously evangelical.

Although no one knows the year that Jesus was killed, it was around the year 35. The origins of Liberty, then, are about 1900 years after Jesus's death and resurrection.

The 1940's

"The official board of the Liberty Circuit met at the school house Jan. 27, 1940 with Bro. W.H. Maddox in charge." Five persons answered roll call. Item 7. states "Sister Virginia Thompson was nominated & elected as committee on charity." Item 9 states "What is the status of membership?" with no responses recorded. Item 9.b. states "motion was made and second to extend Bro. Madisons (sic) probation" (p.12).

The next record in the *Account Book* is a board meeting April 30, 1940 "with Bro. W.H. Maddox in charge." Six persons answered roll. "… James Thompson was recommended and accepted for full membership." "Moves & seconded to dismiss Mr. Madison from probation." $2.00 was received for Missions and $1.00 for Christian education. "The Sunday School was reported to have increased in number" (p.13). It would be interesting to know the number of children participating.

The next board meeting is July 16, 1940 "with Bro. W.H. Maddox in charge." "The meeting was open with prayer by Bro. Maddox." Six answered roll call including Bro. Nelson. Presumably he is still the pastor. 8.a. "There have been five received on probation Donald Wayne Thompson, Orville Allen Murray, Lois Jean Murray, Norma Ruth Rush & Betty Marie Thompson." Item 5 states "Motion was made & seconded to renew Bro. F.M. Rush and C.N. Thompson's exhorter's license." "10. The Charity Committee reported clothing for some children in the neighbor(sic) have been provided" (p.14-15).

The next record is for a "Circuit and Society meetings July 18, 1940 at the Liberty School House with Bro. Nelson as chairman." Eight answered roll call. "8. Motion was made & second to continue the Circuit meeting into the Society meeting."

The next record is the quarterly board meeting of Sept. 28, 1940 "for the first quarterly meeting since conf. Bro W.H. Maddox in charge" (the same statement had been made in the Nov. 1939 meeting). It seems likely that pastor Walter Nelson, "Bro. Nelson," has left, and superintendent Maddox was "in charge" in the sense that he was functioning as pastor. Five answered roll call. Five persons were "received on probation" (p.16). "Flossie Rush, Louise Nelson, Gayla Thompson, Orville Murray, & Jean Murray have been baptised (sic)." "Other money received $9.25 for evangilism (sic)."

The next record is the board meeting of Dec. 21, 1940, "Bro. W.H. Maddox appointed G.W. Bugg to have charge." Five answered roll call. Following "status of membership," "9 members over 16 – 1 under 16" (pp.17-18). This is the one and only reference to G.W. Bugg. In this case to "have charge" does not unequivocally indicate a new pastor, e.g., he is not referred to as "Bro." or "Rev.," and therefore I have not included G.W. Bugg in the list of pastors. If he was pastor, it was for a short time.

The next record is a board meeting March 1, 1941 "with Bro. W.H. Maddox in charge." Five answered roll call. 8. C. "None received in full connection" and "D. None died." Virginia continues to be the secretary (pp.18-19).

I note that at this time the nation is in the middle of World War II and is fighting desperately in both Europe and the Pacific. It is possible the above "none died" (the first such reference) shows some local impact of the war, but this might be a stretch.

"The official board of the Liberty Chapel Circuit met June 20, 1941 at the school house with Bro. W.H. Maddox in charge." "Bro. Martin, Charley Thompson, Beulah Thompson, Lillie Murray & Virginia Thompson" answered roll call. Six were extended on probation. "None received into full connection." "None have died" "Louise Nelson was transferred by letter." "Charley Thompson was recommended to the Quarterly conf. to receive local preachers (sic) license." Item 8. (d) states "for central college $5.00" (pp.19-20).

"The society of the Liberty Chapel Circuit held their annual meeting at the Liberty School House July 23, 1941 with Bro. Milo Martin in charge." Eight persons answered roll call. The usual elections were held. I assume Bro. E. Milo Martin is the new pastor (1941-1942). I do not know if he was related to A.R. Martin.

The next board meeting is Aug. 25, 1941, at the schoolhouse, with Bro. Ralph Butterfield in charge. Virginia Thompson, who was the first elected secretary (1937), is re-elected in that capacity, an excellent choice as she is almost always present, and her hand-written minutes are generally excellent. Six answered roll call. A "charity committee" with three members was elected. "Orville Murray, Jean Murray, Donald Wayne Thompson, Norma Ruth Rush, & Betty Marie Thompson were taken in full connection" (p.21). Ralph Butterfield was District Superintendent 1941-48.[15]

The board met Nov. 21, 1941, "with Bro Ralph Butterfield in charge." Six answered roll call. It was mostly business as usual, except "The motion was made to start our revival with Bro. Crown the first of the year" (p.22-23). This is the only reference to Bro. Crown.

The board next met Feb. 21, 1942, at the schoolhouse, "with Bro. Butterfield in charge." Six answered roll call. The treasurer reported "pastor's support $70.19," "Elders support $3.51," "$14.00 for evangelism (sic)," and "Bal. in treasure .30" (pp.24-25).

The next board meeting was May 15, 1942 "at the School House with Bro. Butterfield in charge." Six answered roll call. Business was as usual.

"The Society of the Free Methodist Class of the Liberty Chapel Circuit met July 22, 1942 with Bro. Milo Martin in charge." "The following answered the roll call, Charly (sic) Thompson, Floyd Rush, Flossie Rush, Beulah Thompson, Esther Martin, & Virginia Thompson Betty Thompson & Norma Rush." The treasurer's report indicated "Pastors support -- $333.71," "Elder claims -- $24.91," "missions -- $3.00," "Central School -- 7.00," "Evangelism – 14.00," "Elders Parsonage – 17.80," "men in service – 3.05," and "conf. claims 30.00." (p.24-25). "… men in service" is the first clear reference to the war.

The board next met Oct. 3, 1942, "with Bro. R.E. Butterfield in charge." Six answered roll call. "The letter of recommendation for Harold Daniels, Lucy Daniels & Ronald Daniels from the Free Methodist Church in Santa Anna California was read. It was voted to receive these three in full connection." "It was voted to renew Floyd Rushes exhorters licenses" (p.26).

The *History of the Oklahoma Conference* states, "In 1939 there were ten members on the [Liberty]circuit with a pastor serving on the field. When the pastor

15. *History of Oklahoma Conference*, p. 31.

sent to this church in 1942 resigned the class was held together by the efforts of C.N. Thompson, a local layman who later joined the conference as an active minister. Under his leadership the circuit has increased to thirty members" (p. 20). It does not say at what date the church had thirty members. Also, in the *Account Book*, the minutes from June 1941 indicate that "Charly" Thompson was recommended to the conference to receive his "preachers license," i.e., soon he was to be ordained, and the conference did ordain him, but I do not know exactly when. Charly (sometimes spelled "Charley" in the board minutes) was recommended for an "exhorter's license" in the May 26, 1939, Board minutes (and Floyd Rush was also recorded as having his exhorter's license renewed that date).

In the *History*, R.E. Butterfield is listed as a District Superintendent from 1941 to 1948, and Conference Superintendent from 1948 to 1949. Possibly, then, the Superintendent had formal charge of Liberty, but was only present part time, while local laypersons ran the church on a week-to-week basis, presumably filling the pulpit on most occasions, in the not unusual situations when they were in-between pastors. However, many of the Board financial records show amounts for "pastor's support," strongly suggesting the money was given to someone. The first such record is for Jan. 29, 1938, "pastor's support for the quarter $31.99." This was presumably for G.J. Eikermann, who was indicated as present. The January 10, 1939, Board minutes record "A.R. Martin in charge," "Pastoral support $47.77," and "District Elder's support $6.36." The latter was presumably for A.R. Martin, but who was the pastor? G.J. Eidermann was not recorded as present, as he was previously, and does not show up in the record thereafter. The amounts designated as "pastor support" could have been given to whomever was filling the pulpit, whether ordained or not (a tradition which continues today) or assigned to Liberty or not. Or it could have been collected for whoever the next pastor would be.

Of the persons listed as "in charge" of Board and Society meetings since 1936 – A.R. Martin, W.H. Maddox, Ralph Butterfield -- all were District Superintendents, except G.W. Bugg in December 1940 (who never appears in the record again) and G.K. Eikermann, "pastor in charge," in the organizing meeting in 1937. However, G.K Eikermann was present Nov. 16, 1937, and July 9, 1938, presumably as pastor, when A.R. Martin was recorded as "presiding." Bro. Nelson was also referred to as "chairman" July 19, 1939, and July 18, 1940, when no superintendent was present. Why was he not listed as "in charge?" According to Dwight Gregory, Ph.D., Assistant to the Superintendent of the Mid-America Conference, in an email Wednesday, April 20, 2022, "Supt presiding does not necessarily mean there is no ordained pastor or no pastor appointed as "in charge." It may mean that, in light of a former provision in Discipline that a pastor could be appointed without being "in charge," meaning the church was technically under the supt, and "pastor" was really there primarily as "preacher."" In my estimation this was likely true for Liberty in at least some of its early years.

Based on the records that I have access to, it is not possible to know for certain who all the pastors of Liberty FMC were, until we get to the 1970's, and even then there are questions. This suggests that pastors, per se, were not essential to the survival of the church. Rather, the members were. For a further discussion of this problem, see Appendix I, Liberty Leadership.

The board next met Jan. 8, 1943 "with Bro. R.E. Butterfield in charge." Five answered roll call. It was noted "Mrs. J.W. Thompson sick."

The next board meeting was March 26, 1943, at the schoolhouse, "with Bro. R.E. Butterfield in charge." Answering role call was Charley Thompson, Beulah Thompson, and Virginia Thompson. Reports indicated "Conf. claims raised in full," and "no pastor's support." "Dist. Elder's support $14.25" (ibid p. 28).

"The official board of the Liberty Chapel Circuit met at the Liberty school house July 16, 1943, with Bro. R.E. Butterfield in charge." "The following answered the roll call, Charley Thompson, Beulah Thompson, Floyd Rush, Flossie Rush and Virginia Thompson." "No sick, none received on probation." "No probation expired." "Motion was made and second to adjourn to renew Bro. Rush's exhorter's license." "Conf. claims raised in full." "No pastors (sic) support." "Elders support $12.90." "Balance in treasury, None" (ibid p.29).

The next record in the *Account Book* is for Nov. 12, 1943 "for the first time since conf." "with A.R. Martin in charge." Answering roll call was Charley Thompson, Beulah Thompson, Floyd Rush and Virginia Thompson. "Conf. claims $18.00." "Pastor's support $46.78." "Other money received, $20.00 church (illegible word). $10.00 for men in service. $10.00 for conf. evangelism." And signing off as usual, "Virginia Thompson, Sec."

A.R. Martin served Liberty three separate times: 1938-39 as superintendent with no regular pastor that I know of; same for 1943-45; and 1953-54 when C.V

McCully (1952-53) and W.E. Heginbotham (1953-54) were pastors. Although the record is not clear, part of this time he was probably the lead or senior pastor, and part he supervised a fledgling pastor. From what I can tell, A.R. Martin either preached, or supervised someone who filled the pulpit (such as an "exhorter") at least four years, and possibly more. Clearly A.R. Martin was a seminal influence in Liberty's early success and development.

On the back page of the "Oklahoma Conference Heritage" is a photo of A.R. Martin, with a caption that states he "served with the WMS as Young People's Superintendent from 1929-1932 ...." The caption also states, "He remains our conference's primary link with its heritage and is currently the chairman of the Historical Committe (sic)." Following his photo is an article he wrote in the *Free Methodist*, Jan. 9, 1942, when he was "District Elder" (in 1943 he was back at Liberty). The short article, about 350 words, is titled "Prairie Queen Dedication and District Meeting." The *History of the Oklahoma Conference* records that he was "District Superintendent of the Oklahoma Conference" 1937-1945. We know that for several years A.R. Martin oversaw formal meetings of Liberty (Society and Board meetings). During these years Charley Thompson, who eventually got his "preacher's license," and Floyd Rush, who was an "exhorter" and privileged to preach at Liberty, typically were recorded as present, and occupied elected positions within Liberty's organizational structure. As mentioned above, the *History* singles out Charley Thompson as someone who held the church together "when the pastor sent to this church in 1942 resigned." My guess is that during those years when the record shows A.R. Martin in charge with no mention of a pastor, Martin was in charge but not always present, for example he would conduct quarterly meetings at the other churches he was supervising. Probably Charley Thompson filled the pulpit some of the time, perhaps with Floyd Rush occasionally preaching.

The next meeting is Feb. 5, 1944 "with A.R. Martin in charge." "Role call answered by Charley Thompson, Beulah Thompson and Virginia Thompson." "Nov. 13, 1943 Mrs. Swiggert was received in full connection" (ibid p.32, 31).

The next record is July 7, 1944 "Rev. A.R. Martin in charge." Answering role call was Charley Thompson, Beulah Thompson, and Virginia Thompson. "Two have been received in full connection. Elzie and Marvel Hemphill by letter from the Pilgrim Holiness Church April 30, 1944." "Esther Martin was given transfer to Oak Glade Society." "On motion Floyd R. renewed exhorters (sic) license." "Conf. claims $21.00." "Pastors(sic) support $90.38." "Dist. Support $17.05." "Other money received, Missions $20.56/ schools $5.00" (ibid pp. 31, 32).

A note is made in the margin of the *Account Book*, "Should of come before last writing." Then "The official Chapel Circuit met at the school house April 28, 1944 with Rev. A.R. Martin in charge." Answering roll call was Charley Thompson, Beulah Thompson, and Virginia Thompson. There is the usual financial report then adjournment (ibid p.32).

"The society of the Liberty Chapel Circuit were called together June 8, 1944 by Bro. A.R. Martin. D.S. in charge." "The following answered the roll call, Charley T., Elzie Hemphill, Marvel Hemphill, Mrs. Swiggert, and Virginia Thompson." In pencil is added "Beulah Thompson" (Virginia Thompson normally uses a blue fountain pen). "Fern Rodman was elected tellar (sic)." "On the third ballot Beulah Thompson was elected delegate to annual conf." "On second ballot Elzie Hemphill was elected class leader." "Moved and seconded to have three stewards. On first ballot, Marvel Hemphill, Fern Rodsman & Virginia Thompson were elected stewards" (ibid p.33).

The next board meeting is Nov. 4, 1944 "with A.R. Martin in charge." Answering the roll call were Charley Thompson, Elzie Hemphill, Marvel Hemphill, Fern Rodman, Floyd Rush, and Virginia Thompson. "On motion the following were received as suitable -- Hubert Rodman., Fern Rodman, Maxine Rodman to be received in full connection Pauline Rodman, Melba Collins, & Gayla Thompson probation has expired." It is unclear here as to who has what status. The treasurer's report states, "Conf. claims $24.00." "Pastors support $87.00." "Dist. Supt. $9.26." "Other money raised for preacher's assist $7.59." "Bal in treasure $3.25." "Motion was made & ordered to comply with the pastor's assistance./ Virginia Thompson./ Sec." (ibid. p.33, 34).

A pencil note in the margin states "Jan meeting held March 7. 1945." Then "The official board of the Liberty Chapel Circuit met at the home of Virginia Thompson March 7, 1945 with Charley Thompson as chairman." Answering the roll were Charley Thompson, Elzie Hemphill, Floyd Rush, Marvel Hemphill, and Virginia Thompson. "On Nov. 5, 1945 [this must be an error, it should be 1944] the following were received in full connection. Hubert Rodman, Fern Rodman, Maxine Rodman, Pauline Rodman, Melba Collins

& Gayla Thompson." In the treasurer's report is included "$15 for Tabernicle (sic). Men in Missions $9.63 Evangilism (sic) $25.00 Preachers assistance $4.88 Balance in Treasure. Bal. in Treasure used to pay Mrs. Swiggerts conf. claims" (ibid pp.34, 35).

The next board meeting is March 30, 1945 "with Bro. A.R. Martin in charge." "The meeting followed the regular service as the devotionals were omitted." Answering roll call were Charley Thompson, Elzie Hemphill, Marvel Hemphill, Fern Rodman, Floyd Rush, and Virginia Thompson. After the financial report is the statement "The Sunday School Supt. Reported increased in numbers at S.S" (ibid p.35).

On April 30, 1945, Adolf Hitler committed suicide. Berlin fell to the allies May 2. On May 7, Germany surrendered, and World War II in Europe ended. It is interesting, though perhaps not surprising, that the minutes of Liberty Chapel, then Church, generally do not reference world, national, or even local events, although these surely effected the congregation in various ways (economically, for example, or in terms of war deaths). Around this time men and women in war service started returning home.

For the next record Virginia has used a black ink fountain pen, apparently with a narrower tip. This compacted her style a bit. The board meeting was at the schoolhouse, July 13, 1945 "with D.S. A.R. Martin in charge." "The meeting followed the regular service." "The following answered the roll call. Charley Thompson, Elzie Hemphill, Marvel Hemphill, Fern Rodman, and Virginia Thompson." "It was moved and second to renew Floyd Rush's exhorter's license." Under the treasurer's report, "Conf claims raised in full." "Pastor's support $198.02." "Dist. Supt. $7.59." "Pastor's assistance fund $6.96." "lamp fund $3.50 paid out for repairs 1.50 leaving bal. 2.00."

"The Liberty Chapel Society were called together July 25, 1945 for their annual society meeting." "Rev. C.N. Thompson acted as chairman." This is the first reference to "Rev." Thompson, although he was ordained in 1941. Presumably Rev. Thompson is now the pastor. "The following answered the roll call. Charley Thompson, Hubert Rodman, Elzie Hemphill, Marvel Hemphill, Beulah Thompson, Flossie Rush, Floyd Rush & Virginia Thompson." The usual elections were held. Also, "The name of Elzie Hemphill was recommended for exhorter's license." Virginia Thompson remained secretary and treasurer (ibid p. 37).

August 6, 1945, the first atomic bomb was dropped on Hiroshima. Three days later another was dropped on Nagasaki. On August 15 Japan surrendered, and World War II was over. The minutes do not mention these epochal events.

Liberty Moves to a New Location and Facility

The next meeting contains the first record of the search for a new church location. "The members of the Liberty Chapel, Free Methodist Church were called together Sept. 26, 1945 in a society meeting, for the purpose of electing a board of trustees and to decide where the new church would be located." "Rev. C.N. Thompson was in charge." "On first ballot Elzie Hemphill, Hubert Rodman and Gerald Johnson were elected as the board of trustees." "Motion was made & second to leave the naming of the new church to the board of trustees." "By majority vote the church was to be put on the Frank Anderson cornor (sic)" (ibid p. 38). It seems probable that the end of the war, the return of the troops, and the prospect for improved economic conditions, contributed to the optimism necessary to move to a new location and church building with its associated costs and upkeep. As will be amplified later, the "Anderson corner" was one hilltop acre at the intersection of two section line roads.

The *History of the Oklahoma Conference* states, "The conference finally recognized the possibilities in the Liberty Community and in 1945 voted to give to the Liberty Circuit an old church building in Perkins, which had been bought from the Congregational Church but had not been successfully used by the Free Methodists. This old building was moved to the Liberty Community and remodeled into a small but attractive chapel, which greatly improves the outlook for the church there. The laymen of this church are a sincere and zealous type and the prospects for advancement in the community are very promising. This encouraging development did not, however, relieve the concern of the conference for an evangelistic advance" (p. 20). According to the memories of congregants in 2022, the "old church" was taken apart and moved in wagons to the current location, where it was re-assembled, minus its square tower.

One of the 2022 members, Lynda Grimes, has an undated, yellowed, newspaper cut-out (3 ½ x 5 ½ inches) which shows a photo of the "Congregational Church" as it existed in Perkins. The caption reads, "Perkins Congregational Church – Many members of the Perkins Congregational Church, pictured above, joined the Perkins Methodist Church when the former discontinued services in 1919.

The church was built around the turn of the century at First and French. It was used for several years as a classroom for vocational agriculture classes from Perkins High School. The structure was dismantled about 1935." Written in ink pen across the top left is "Now Liberty Free Methodist Church." "about 1935" may be off by a decade or it may be an error for 1945. In the photo the church has a square bell tower that extends about fifteen feet above the roof line and is about forty feet off the ground. That tower does not currently exist and presumably was not re-assembled when the church was moved to the current location at Worthy and Union roads, across the county line into Lincoln County. The original church was apparently built around 1899 and therefore is, in 2022, well over a century old. A few rooms (including bathrooms and classrooms) have since been added on to the original structure, about doubling the space. The original space, which is currently the sanctuary, holds about eighty people comfortably, and perhaps a hundred maximum.

In 2022 Sam Savory is treasurer for Liberty as he has been for decades. He joined the church in the 1970's and is one of the persons who maintains the physical integrity of the building. He says the church originally was just the current sanctuary and foyer. The rooms to the east of the sanctuary were added in the 1980's, and the bathrooms and rooms to the north of the sanctuary were added in the 2000's (more about this later). Prior to this, the only bathrooms available were in the auxiliary building to the north and/or outhouses. There were still outhouses in pastor Harry Adams' time (late 1960's) which he told me surprised his daughters. The auxiliary building was originally a house, and it was also moved to the current location. It was originally used by the church as a parsonage. In 2020 it is mostly used for Sunday School and meals. No one remembers when the change from parsonage to auxiliary occurred, although Bill Grimes remembers that pastor Joseph Simpson (1954-56) lived there. When the building was converted to auxiliary use, the two bedrooms were deconstructed.

In 2019 Liberty bought new chairs for the sanctuary, and sold the existing eighteen wood pews, most of which were nine feet long (a few were about half that length). According to Bill Grimes, those pews were there when he attended Liberty FMC as a child in the 1950's. It is possible that these pews were the original pews in the church in 1946. They were probably used at that time. They were stained (dark red or brown), clear pine (some about eleven inches wide), and at some point, had cushions added (the last set of cushions was removed in 2018). Sometime in the past the pews had been elevated about one- and three-quarter inches by adding boards to the bottoms of the supports. The construction was simple. Nine-foot boards, eleven inches wide, of straight, clear pine (no knots), would be difficult to find in 2022. The new chairs are considerably more comfortable, as noted by the members of the Tryon Ministerial Alliance when they attend meetings at Liberty, but they will not last half as long as the old pews, and they are more difficult to clean.

The next record, Oct. 26, 1945, "was the first meeting after conf." It was at the schoolhouse, and "Bro. L.B. Vanderhoofen was in charge." Answering the roll call were Charley Thompson, Elzie Hemphill, Fern Rodman, Marvel Hemphill, Floyd Rush, Flossie Rush, Hubert Rodman, Gerald Johnson, and Virginia Thompson. Various were received "on probation." "Elzie Hemphilll was recommended by the society as a suitable person to receive exhorers (sic) license. On motion the license was granted." "Gerald and Kathleen Johnson, Clausine and Maxine Bales and Elmer Leon Hemphill have been baptized." Given the date of October, it would be interesting to know where they were baptized, although they might have been baptized considerably earlier (ibid p. 39). L.B. Vanderhoofven was District Superintendent 1945-1948 (concurrently with R.E. Butterfield).[16]

The next meeting is still at the schoolhouse, Feb. 1, 1946, "With Bro. L.B. Vanderhoofen in charge." Nine persons answered the roll call (ibid p. 40).

The next record, in the top margin of p.41 in the *Accounting Book*, is in pencil and states "Our first service in the new church June 30, 1946. Our first revival July 8—14 with Bro. L.B. Van. as evangilist (sic). First Dist Meeting July 11-14—1946." In 2022, then, the structure has been in use seventy-six years at the present wind-swept, hilltop location, and is about a century and a quarter old. Whoever originally built it, probably associated with a Congregationalist Church, might be surprised at how many services have been conducted in the building.

"Warranty Deed No. 113/ Lincoln County Republican, Chandler, Okla." shows that one acre of land was deeded "from Frank T. Anderson and Lillie M. Anderson to The Liberty Church of the Free Methodist Church of North America." The "instrument" was filed "for the record" "the 12th day of November 1946." The property was exchanged "in consideration of the sum

---

16. *History of the Oklahoma Conference*, p. 31.

of Fifty & No/100 ... dollars." The description reads in part, that the property shall be "In trust for the use and benefit of the membership of the Free Methodist Church of North America ....subject to the Disciplin (sic), usages and ministrial (sic) appointments of said church ... that in the houses of worship now erected or that may hereafter be erected on said premises hereby conveyed, the seats shall be forever free; and in further trust and confidence that the said trustees and their successors in office shall permit at all times the preachers who may be duly authorized according to the Discipline of the said free Methodist Church, to hold religious services in said houses of worship according to said Discipline." One defining trust of the "Free" Methodists is that "the seats shall be forever free." Also, individual congregations must permit those "dully authorized according to the Discipline" to occupy the pulpit. Of course, there is give-and-take between the Conference and the congregation, as to who the pastor is going to be.

The 2022 "Property Assessment Information" from the Lincoln County Assessor shows the school district as "Perkins-Tryon." The legal description is "1 AC MOL 23-17-3 TR SW/C SW/4 SW/4 17-3-23-300-002" and the property location "740990 S 3390 RD."

The *Account Book* continues, "The Society of the Liberty Free Methodist Church met at the church July 2, 1946, for the purpose of voting on whether we would have a musical instrument in the church or not." "The meeting was opened by singing No 306, Are You Washed in The Blood of the Lamb. Was led in prayer by Bro. Gerald Johnson." Eleven answered roll call. "The name of James Thompson was recommended by the society as a suitable person to receive exhorters (sic) license." "Ten votes were cast. Nine (9) voted to have a musical instrument & one (1) against." Although not certain, it seems likely that before this no musical instruments had been used in services. There was no treasurer's report (ibid p. 41). The only instrument that is ever mentioned is a piano.

In the last year or so, Virginia Thompson's records have increased in length. It seems more persons were attending church, and slowly revenues increased, though probably the pastors remained bi-vocational as the funds would not have been enough to support a pastoral family. World War II has been over about a year, the men and women in service were mostly home, and the economy was improving.

The next regular board meeting was July 11, 1946, "with Bro. L. B. Van in charge." Eight members of the board answered roll call. Delbert Bales, Orpha Bales and Clausine Bales' "probation is expired" and they were "received in full connection." "James Thompson is recommended by the society as a suitable person to receive exhorters license. Motion moved and second to grant exhorters license." "Motion made & second to renew Floyd Rush exhorters license." Included in the treasurer report is "Home of Redeeming Love $3.00" (ibid p.42).

The annual society meeting "met at the church July 24, 1946." "Bro Thompson acted as chairman." "The roll was called, and eleven members present." Following this statement in the *Account Book* is a vertical list of eighteen persons with three columns to the right of the list. Each of the persons on the list shows, in each of the columns, a "P," or "A," or the column space is left blank. The first column has twelve "P," the second nine "P," the third nine "P," none of which match the recorded "eleven members present." The names are, in the original order: Charley Thompson, Beulah Thompson, Elzie Hemphill, Marvel Hemphill, Gerald Johnson, Kathileen Johnson, Hubert Rodman, Fern Rodman, Flossie Rush, Floyd Rush, Maxine Bales, James Thompson, Don Thompson, Delbert Bales, Orpha Bales, Gayla Thompson, Mrs. Swiggart (followed by a superscript "alice T."), and Virginia Thompson. It is not clear why the list is in the order it is, though roll calls usually have Charley Thompson first, and his sister-in-law Virginia Thompson (secretary) last.

Following the list is the statement: "Edah Crawford was elected tellar (sic). On first ballot Elzie Hemphill was elected delegate to annual conference. On second ballot Gerald Johnson was elected as reserve delegate to annual conf. Motion was made & second to have three stewards. Marvel Hemphill, Fern Rodman & Flossie Rush were elected stewards. On third ballot Elzie Hemphill was elected Sunday School Supt. On third ballot Gerald Johnson was elected assistant S.S. Supt. Flossie Rush, Kathileen Johnson & Marvel Hemphill were elected as nominating committee. [In the margin on the left is written "Sunday School Board"]. Moved & second to adjourn/ Virginia Thompson/ Sec" (ibid pp.43, 44).

Edah Crawford is not on the list of eighteen persons, though since she was elected teller she would regularly attend church; she could be on probation (not yet "in full connection"), or she could be attending and not be a formal member. It appears that at this time Liberty FMC had about twenty adult members either on probation or in full connection. The church has an active Sunday School, and given the various child-related positions, possibly would have had a dozen or more children. The church likely also had attendees who were not on probation or in full connection. Liberty FMC is now about eleven years old.

"The official board of the Liberty Free Methodist church met at the church Aug. 27, 1946 for the first meeting since conf./ The meeting was opened by singing 'The Blood Has never Lost Its Power.' Was led in prayer by Bro. L.B. Van. Dist. Supt." "Motion was made and second to renew the exhorters license of Elzie Hemphill." "On motion a committee of three were elected to set the Pastor's salary. Floyd Rush, Gerald Johnson & Elzie Hemphill were elected. The committee reported our goal of the pastor's salary to be $720.00. On motion the report was received." This appears to be the first time the church has provided a regular salary for the pastor. The minutes note "The legal documents of the church property are in the pastor's possession." I believe the pastor was the Rev. Charlie Thompson. "On motion it was ordered the board of trustees be instructed to investigate the matter of insuring the church property" (ibid p. 45). Both the institution of a regular salary for the pastor, and the movement to purchase insurance for the church, indicate increasing income, and probably increasing numbers of congregants.

The next society meeting was Sept. 3, 1946. "The meeting was opened by singing Love Divine & led in prayer by Hubert Rodman./ Nine members answered the roll call." Elections were held for "Secretary and Treasurer of the Sunday School"; "teacher for the Young People's class"; "Sunday School Superintendent"; "teacher of the Bible Class"; "teacher of the Juniors"; "teacher for Primary Class"; a three-member board of trustees with a chairman, and a "treasurer of the trustee board"; and "Class Leader" (ibid p. 46).

The next board met Nov. 23, 1946, "with Bro. L.B. Vanderhoffen in charge." "Eight members answered roll call." "The name of Don Thompson was given as married to Alice Andres Aug. 30, 1946." The treasurer's report shows "Conf. Claims $7.00"; "Pastor's Support $186.65"; "Dist. Supt. $13.80"; and "other money received & disbursed $208.57." The report also indicates that funds "paid out" include: "Preacher's Assistance $13.80"; "Radio Program 17.00"; "kerosene 7.80"; "S.A. Missions 11.43"; "Men & Missions 10.00"; "Recording deed 1.00"; "telephone calls .30"; and balance of $147.24." "Total taken in since Conf. $409.02" and "pd. out 261.78." "By motion the board of Trustees were ordered to put a $2000.00 insurance on the church building." "On motion the Trustee Board were authorized to contract for the insurance on their own judgment." "Plans are being made to organize a W.M.S" (ibid pp. 47-48).

Again, we see the increasing prosperity of the church. This is the largest amount of funds reported by the treasurer in the church's history. They have the funds to insure the church for $2000.00. In 2019 the insurance valuation of the church was about $160,000, the auxiliary about $50,000. The cost for insurance in 2019, $3,273 annually, is more than the original valuation of the church in 1946.

The next official board meeting is Feb. 16, 1947, "with Bro. L.B. Vanderhoofen in charge. The meeting followed the regular service, so the devotionals were omitted. The following answered roll call. [listed vertically] Charley Thompson./ Beulah Thompson/ Elzie Hemphill/ Hubert Rodman/ Flossie Rush/ Marvel Hemphill/ Kathileen Johnson/Virginia Thompson./ The sick were reported. None been received on probation. Seven been received into full connection. Six by letter & one whose probation had expired. The names of those received by letter are Mrs Alice Thompson in Dec. 1946 Mrs Nora Connelly, Mr J.D. North & Mrs Mary North on Feb 2. 1957. Mrs. Lillie Johnson Feb 2, 1947 and Clausine Bales Dec 15, 1946 by expiration of probation. Trea Report. Con Claims 10.50/ Pastor's support. 172.50/ Preachers assist 13.80/ Other money received 142.43./ Pd on ceiling $71.90/ Stove pipe supplies 3.15/ kerosene 11.93/ Pd on Christmas gift. 5.46/ Pd Evangelism McGill 50.00/ total of 142.44/ On hand at beginning of quarter 147.22/ took in since quarterly meeting $214.89/ Making total took in 362.13/ total pd out 342.54/ total in treas. $19.59/ The property has been insured for $2000.00/ A W.M.S has been organized. On motion we adjourned. Virginia Thompson/ Sec & Trea."

Kerosene appears regularly as an expense item, so perhaps the church was heated with a kerosene stove. It was also commonly used in lamps. The church was not insulated. In the twenty-first century, on very cold days (in the teens or lower) the central heat is unable to warm the building to a comfortable level. Before central heat, the church would have remained quite cold during services.

"The next official board of Liberty Free Methodist Church met May 31, 1947 at the church with Bro. L.B. Vanderhoofen in charge." "Ten members answered the roll call" but only nine are marked as "P", and two with an "A" for absent, that is, James Thompson and J.D. North. "Maxine Bales was reported as sick." "One reported died Mrs. J.D. North March 14, 1947." "Bro. Hemphill & Bro Rush exhorters license to be renewed. James Russell Thompson is recommended as suitable person to receive local preacher's license. None married or baptized." The treasurer's report follows. "Conf. Claims. $38.50/ Pastor's support. 217.50/ Dist Supt. Support 18.40/ Pledges received 40.00/ Other money received & disbursed/ Preacher's assist. 1840/ kerosene 4.04/ enamel .70/ Home of Redeeming Love 5.27/ Gen. Evangilism (sic) 10.53/ total 38.94/ total in Treas. $25.47." "Sunday School Supt. Reported some drop in average attendance. The W.M.S. Supt. Reported three meeting held. The Y.P.M.S. Supt. reported services held each Sunday evening."

The Society met July 30, 1947. "On motion the society & circuit meetings were combined. Bro. C.N. Thompson was chairman. Ten members answered the roll call. Elmer Hemphill was elected tellor (sic). On second ballot Don Thompson was elected delegate to annual conf. On first ballot Virginia Thompson was elected reserve delegate. On motion Marvel Hemphill, Fern Rodman & Kathileen Johnson were elected stewards. Virginia Thompson elected church Treasurer. Gerald Johnson elected Sunday School Supt. Marvel Hemphill, Elzie Hemphill & Hubert Rodman elected Sunday School Board. Virginia Thompson elected Supt. of Y.P.M.S. Hubert Rodman reelected member of trustee board. Marvel Hemphill elected class Leader." Virginia Thompson, Sec., signs off in her neat hand (this time in pencil).

The next Board meeting was Oct. 3, 1947, with Bro. Vanderhoofven in charge. Six out of eleven persons on the roll answered present. Ray Hudson was received on probation. Mrs. Ada Stratton was received into full connection by letter. Ray Hudson was baptized. The Treasurer's Report was given. "... on motion it was ordered that we pay our pastor on basis of $15.00 a week." "The church title is secure." "The legal documents of the church property are safe in possession of the pastor. The church property is insured." I note that pastors do not always return all the church's documents when they leave.

The *History of the Oklahoma Conference*, whose data ends with 1947, reports that in 1935 the conference had 28 active pastors and 10 inactive; it had 936 members, 30 Sunday Schools, and 1822 enrolled in Sunday School. In 1947, it had 27 active pastors and 14 inactive; it had 812 members, and 1686 enrolled in Sunday School (p. 29).

The next Board meeting was Feb. 11, 1948, with Bro. C.N. Thompson in charge. Six members answered the roll call. Ray Hudson was received into full connection. "Mrs. Mary North reported died Dec. 26, 1946. Maxine Bales married Jan. 31, 1948." The Treasurer's Report includes "Con Budget. $184.75/ Pastor's support $270.00." "Total in Treas. $107.19." Also, "The building committee reported they had enough money to make the sign board after paying for the paint. The W.M.S. President reported one box of used clothing sent to Japan. The Y.P.M.S. Supt. Reported the Y.P.M.S. meets every two weeks for Bible Study & once a month for cottage prayer meeting. They also sent three boxes of canned foods & candles to Japan."

The next Board meeting is June 4, 1948, with Bro. L.B. Vanderhoofven in charge. "The meeting followed the regular service." "Nine members answered the roll call." Elzie Hemphill and Floyd Rush had their exhorter's licenses renewed. A brief treasurer's report follows. "The Sunday School Supt. reported a small increase." "The Y.P.M.S. Supt. Reported a (B) rating for the society." I am not sure what a "B" rating refers to. Virginia Thompson signs off.

The Society meeting was July 7, 1948, "with Bro. C.N. Thompson, pastor, in charge." "The song "Take The Name of Jesus With You" was sung & the congregation was led in prayer by Bro. Elzie H. after which Bro. Thompson reads a portion of second chapter of second Tim." "Thirteen members answered the roll call." Elections were conducted. The Treasurer's Report included "conf. Budget $205.25/ Pastors – $725.00 up to including July 12./ bal in Treas. $54.94 Up to July 12./ Paid out 172.01./ 72.81 carried over./ 889.14 took in./ 725.00 pastors support."

Another Society meeting was held Sept. 8, 1948, "to hold the first society meeting since conf. Bro. A.F. Dile was in charge." "... the meeting followed the regular prayer service." Eleven answered the roll. Not surprisingly, "Virginia Thompson was elected Sec. of the Society meeting by acclamation." The offices of secretary and treasurer were divided "four voted to divide it & four against." "Kathileen Johnson was elected Sec. of the Church and Virginia Thompson was elected Treasurer." This removes, or perhaps relieves, Virginia from her long role as secretary. "It was voted to change the fund for Sunday School rooms into a fund for a parsonage. An offering is to be taken each quarter for the radio program." Once again Virginia Thompson signs off with her neat, forward slopped hand. However, the next entry is in Kathileen Johnson's hand.

At least starting in September, A.F. Dile is the new pastor. Charley Thompson was pastor in July. He has probably pastored Liberty starting 1945 and preached there many times before that. To date he has been Liberty's longest serving pastor. A.F. Dile will pastor one to two years. It will not be until 1965 that someone will again pastor Liberty more than two years (not counting superintendent A.R. Martin). Why was pastor Thompson moved from Liberty after three years, more or less? Probably because the conference needed an experienced pastor at some other church, and Liberty appeared to be stable and able to function without him. Charley Thompson will return to pastor Liberty in 1971. In all, Charlie Thompson will pastor about fourteen years, and is the longest serving pastor in Liberty's history, although Edsel Hall (1997-2009) will fill the role for about twelve years, and Harry Adams for eleven (five different times – Harry has the record for the most times served as pastor). These calculations could be off by a year or so.

Another Society meeting was held Sept. 15. "A. F. Dill was in charge of the service." "This meeting was called to elect our Sunday School teachers." Also, "It was voted & passed to pay the janitor $5.00 a month." Teachers were elected for "Young People," "Juniors," "Beginners," as well as "Sec. & Treas.," "Usher," "Librarian," "Song Leader for Sunday School," and "Song Leader for Church," "Pianist for Sunday School," and "Pianist for Church." "It was voted to pay the Pastor $20.00 a week & to bring in food." Kathleen Johnson signs off as "Secretary."

On the back of the first, not numbered page of the *Account Book,* is a list titled "Roll Call Of Liberty F.M. Church 1948." It is written in ink. It lists: Elzie Hemphill, Marvel Hemphill, Floyd Rush, Flossie Rush, Hubert Rodman, Fern Rodman, Lillie Johnson, Gerald Johnson, Kathileen Johnson, Delbert Bales, Orphia Bales, Ada Stratton (followed by, in pencil, "given letter 53"), Virginia Thompson, Donald Thompson, Alice Thompson, Maxine Rodman, Ray Hudson (followed by, in pencil, "dropped 52"), Betty Thompson (followed by "Hudson" written in a different hand) followed by, in pencil, "given letter 52", Gayla Thompson (followed by "Green" written in pencil, then "given letter"), T.D. North, Mrs. Nora Connelly, Mrs. Anna Swiggart (crossed out and followed by "Deceased"), Elmer Hemphill (followed by, in pencil, "dropped 52"), Norma Rush, Pauline Rodman, Beulah Thompson (followed by "transferred removed by letter") then written in a different hand, Edah Crawford, Sarah Jane Grover (followed by, in pencil, "removed without letter"), Marjorie Dill (followed by, in pencil, "removed by Letter") and Minnie Heginbotham. Beulah Thompson was Charlie Thompson's wife. Presumably she moved to the church where her husband had been transferred.

The next Board meeting was Jan. 5, 1949. The minutes are in dark blue ink. "A.F. Dill was in charge of the service." Eleven members answered present. Harvey and Erma Brixey were received on probation. Anna B. Swiggart died Dec. 14, 1948. For the Treasurer's Report, the balance left in the account was $40.61. "Money took in since Oct. 31, $236.99." "Money pd. Out $267.83." "Motion was made to sign up for electricity for the church. Motion was recorded." "Motion was made to adjourn." Kathleen Johnson signs off.

Next in the *Account Book,* a short entry is made in pencil as follows: "Feb 1, 1949/ Motion was made & seconded that $40.00 be took out of the parsonage fund to pay off propane note. Kathleen Johnson Sec." Apparently, the church is now using propane for heat, etc.

The Society next met July 12, 1949. "A.F. Dill had charge of the service. Hymns no. 85 & 77 were sang (sic). Scripture lesson was read by Marvel Hemphill __ Gal. 5 & prayer was held around the altar. 11 members answered the roll call." The various elections were conducted. "Elzie Hemphill was elected church treasurer." Adjournment was recorded but the secretary did not sign her name. However, the hand is Kathleen Johnson's.

Summary of the 1940's

As Liberty FMC enters the 1950's, the Society has a church building and an active congregation. The building does not yet have electricity but it will soon. The church members are engaged and often wear multiple hats. Church membership has grown noticeably since the late 1930's. A 1948 "roll call" of the church in the *Account Book* lists thirty names, twenty-one of which are women. Tithing, and probably donations, have increased slowly but surely. Even so, the church's finances are limited, and the church depends on volunteers and a few paid staff, such as the pastors and janitors, who are willing to serve for minimum remuneration. It has a Sunday School program with multiple classes and teachers. It remembers the sick. It has a focus on missions, including over-seas missions and, after the war, particularly Japan. It appears to have a strong, regular connection to the conference, but it is obviously a self-sufficient church that does not depend much on others. It has membership requirements, and appears to abide by them, and is at least somewhat strict as to who is admitted to full fellowship. It baptizes occasionally. Several church members are privileged as "exhorters." The congregants are resilient, self-sufficient, generally without much cash although there might have been exceptions. Many are related to each other by family or marriage. They seem to depend heavily on each other and are faithful to each other and to the gospel that they preach.

The minutes in the *Account Book* tend to be technical. We cannot know much about the church's involvement in the community or nation, or the trials and tribulations it faced in getting the church started and keeping it going, or the trials and tribulations of individual members. Nor can we know much about the personalities involved. The minutes are not very imaginative, so perhaps the members are not either (at least the minute-takers). Also, interestingly, there is almost nothing about theology or dogma. Nor is there any indication of church "troubles" (such as Paul addressed in his letters to the Corinthians). Also, interestingly, there is almost no direct evidence of the great events in the outside world, such as the depression, the rise of Nazi Germany, the attack on Pearl Harbor and the beginning of World War II, the dropping of the atomic bomb, the end of World War II, nor of American national events, such as the election of presidents, the death of Franklin Roosevelt, and so on.

The *History of the Oklahoma Conference,* published in 1949, says that in the 1940's, "with the coming of the demand for war workers and the taking of the young men into the armed services there was a decided drop in Sunday school enrollment and a gradual loss in church membership. This membership reached a low of 812 in 1947" (p.19). "All the losses of this period cannot, however, be attributed to natural causes." Among the causes delineated are, a wayward minister who had transferred from another denomination who had "a critical and divisive spirit and caused serious divisions and losses on the circuit which he served before withdrawing from the church under charges of insubordination and misrepresentation." Also, "two of the outstanding leaders of the conference, L.E. Cook and R.H. Shoup, transferred to another conference. This left more places to be filled by inexperienced men ..." (p.19). The *History* adds, "Most of these new additions to the ministry were young men without previous experience or specialized training" (p.20). This latter statement probably gives some insight into Liberty's problems getting and keeping a pastor, and why the Superintendents figure prominently in church minutes. If an unusually good pastor would have been at Liberty, he (or she) probably would have been placed in a larger church, which is what appears to happen to Charley Thompson. He was a home-grown pastor who, by all accounts of the current memories of Liberty members, as well as the evidence of church growth, became an excellent pastor, and he was soon transferred to other churches. Walter Nelson, writing in a 1949 postscript in the *History*, says that one serious problem of the conference churches is "the general complaint of laymen that many of the pastors neither give full time to their work nor approach their work in a professional manner" (p.33). The reason for this, he thinks, are "inadequate pastor's salaries" (ibid).

The conference made various efforts at increasing over-all church membership. It concluded that "successful evangelism is more in a consistent year around program than in the special programs over a shorter period of time. As a result the conference has been giving more attention to the needs of the local churches. One of the evident weaknesses has been the inadequacy of the financial support for many of the preachers. Consequently, in 1941 the conference adopted a plan for increasing support for both pastors on the weaker circuits and the district superintendents. The amount guaranteed for pastors was increased from $500 to $720 annually during the next three years and in 1947 the salaries of the superintendents were increased to $1,800 annually. (62) These amounts are still inadequate but do indicate a hopeful trend in the conference" (p.21). The *History* also notes that "The enrollment in the church schools has, since 1923, averaged about 200 per cent of the church membership" (p.22).

The conference tried re-redistricting the churches to improve "evangelism." It had some success and some failures. One challenge was to "conserve the time of the superintendents, who are required by the General Church to hold four district conferences each year in each of the districts under their supervision" (p.23). Another "perplexing problem" was "the unsystematic methods of collecting funds for superintendent's salaries, annual conference missions, expenses on the camp ground and for evangelism" (p.23). The Liberty minutes record regular donations for superintendents, missions, the campground, and evangelism. It is accurate to call those donations "unsystematic," and they often were small amounts.

A solution the conference devised was to combine all the assessments and to apportion them "on the basis of $12.25 per member" (p.23). One would suspect that such a move, while no doubt facilitating the budgeting process, would not be conducive to increasing the number of churches "members." This might be a reason someone would want to retract their official membership, and yet continue attending church, as happened at Liberty. In fact, in a postscript, the *History* notes "The Oklahoma Conference concluded its forty-ninth year with a net loss of sixty-one members. (80) This was due largely to the dropping of the names of non-participating, non-resident members because of the heavy per capita assessments of the conference budget" (p.32).

The *History* notes, regarding its first fifty years in Oklahoma, "that the church has failed to advance in membership as it should is a fact beyond question. The leading factors given by ministers of the conference who have been full members in active service for ten years or more are (78) changes in economic conditions causing an adverse migration; failure to change methods as social conditions change; breakdown of positive preaching of the doctrine and standards of the church together with too much of an untactful, negative emphasis, which resulted in a heavy loss of young people from Free Methodist homes; laxness of public morals after the first world war; dependence on professional evangelists rather than the pastors in the evangelistic programs, and, migration of conference leaders" (p.25).

I think it is worthwhile to quote at length the plan the *History* proposes for growing the church, for the plan still seems a sound one today, over seventy years later. "The plan which worked so well when Oklahoma was a frontier country is not producing desired results at the present time. This plan was built around mass revivalism, but it does not work well when the chief problem is to get persons to attend church. No church can grow successfully without reaching the unchurched people of the community. The church must, therefore, place its emphasis on a year round program of personal contact that enlists the laymen as witnesses of the messages of the church, rather than on a ten day meeting with a professional evangelist. In addition, the church must provide social activities, especially for the youthful members of its congregation or lose them to secular life altogether. The program of contact must, then, be followed with a positive and optimistic preaching of the doctrines and ethical standards of the church, rather than a negative and pessimistic preaching, for the latter, too often, is misinforming and alienation instead of indoctrinating and confirming in its effect" (p.25).

Liberty, and other churches in the conference, today continue to have a problem "to get persons to attend church." Liberty's last Easter service, like most of its Christmas and Easter services, was standing room only (90 to 100 persons including children). However, most Sundays (after the covid pandemic) about a dozen or fifteen people are present, the same ones who show every Sunday. It is true that this number is half of what it was before the covid pandemic of 2020, and the pandemic is on-going though now in the "endemic" stage. Nonetheless, the problem remains how to "to get persons to attend church" on a regular basis.

The *History* adds, "The laymen are loyal and believe in the church and are willing to give liberally of their finances to promote its program. In spite of losses in membership the finances of the church have made a continuous increase except for the temporary reverses of the depression. The annual per capita giving of the conference members reached an all time high of $63.41 for 1947. In addition the investment in property amounts to $166,050. These figures are a tribute to the loyalty and earnestness of the laymen" (p.25-26).

There is no church without lay people. Not unusually lay people can manage without an ordained leader. They can manage with little money and a temporary place of worship (like Sandyland School). Liberty was started by a lay couple. It would be interesting to know whether more churches have been started by official leaders or lay people. My guess is the latter. Another interesting question is whether more corruption in a church has crept in through leadership or laity. All leaders of course were once lay, and I am not saying that leadership is not important. Jesus clearly says that the flock needs a shepherd. I am an ordained minister. The history of Liberty shows that its lay men and women were undoubtedly loyal and earnest in their commitment to the gospel of Jesus Christ, their particular church and the members thereof, and missions. The history also shows that they could persevere without an official pastor. They were an exceptional people, but so are their countless peers in countless small churches going back 2,000 years.

The 1950's

The next entry in the *Account Book* is for June 28, 1950, "for an official board meeting." "W.E. Heginbothum was in charge of services." We will meet him again, with his name spelled in various ways. He is the new pastor after A.F. Dile. "Our scripture lesson was brought from St. John 1:1-18." "Kathleen Johnson was elected secretary." "11 answered the roll" but the names were not recorded. Various elections were conducted, including "Elzie Hemphile was elected Treasurer" and "Flossie Rush was elected auditor." "None were reported sick." "Status of membership reported good." "To anyones (sic) knowledge, there has been no violations of church rules." An increase was reported in youth Sunday School. Under "Treasurer's Report" there are eight blank lines, i.e., no report was recorded. Kathleen Johnson signs off. Also recorded is "Minnie Heginbotham was received by letter into full connection." Mrs., Sister, or "Minnie" Heginbotham (as she may be called) will be an important member of the church and will eventually make a key contribution to its survival, as will be noted later.

"The members of the Liberty Free Methodist Church met for a circuit meeting March 14, 1951. Rev. W.E. Heginbothom was in charge of the service." They sang hymns 135 and 188, and the scripture lesson was Second Timothy chapter two. Six members answered the roll call. Elections were conducted. "Wiley Springer was baptized." "The treasurer reported that the conf. Claims are 40% paid ...." "Motion was made & approved that the janitor's offering be taken out of the Sunday School treasury once every month. $5.08 was set as satisfactory." "Superintendent reported that there could be more interest in the S.S. Work but attendance fair under circumstance." They adjourned and Kathleen Johnson signed off.

The next board meeting was April 3, 1951. "Rev. Heginbothom was in charge of the service." "Kathleen Johnson was elected secretary." Elections were conducted. Funds received were $1,000.67. "Donald Thompson & Elzie

Hemphill were appointed as a committee for wiring the church house for electricity." Did Elzie help wire the church? Electricity has finally come to rural Lincoln County and plumbing is to follow soon. "Sunday School Supt. Reported a drop in attendance due to bad weather." The terms of the board of trustees were listed, Donald Thompson three years; Hubert Rodman two years; and Elzie Hemphill one year. "Circuit meeting was held jointly with the Official Board meeting." Elections were conducted and the meeting adjourned (without the secretary's signature).

On page 152 of the *Account Book* is an entry titled "Official Board Roll 1950-51." It lists W.E. Heginbothum, Elzie Hemphill, Marvel Hemphill, Gerald Johnson, Flossie Rush, Lillie Johnson, Kathleen Johnson, Floyd Rush, and Hubert Rodman.

On May 29, 1952, a Society meeting was held, with Rev. B.L. Wayman in charge of the service. Rev. Byron Wayman became Liberty pastor sometime after April 1951. "Our songs were numbers 44, 125, 444, selected from the Light & Life hymnal – Songs of the Living Faith. Our scripture lesson was from the book of Luke. We all met for prayer around the altar." "We have met for the purpose of discussing the erection of a parsonage. A building has been bought for the sum of $200. Which will be used in the construction of said building plans have been drawn up, have been discussed and approved. Construction will begin as soon as funds are available." "C.N. Thompson & B.L. Wayman have been elected as a canvassing committee. The following we're (sic) elected as a building advisory – [unreadable] Johnson, Ira Crawford, Gerald Johnson, Donald Thompson, Harvey Brixey, Raymond Farnsworth, & Will Kelty." "Will" (for Kelty) was written in pencil and lightly underlined, the rest is in dark blue ink. C.N. Thompson of course was a previous pastor. Is he still helping out at Liberty while pastoring another church? "Harvey Brixey was elected as treasurer of building funds. Motion was made & seconded we be adjourned." Kathleen Johnson signed off. The minutes are not clear, but the memory of church members in 2020 is that the parsonage was a building purchased and moved into place. Probably the reference to building funds is to convert the building to a parsonage. Later the parsonage is converted to an auxiliary building. In 2022 it is primarily used for Sunday School and for meals.

The next Circuit meeting is July 31, 1952. "Scripture – Matt 7-7-12. Led in prayer by Floyd Rush & Alice J. Song – Leaning On The Everlasting Arms." Following are elections for treasurer, auditor, Sunday School Super, Nominating Committee, Trustees, and Budget committee. Below this is drawn three lines, then the following is a complete transcription of the rest of the minutes:

"Myron Rush & Clarence Hemphill we're (sic) elected tellers."

"Marvel Hemphill was elected Class leader on second ballot."

"Virginia Thompson was elected Treasurer." After several years, she returns to elected office.

"Don Thompson was elected asst. S.S. Supt."

"By unanimous vote Lillie Johnson was elected SS. Sect & Treas."

"[unreadable] Heginbothom was elected Bible Teacher. (Mazzie Kelty asst. Teacher)."

"Marvel Hemphill was elected young people teacher."

"(Virginia Thompson asst Teacher)."

"Kathleen Johnson was elected Junior Class T."

"Orpha Bales was elected primary class T."

"Alice Thompson was elected beginners Class T."

"Lillie Johnson, Alice Thomson & Maggie Kelty were elected Stewards."

"Don Thompson, Gerald Johnson we're (sic) elected as pulpit Comm."

"It was noted to pay the pastor $20.00 a week when present & $10.00 a week while holding revival meetings."

"It was noted to have a spring revival [there probably should be a period here] Rev. C.V. McCully is to hold an evangelistic campaign in Nov."

Apparently, C.V. McCully is the pastor. The minutes end at this point, without an indication of adjournment or the secretary's signature.

On page 152 of the *Account Book* is an entry for "Official Board Roll" for "1951-52." It lists Elzie Hemphill, Alice Thompson, Kathleen Johnson, Lillie Johnson, Don Thompson, Edah Crawford, Marvel Hemphill, and Hubert Rodman.

A short meeting was held March 18, 1953. The minutes do not indicate what kind of meeting it was. The meeting followed the regular service. A complete transcript of the rest of the minutes are as follows.

"On motion Gerald Johnson was unanimously elected as member of board of Trustee to fill Hubert Rodmans place."

"Treasurer report was given & approved.

    Money rec. $775.81

    Money dispersed $737.26

      bal in Treas $38.25"

"Treasurer was informed to have parsonage insured."

There is no record of adjournment or secretary's signature. It is possible, perhaps likely, that the parsonage has been completed or near to it, given that they ask the treasurer, Virginia Thompson, to insure it. Probably C.V. McCully is still pastor.

A "circuit-society meeting" was held July 29, 1953. "Bertha McCully was in charge of the service." "Rev. W.E. Heginbotham led in prayer. Scripture Lesson was found in Psalm 122." Various elections are noted. Three stewards were elected for the year. "Pastor recommended that Hubert Rodman, Fern Rodman & Pauline Rodman be removed from the Church records." "Artie Grimm & Johnny May Grimm we're received by letter July 26, 1953." "Motion was made & recorded we adjourn. Kathleen Johnson." Probably sometime in 1953 C.V. McCully leaves his post as pastor. W.E. Heginbotham (spelled various ways) has previously been pastor (1950-51). Possibly he is now temporarily filling the pulpit while Liberty and the superintendent (who was, once again, A.R. Martin 1953-54) search for a new pastor.

"The Liberty Society of the Free Methodist Church, Perkins, Okla. met at the Church Wed Evening Aug. 26, 1953 at 8-P.M. A.R. Martin presiding." A.R. Martin, conference superintendent, has presided over Liberty affairs during at least two previous terms, 1938-39 and 1943-45. Various officers were elected, including assistant superintendent, adult teacher, young people teacher, junior teacher, primary teacher, beginners' teacher, temperance superintendent, secretary, song leader, flower committee, finance committee (three persons), "on motion Virginia Thompson was elected janitor, & that she be paid $4.00 per month," building committee, and "Virginia Thompson was elected as church Treasurer for new year."

The Church Board met Oct. 10, 1953, with A.R. Martin presiding. "Three members were present. Don Thompson, Virginia Thompson, and Minnnie Hegginbotham." "Pastor requested privalige (sic) of holding two meetings during year. This was granted. The pastor offered to hold the first revival. It was accepted." It is not clear who the pastor was. The most obvious candidate is W.E. Heginbotham.

On page 152 of the *Account Book* is an entry for "Official Board" for "52-53" (this list follows others on the same page for 1950-51 and 1951-52). It lists Virginia Thompson, Kathleen Johnson, Don Thompson, Gerald Johnson, Hite Johnson, Lillie Johnson, Mrs. Kelty and Alice Thompson.

"The official board met Jan. 9, 1954 at 2:30 p.m. at the Liberty Free Meth Church with Rev. A.R. Martin presiding. After a devotional period, scripture and prayer the meeting was called to order. Four answered the call. Virginia T., M. Hegginbotham [no comma] Don and Alice T." New trustees were elected, and the treasurer's report was given by Virginia.

A combined Society and Board meeting was held June 9, 1954, with Bro. A.R. Martin presiding. Answering the call were Delbert and Orpha Bales, Don and Alice Thompson, Sis Heginbotham, and Virginia Thompson. Various elections were held with some occupying several offices. It took five ballots to elect Virginia Thompson as reserve delegate to the conference. Election of the finance committee was moved until after conference.

A Society and Circuit meeting was held Sept. 3, 1954. "Singing was omitted." Answering the call were Don Thompson, Virginia Thompson, Alice T. and Johnnie Mae Grimm. Various officers and positions were elected. It is not clear who was pastoring at this time. It was probably W.E. Heginbotham or Joseph Simpson.

The board met Sept. 9, 1954. "Redeemed" was sung, and Rev. Joseph Simpson, the new pastor, read scripture. Three answered the roll call: V. Thompson, Don Thompson, and Alice Thompson. "By acclamation Alice T. was elected as Sec of the official board." The treasurer's report indicates the year was begun with $60.78 and $94.53 was on hand. Various elections were made, including "librarian." "Class and School literature was discussed and plans for new material discussed." Meeting was adjourned. This is on page 79 of the *Account Book*.

On page 153 is a typed sheet attached to the page with a sewing pin and written in barely legible pencil at the top is "Roll for 53-54" (on the previous page were rolls for 50-51, 51-52 and 52-53). Twelve persons are listed, from

Tryon unless indicated otherwise: Mrs. Lillie Johnson, Don Thompson, Alice Thompson, Elsie Hemphill of Tulsa, Marvel Hemphill of Tulsa, Delbert Bales of Perkins, Orpha Bales of Perkins, Will Kelty, Mrs. Will Kelty, Mrs. Virginia Thompson, Floyd Rush, Flossie Rush, Norma Rush, Mrs. Ira Crawford of Perkins, Gerald Johnson, Kathleen Johnson, Nora Connelly of Wellston, T.D. North of Meeker, Mrs. W.E. Heginbotham of Carney, Artie Grimm of Perkins and Johny (sic) Mae Grimm of Perkins. Immediately below are "Probationers": John Wiley of Perkins which appears to have been crossed out, and "Wiley Springer" penciled in, then Clarence Hemphill of Tulsa, and written by hand "Bro Wayne Lawton June 1957." I presume that Wayne Lawton, who was pastor 1956-58, compiled these lists from documents he had in 1957, and wrote them in the *Account Book*.

On the wall in a back room of Liberty is a plaque that reads "Christian Life Magazine awards" for an "International Sunday School Attendance Contest October 10—November 14, 1954." "Liberty Free Methodist Church/ Tryon, Oklahoma/ FOR ACHIEVEMENT IN INCREASING ATTENDANCE AND EMPHASIZING THE MINISTRY OF THE SUNDAY SCHOOL IN LEADING MEN AND WOMEN, BOYS AND GIRLS TO PUT THEIR FAITH IN CHRIST." Liberty was given "Honorable Mention, class F."

The next entry is for a circuit and Society meeting July 13, 1955. "The 146 Psalm was read by Bro. Simpson and several led in prayer." "Seven answered roll call – Eda Crawford – Johnnie Mae Grimm – Mrs. Hegginbotham – Lillie Johnson Don Thompson – Virginia Thompson and Alice Thompson." The treasurer reported "Took in 1264.58" and "Pd. Out 1221.77" with "Balance $42.81 in Treas." Various elections were made. "On motion we adjourned." This is at the bottom of page 81.

At the top of p. 82, "The official Board of the Liberty Church met July 13, 1955, in connection with prayer meeting & Soc. & Cir. Meeting. Devotions were omitted." "Four answered roll call. Lillie Johnson Minnie Hegginbotham, Virginia Thompson [no comma] Don T." "Norma Rush was dropped from membership on her own request since moving to another state. Sis. Simpson was received by letter." The treasurer's report shows "Raised 1264.58" and "Pd. Out 1221.77 Balance 42.81 in treas." "Church property is insured." "On motion we adjourned."

The first meeting on this date was for the "circuit and Society" meeting, while the second was for the "official Board" meeting. There are redundancies between both meetings.

Among Liberty's records is an insurance policy from "The Church and Parsonage Aid Society of The Free Methodist Church of North American" with "Executive Offices" at Winona Lake, Indiana. The policy is for April 23, 1955, to April 23, 1956. The policy pays out a maximum of $2,000, and the cost of the policy to the church appears to be $16.08. An existing receipt dated April 26, 1955, for $16.08, for the "Church and Parsonage Aid Society" is "Received of Mrs. Virginia Thompson" of "Tryon, Oklahoma." It is signed by G.E. Vincent.

A Society meeting was held Aug. 17, 1955. Rev. J.T. Simpson (the pastor) presiding. Eda Crawford, Virginia Thompson, Don and Alice Thompson, Johnnie Mae Grimm, Mrs. Heginbotham and Lela Simpson answered the call. Various elections were held. "On the fourth ballot W.E. Hegginbotham was elected treasurer. By acclamation Sis. Lela Simpson was elected auditor." "On motion it was ordered that the parsonage fund treas. be eliminated and that all such monies be channelled (sic) thru the reg. Treas." Motion to adjourn.

The next Circuit and Society meeting was Aug. 24, 1955. Rev. J.T. Simpson presided. Five answered roll call. "On motion it was ordered we divide the offices of SS. Sec. & Teas." Various elections were made. "On motion it was ordered we have class meeting the 1st Wed. nite (sic) of each month." "... elected chorister & pianist for church worship services: Johnnie Grimm & Virginia T." The Sunday School Board "held a short meeting following the Soc. Meeting ...." Among other business, "On motion it was ordered we have Temperance Sunday once a quarter." "...ordered we instruct the treas. To buy a birthday bank & gifts for children in S.S." Motion to adjourn.

The next Society meeting was recorded in the *Account Book* as April 21, 1955, 8 p.m. – but "1955" is an error and the year is 1956 because the statement is made that "Flossie Rush passed away April 8th. 1956." Flossie was one of the four charter members of Liberty. The Society meeting was held "on the camp ground near Perkins, Okla with Rev. L.B. Vanderhoofen presiding." Answering the roll was Delbert and Orpha Bales and Lela Simpson. The treasurer's report showed: pastor's support $700; Parsonage $6.56; Conference budget $100.00; Flowers $6.04; Butane $43.00; Easter offering $3.28; Lights $12.00; Postage .66; Insurance $16.22. Collected was $943.61 and paid out was $942.44. Bro.

Vanderhoofven "spoke words of counsel & encouragement to those present." Motion to adjourn, "secretary pro tem Lela Simpson."

A Circuit and Society meeting was held Wednesday night, June 13, 1956. Four answered the roll call: Minnie Heginbotham, Lela Simpson, Alice Thompson and Edah Crawford. Various elections were held, Virginia Thompson's name does not appear. Meeting adjourned, the secretary signing was Alice Thompson.

Among Liberty's records is an insurance policy from "The Church and Parsonage Aid Society of The Free Methodist Church of North American." The date of the policy is from July 2, 1956, to June 25, 1959. The maximum value of the policy is $2,000, and the cost of the policy to the church appears to be $41.80, made in two installments. A receipt from "Winonna Lake, Ind" dated June 29, 1956, "No. 7206," is "Received of W.E. Heginbotham c/o Rev. Jos. T. Simpson Rt 1 Tryon, Oklahoma." The amount is shown as $16.08 followed by "Church and Parsonage Aid Society." It is signed by S. Vysacke.

W.E. Heginbotham (probably the correct spelling since it is his receipt) has shown up occasionally in the minutes in the last several years. Minnie Heginbotham has more often, who is probably his wife. Here is a clear example of someone who does not always show up in the minutes, but who probably comes to church regularly and is indeed a key member. Furthermore, he has previously filled the pulpit, and I have included him in the list of pastors. And he will pastor again 1962-63. He was replaced as pastor in 1954 by Joseph Simpson, and yet he seems to still be attending the church, since in July 1956 he signs a receipt for insurance on behalf of pastor Simpson. The answer to this conundrum, I think, is that W.E. Heginbotham is a home-grown pastor. He stepped up to fill the pulpit when the church was having difficulty finding someone to do so. When an acceptable pastor was found, he steps back into the laity. But he is ready to step forward again, as needed. He may or may not be ordained. My guess is that he is not. My assumption is that the willingness of someone local to the congregation to become interim pastor or at least preach has repeated itself many times in Liberty's history, as it has in the history of many such small churches.

An official board meeting was held Aug. 1, 1956. Devotions were led by Bro. Simpson, the pastor (sometimes referred to as "Rev" and sometimes "Bro"). Five answered the roll call. "By personal request Johnnie Mae & Artie Grimm were dropped from the roll." "Dismissed by Alice Thompson, sec."

The next Society and Board meeting was August 20, 1956 "with the appointed pastor, Wayne Lawton presiding." Sung were "Jesus Plant & Root in Me," and verses 4—8 of 1 Cor 13 were read "and testimonies were given by each member present." "Four members answered to roll call: Eda Crawford, Minnie Hegginbotham, Lillie Johnson & Lela Simpson. "The nominating committee presented its slate of electors, which was accepted." "First Sunday of each month is Peney (sic) a Day." "One dollar per week has been allotted to the janitor fund and may be raised by special offering or other-wise taken from S.S. Offering." Lela Simpson signs as acting secretary. I note that these minutes consisted of about a page and a quarter of medium to large script, with a treasurer's report approximately five inches by seven inches attached by a sewing pin to the page. On August 1, the pastor had been Joseph T. Simpson (*Oklahoma In Action* shows him as pastor 1954-1956). On August 20, 1956, a new pastor has been appointed, Wayne Lawton, who *Oklahoma In Action* shows as pastor to 1958.

The next entry in the *Account Book* (p. 90-93), for "an official board meeting July 31, 1957 at 8:00 p.m.," is four pages of fairly small script. It has considerably more detail than previous minutes and follows a carefully arranged numerical scheme. "Bro. Wayne Lawton who was in charge offered prayer after which Lillie Johnson was elected secretary." Presumably the minutes are in her hand (she did not sign off at the end). Eleven persons were listed as on the roll: Delbert Bales; Orpha Bales; Nora Connelly; Edah [this time spelled with an h] Crawford; Minnie Hegenbotham; Lillie Johnson; T.D. North; Floyd Rush; Alice Thompson; Don Thompson, and Virginia Thompson. All were absent except Edah, Minnie and Lillie.

The minutes for the July 31, 1957, Society and Board meeting have agenda items numbered. There are seventeen agenda items for the Society meeting, and nine for the board meeting, with numerous sub-categories in both. Some examples follow. "(5) Edah Crawford was elected Treasurer for the coming year." "(6) To audit the books, Ira Crawford and Amos Sadler were elected." Note that neither of these apparently are full members of Liberty, although the treasurer Edah Crawford is. "(7) Sister Heginbotham is chairman of the committee on charities." "(8) 2. b. There were no converts reported." "(8) 2. f. Don & Alice Thompson transferred to McPherson KS. Lela Simpson transferred to Geary,

Okla." "(8)3. There are none violating our rules as far as we know." "8). 6. Wayne Lawton was recommended at the last Quarterly Conference by the Conf. Supt. & therefore needs no recommendation at this time from the society for Local Preach." I assume this means that Wayne Lawton is not ordained and only has a license to preach "locally," that is, probably in his home church (see also below), or he might have a conference license. "(8) 7. Floyd Rush was united in holy matrimony to Miss Irva Wickman." Floyd Rush (and his previous wife Flossie) was one of the charter members in 1937. "(8) 8. W.E. Heginbotham submitted the following report …." This is the finance report which I will summarize as follows. The Conference assessment is $175 and $72 was raised so far. The Pastor's salary is $638.90. "Received during the year" were "local expenses $30; Flowers and Gifts $41.54; Parsonage Debt $130.55; Sunday School $72.82; Missions $41.34; Benevolences $18.20; Parsonage Rent $240.00; Pastor's Other Income $100.00." Total money raised was $1,381.83.

Agenda 10. a. states "Committee on charities reported 75 garments distributed." "11. New Business-- On motion it was decided that we would donate the old communion set to Light & Life Mission in Oklahoma City." "12. Reports. a. Bro. Heginbotham reported for the S.S. Our average fell below the previous year but there is still interest in the S.S." "14. The title of the church property is secure." "15. The legal documents for the society are kept in the conference safe at Stillwater, Okla. The official records are being kept and are in the hands of the pastor." "16. The church property is insured." "17. The advices (sic) regarding vocal music are not being particularly observed and it was suggested that in the coming year we organize a singing school to teach the songs in 'Hymns of the Living Faith'." The final entry for this date is "We adjourned!" It must have been a long meeting.

As mentioned above, item six on the agenda states "Wayne Lawton was recommended at the last Quarterly conference by the conf supt & therefore needs no recommendation at this time from the society for Local Preach." He is the pastor of Liberty. Normally the first step in seeking ordination is to be given an "exhorter's license" by the local church, which allows the candidate to preach in his or her church. The next step is to obtain a "Local License," through the conference, which typically allows preaching in conference venues. The last step is ordination. Typically, years pass between each step. In a young conference or one with challenges, exceptions can be made. The conference at this time apparently suffered from a lack of candidates for pastor, no doubt partly because most churches were poor and could not afford to pay a living wage. Apparently, Liberty had difficulty in procuring a pastor (I note that "Bro. Heginbotham" – who is recorded as "W.E. Heginbotham" in the August 28, 1957 minutes, elected as "Librarian" – is one of the previous pastors), and Brother Lawton was advanced through the process by the conference superintendent, as probably W.E. Heginbotham was before him. *Oklahoma In Action* records that Wayne Lawton was pastor 1956 to 1958. The minutes in the *Account Book* show that Lawton's first Sunday of service was August 30, 1956.

When Liberty Church was organized in 1937, the "full members" were listed as Floyd Rush, Flossie Rush, Beulah Thompson, Virginia Thompson, and "Mrs. Lucia M. Eikermann presented her letter from Wisby society." Twenty years later in 1957, of the eleven members on the roll, only Floyd Rush and Virginia Thompson remain of the chartering group. However, Beulah will return again, with her husband Charlie.

The next Society meeting was August 28, 1957. "Wayne Lawton read Psalm 66; 14-19 and Lillie Johnson led in prayer." Answering the roll were Edah Crawford, Minnie Heginbotham, Lillie Johnson, and Wayne Lawton. "It was decided that instead of a nominating committee we would just nominate from the floor and then vote following the nomination for the Sunday School offices." Elected were secretary Wayne Lawton [it is unusual but not unheard of for the pastor to be secretary], assistant secretary Bertha Brake, treasurer Lillie Johnson, librarian W.E. Heginbotham [a previous and future pastor], Cradle (?) Roll Supt., Nora Sadler, Home Dept. Supt., also Wayne Lawton, Temperance Supt., W.E. Heginbotham, Penny-a-day Supt., Orpha Bales, teachers for Bible Class, W.E. Heginbotham, Youth Class, Wayne Lawton, Junior Class, Orpha Bales, Junior Class Asst., Lillie Johnson, Primary Class, Edah Crawford, Primary Class Asst., Nora Sadler, Beginners Class, Minnie Heginbotham, and Beginners Class Asst., Mrs. Harley Holman." Following was adjournment. These minutes are written in blue ink, in the same small, neat hand of pp.90-94, and fill p. 94 of the *Account Book*. They might be by the pastor Wayne Lawton who is listed as secretary.

Somewhat unexpectedly, this is the last entry until 1962. It is ironic, or perhaps portentous, that the last two sets of minutes before a four-year hiatus are among the most organized, detailed, and lengthy of the minutes to date.

In Liberty's records is a set of six loose-leaf pages (faded white, yellow, or blue), stapled together and held with a sewing pin, about 8.5x11 inches (but with an inch or so on both margins in rough shape). The pages are not in chronological order. The fifth page is a letter of transfer, on letterhead, titled "Free Methodist Church/ "The Church of the Light and Life Hour"/ Oklahoma Conference/ Church Address/ N.W. 13Th & Kentucky/Phone Jackson 5-3877." Below to the left is "H. Harold Helser, Minister/ Parsonage 4312 N.W. 44th", and to the right "Parsonage Phone/ Windsor 2-5103." It is dated November 18, 1958. It reads, "Mr. Kennison Lawton, the bearer, wishing to remove from this society, we hereby certify that he is an acceptable member of the Free Methodist Church in Oklahoma City, Oklahoma, and cordially commend him to the Free Methodist Church in Liberty Oklahoma, or in any other place. When admitted to another society his membership in this society shall cease. This certificate is good for one year only, unless renewed." It is signed by H. Harold Helsel, Pastor. The last piece of paper is the same letter head as immediately above, and is for Mrs. Audrey Lawton, and reads like the previous letter, except it adds "Mrs. Lawton holds an annual Deaconess license in the Oklahoma City Free Methodist Church." It is again signed by H. Harold Helsel, pastor. According to *Oklahoma In Action*, Kennison Lawton was pastor of Liberty 1959-1960. It seems likely he is related to the previous pastor, Wayne Lawton (pastor 1956-58). He, and presumably his wife, are transferring to Liberty. Whether he is transferring to be the pastor, is not clear. There seems to be a gap between when Wayne Lawton left, and when Kennison Lawton becomes pastor, but this is not certain.

From August 1957 until August 22, 1962, except for a "roll call for 1961 -1962," and the loose pages mentioned above, there are no significant records that I know of. The "Celebrating 80 Years" pamphlet shows 1958 as "under the Superintendent"; the 1959 pastor as Kennison Lawton; and 1960 to 1964 as "under the Superintendent." *Oklahoma In Action* records Kenniston Lawton as pastor 1959-1960; no pastor for 1961 to 1963 (presumably then under a conference superintendent); and T.F. King pastor 1964-1968. See below for what the minutes say about pastors starting August 1962. The August 1962 "official board meeting" was held at the home of W.E. "Hegibothan" (another unique spelling) who also "conducted" the devotional. He was a long-time member of the church who served as pastor previously.

In Liberty's loose records is a copy of a letter from the Internal Revenue Service, Department of the Treasury, P.O. Box 2508, Cincinnati, OH 45201, to "FREE METHODIST CHURCH OF NORTH/ PO BOX 535002/ INDIANAPOLIS IN

46253-5002" dated January 22, 2007. Among other things the letter states "In June 1958 we issued a determination letter that recognized your organization as exempt from federal income tax. Our records indicate that your organization is currently exempt under section 501(c)(3) of the Internal Revenue Code and is not a private foundation within the meaning of 509(a) of the Code because it is described in section s 509(a)(1) and 170(b)(1)(A)(1)." This letter of course is not to Liberty per se, but the Free Methodist Church as a whole. It does indicate that Liberty is recognized as a 501(c)(3) not-for-profit corporation and that contributions to it are therefore tax deductible.

Summary of the 1950's

A lot happened at Liberty FMC during the 1950's, good and bad. Electricity and presumably plumbing were added to the church. A parsonage was added. Church and parsonage were insured. The evangelistic commitment continued, as well as commitment to Sunday School. During the early to mid-1950's the church seemed to have grown and been preparing for further growth. The 1948 roll lists thirty adults. Then it begins to lose members. At this time many local rural populations in Oklahoma were diminishing as people moved to the cities for jobs, and this may be a factor in the loss of members. Several members were recorded as transferring to larger communities. From 1951 to 1957 annual church income was from $1,000 to $1,381, not bad, but not enough to keep a pastor and family. Men and women continue to wear multiple hats. Fewer people were baptized and there is less mention of children and youth. From the minutes at least, there is no information about local, state, national or world affairs. The order of service remains the same although they now have musical instruments, apparently primarily, or only, a piano. In 1950 eleven people answered the roll. In 1957 apparently four people did, although of course many more were on the rolls and had church positions. Clearly a few key people kept the church going while others came and went, and the faithful few should be recognized and commended. Pastor turnover is significant. There seems to have been seven pastors in the 1950's, and as many as three may have been "under the Superintendent" as the "Celebrating 80 Years" pamphlet indicates.

Attendance at Board meetings are: eleven on June 28, 1950, at what was apparently a combined Society and Board meeting; thirteen on April 3, 1951; no information is given for roll calls in 1952; three on October 10, 1953; four

67

and three in 1954 (two meetings); four in 1955; two and four in 1956; three in 1957; and no records thereafter until 1962. The number of members in "full connection" dwindled in the 1950's. As previously noted, the financial requirements for full members may have contributed to the reduction in numbers. Almost certainly at some meetings persons were present who were not official members, and of course the pastor is there, who is not usually on the roll (except Wayne Lawton is one of four who answer the roll August 28, 1957). The quality and quantity of minutes generally also diminishes during the 1950's, and we begin to see minutes in which a roll call is not documented, probably because it was not made. Roll call is a tradition that gradually passes away, not just at Liberty. In 2022, I cannot remember the last time a "roll call" was taken at Liberty (or at the other small churches I am familiar with, Free Methodist and otherwise). In the twenty-first century it is no longer as clear, or at least it is not as often publicized, who the formal members are, and, obviously then, formal or "full" membership is not as important as it used to be. Today there is less emphasis on doctrinal purity and unity. This might be good, or bad. It is at least partially a function of generally diminished church attendance, generally diminished religious education in the home, and the rejection of religious practice in the schools.

From 1953 through 1956 the persons answering the roll in Board meetings (and Society meetings) were always or almost always Don Thompson, Virginia Thompson, Mrs. or "Minnie" Heginbotham, and Alice Thompson. In the Society meeting April 21, 1956, the roll was answered by Minnie Heginbotham, Alice Thompson, and Edah Crawford. On August 20, 1956, Lillie Johnson also answers, and in 1957 Lillie Johnson and Minnie Heginbotham are typically present. The disappearance of Don and Virginia from the roll is remarkably sudden and continues until June 18, "1967 & 68" when "Treasurer Virginia Thompson" appears.

Oklahoma In Action has a two-page section on Liberty (as on the other churches reported), which includes a chart for "15 Years of Sunday School Attendance and Church Membership" (the pages are unnumbered, the churches are listed alphabetically). It is a line graph, running from 1955 to 1970. It shows a straight decline in Sunday School and Membership for 1955-58. Sunday School drops from about fifty to twenty-two attendees. Membership drops from fifteen to six or seven. This does not include "Non-Members Attending." From 1958 to 1960 Sunday School increases to thirty, and Membership to about eleven. For the time covered, 1955 to 1970, the low in Sunday School is ten in 1963, ten again in 1967, and for members about six in 1963, 1964, and 1967.

During the middle of the 1950's Liberty's growth slowed and reversed, some key members left, Sunday School diminished, and record-keeping which here-to-fore had generally been excellent, apparently ceased. The reasons for the relatively sudden and unexpected decline are unknown to the author and the 2022 Liberty congregants. The loss of certain key persons may have contributed significantly to this decline. A long-term, stable pastor may have been able to stave off the decline, but this Liberty did not have in the 1950's.

The 1960's

As mentioned above, in Liberty's records is a set of six pages (faded white, yellow, or blue) both stapled together and held with a sewing pin, about 8.5x11 inches (but with an inch or so on both margins in rough shape), not in chronological order. The first page is undated. The second page, mostly written in pencil, is titled "roll call for 1961-62." It reads Lillie Johnson, Edah Crawford, Minnie Heginbatham, Virgina Thompson, Sister Connley, Kenneth Lawton scratched through, Audra Lawton scratched through and to the right "join another church," Wayne Lawton, scratched through and to the right "member conference," Mary Lou Lawton scratched through, Delbert Bales, Orpha Bales, Margaret Martin scratched through and to the right "Stillwater," Floyd Rush scratched through and to the right, also scratched through, "in ? since he has join up thre [there]," and finally "on six month Rhoda Butler."

The next (third) page is titled "On the 27 day of Aug. 19.61." "No 247 Guide Me O Thou Great Johavah (sic)." "... received in church Sister Rhoda Butler by Bro H on six month." Also, "received in church Sister Margaret Martin by letter. By Bro Hegginbathan." "Song no 233 Rock of Ages Cleft for me." "... prayer by Bro Hegginbathan." Probably "Bro H" is W.E. Heginbotham, who has twice previously served as pastor and who is a long-time attendee of the church. He may be filling the pulpit. *Oklahoma In Action* shows no pastor for 1961 to 1963, and in my list of pastors (Appendix 1) I have this period as "under the superintendent" who, according to a list provided in 2022 by Dwight Gregory, assistant to the conference superintendent, was L.B. Vanderhoofven (superintendent 1955-1963). Nonetheless, Liberty does have a previous pastor in the congregation, and my reading of the minutes is that he functions as pastor 1962-63.

The fourth page is a "Letter of Transfer" written on blank paper (not letterhead), headed "August 31, 1961." It reads, "Marguritte Martin, the bearer, wishing to remove from this society, we hereby certify that she is an

71

acceptable member of the Free Methodist Church in Stillwater, and cordially commend her to the Liberty Free Methodist church or an any other place. When admitted to another society her membership in this society shall cease." It is signed Rev. Tom Kegin, Pastor (of the church in Stillwater). And, as mentioned above, the fifth and sixth pages are also letters of transfer, on letterhead, both dated November 18, 1958, one regarding Mr. Kennison Lawton, the other Audrey Lawton.

In the *Account Book,* on p. 95, is "The First Liberty Official Meeting for year 1962. The first official board meeting was held at the home of W.E. Hegibothan Aug 22 1962." It is written in pencil. There is a gap of five years in the *Account Book*, from August 28, 1957 to Aug. 22, 1962. In the August 28, 1962, meeting, three persons answered the roll: Lillie Johnson, Edah Crawford, and Minnie Heginbothan. The agenda is numbered, and "9. what is state of membership. Good." Item 14. notes "Mr Bob Baker left $500.00 to church." The Sunday School Superintendent's report simply states "good." Item 19 asks, "Is the church property insured" and then "pars is insured for 1 year. The church is not insured." Although *Oklahoma In Action* indicates that 1962-64 is a low point in both Sunday School Enrollment and membership, the minutes do not indicate any particular concern, although the fact that they have allowed the insurance to lapse probably reflects diminished tithes.

Several of the 2022 members of Liberty, one of whom attended Liberty as a child in the late 1950's (Bill Grimes), and others who were adult members in the 1970's, tell a story that was related to them by Lillie Johnson. Attendance had dropped, there was no regular pastor, there seemed to be no future, and they decided to close the church. Lillie and Minnie Heginbotham went to church and began to roll-up the carpet. One looked up and asked the other, "do you really want to close the church?" The other said "no." So, they left the carpet as was, and continued to have services, perhaps with as few as two people, and perhaps without an official pastor or preacher. In 2022 the members could not remember, or maybe never knew, the date of this event. The last mention of Sister Heginbotham in the minutes is May 22, 1966 (Lillie continues to be mentioned). It seems logical that this event was between 1958 and 1964. The story is well known to the members at the time of this writing (2022). Several members thought that W.E. Heginbotham was the pastor when this happened. He was pastor 1953-54 and 1962-63, immediately after the church was "under the superintendent" (1960-63, probably L.B. Vanderhoofven).

In any case, this event shows the power of faith. Just one or two persons of faith can keep a church open, ministering, and serving, in this case for at least another sixty years or so (to the present), benefiting not only themselves and their families, but the local community, the conference, and missions around the world. The consequences of these two ladies' faith and perseverance has produced a great amount of good and contributed significantly to the building of the Kingdom of Heaven on earth. These sisters in Christ have provided the opportunity for others to stand on faith, as they did. And that may be the greatest opportunity of all, an opportunity to bear fruit for eternity. Who knows if this was not a test of faith from God?

This story is also a caution to anyone who would write history. There is nothing in church records about a threatened closure during this time, or any other. It is clear that Liberty went through some challenging times in the late 1950's and early 1960's, but the minutes never project a sense of insipient failure. The story nonetheless is powerfully attested as truth by a half dozen of the members in the twenty-first century. Minnie seems to have been the wife of W.E. Heginbotham. Where was he when the two women went to close the church?

There is one entry for 1963, "Liberty Society meeting Oct. 9, 1963." "Devotional was conducted by Bro Hugh Waymon." "Prayer by bro Beck." Elections are noted for secretary (Lillie Johnson); treasurer (Sis Edah Crawford); auditor (Bro Beck); class leader; and Stewart (sic) "Sis Beck, Sis Heginbotham and Sis Crawford." This entry is about a half page. Bro. Waymon seems to be the new pastor. W.E. Heginbotham, the previous pastor, is not in the minutes, but "Sis" Heginbotham is, probably his wife. W.E. will show up in the 1964 minutes.

Hugh Waymon will become a long-serving conference superintendent. According to records provided by Dwight Gregory (see above) Hugh was superintendent 1963-1978 (one of several during some of these years). His brother, Byron Wayman, served as pastor to Liberty 1951-52. As previously mentioned, he is the author of *The Free Methodist Church/Oklahoma In Action/ Past Present Future* which is quoted herein. He is responsible for preserving a significant amount of history of the Oklahoma Conference. *The 124th Session of the Mid-America Annual Conference (MAM) Sunday, July 24, and Monday, July 25, 2022*, notes "That the following persons are deceased as of this annual conference: Hugh Wayman" (p.93). It also notes "that the following persons be received by transfer: Danny Wayman" (p. 92). Danny Wayman is the son of Hugh Wayman, and I spoke with him at the Conference. Raised as a Free Methodist, after attending Seminary, Danny found a church with the United Methodists. Whereas his father primarily served Free Methodist rural churches, Danny mostly pastored United Methodist urban churches. At the end of his career, Dany chose to return to the church of his father.

The next entry, in pencil, is simply titled "1964." The Board of Trustees consists of Hite Johnson, Bro Hegibotham, and Ira Crawford. The Sunday School Superintendent is Sis Thompson, and the assistant is Bro Hegibathan (several secretaries have had problems spelling this name). The stewards are listed as Sis Hegibathan, Sis Thompson, and Sis Crawford. The treasurer is Sis Crawford and the secretary Lillie Johnson. "... prayer by Bro Waymon." This entry is twelve lines long. "Sis Thompson" may be Virginia Thompson, the original charter member, and if so, this is her first mention since 1957. But several Thompsons attended Liberty.

In the same hand, in pencil, is "May 23, 1965." "... prayer by Bro King." The minutes are read by Secretary Lillie Johnson. Seven items are listed on the agenda. The first is "Voted on pastor" without the pastor being named. The pamphlet "Liberty Free Methodist Church Celebrating 80 Years" lists the pastor for 1965-67 as T.F. King, as does *Oklahoma In Action* for 1964-68. Item 2 is "Del Sis Hegibatham res Lillie Johnson." "3 Supt Sis Thompson." "4 Church Treasure Sis Thompson." "5 Sec Lillie Johnson." "6 Board of Trustee Bro Hegibathan Ira Crawford Hite Johnson." "7 Steward Sis Crawford Sis Thompson Sis Hegibathan." "Sunday School Supt Sis Thompson," Bible Teacher Bro Hegibatan," "Junior Sis King," "primary Sis Heginbathan," "penny day Director Sis King." "... dismissed by prayer."

There is one entry for 1966, "Liberty Society Meeting" of May 22. "... prayer by Bro King," probably the pastor. Lillie Johnson read the minutes. Elections are conducted. A treasurer's report was given, presumably by the treasurer who is listed as Sis Thompson. One entry is "pd Bro King 360.00." "Light Bill $15.20." "gas Bill $14.67." "Money in Bank $104.50" and "money in purse $1.26." "Total Money raised" listed as $531.52, which is roughly half of what was typically raised in the 1950's.

On the back of the last page (not numbered) of the *Account Book* are three lists. The first, in blue ink, is headed "Year 19.66 May 22" followed by: Sis Edah

Crawford, Sis Minnnie Hegiobotham (followed by "deceased" in pencil), Sis Virginia Thompson, Sis Nora Connley, Sis Lillie Johnson, Bro Delbert Bales, Sis Orpha Bales, Bro Floyd Rush (followed by a check mark) and, in pencil, Sis King – seven women (one deceased) and two men. Sis King is probably related to the pastor, T.F. King, and may be his wife.

A Liberty Society meeting for "June 18, 1967 & 68" (combined meetings) occurs next (after the May 22, 1966 entry) in the same hand as the previous entry, presumably Lillie Johnson, and in blue ink. Delegates are Sis King and Lillie Johnson. Superintendent Sis King, Song Leader is Sis Barnard, treasurer is Virginia Thompson (who presumably was listed as "Sis" Thompson in previous entries) and Secretary Lillie Johnson. Board of Trustees is Harry Thompson (Virginia's husband), Ira Crawford and Hite Johnson. Stewards are Sis Crawford, Sis Thompson and (I think) Sis Barnard. Bible Teacher is Sis King, and "young people" teacher Sis Johnson. "Money raised" is $701.89, with a curious reference to Central College $11. The pastor was paid $427.00. These entries are on page 99 of the *Account Book*. On page 100 is "Treasurer's report to & including June 30 – 1968." Sunday offerings is $485.71; "from friends" $61.00; Central College $11.00; "W.M.B." $200; "pastor's support" $477.00; "Miss. Expence (sic)" $30.44; and "cash on hand" $112.70. Board of Trustees are Hite Johnson, Harry Thompson, and Ira Crawford. Stewards are Sis Crawford, Sis Thompson, Sis King. The Delegate is Lillie Johnson, treasurer Virginia Thompson, Secretary Lillie Johnson, and song leader Sis Barnard. Because Sis King is mentioned, I assume the pastor continues to be T.F. King.

The last list on the back of the last page of the *Account Book* is titled "year 1967." It includes Sis Edah Crawford, Sis Virgina Thompson, Nora Connley crossed out and with a check mark afterward, Sis Lillie Johnson, Sis Orpha Bales, Bro Delbert Bales, Sis King followed by "gave letter of transfer to United Methodist Sept. 9-75," Elixabeth (sic) Jones crossed out and followed by "Dec 10 1967 by Letter," Beulah Thompson followed by "Aug 1969 by Letter." Beulah Thompson is the wife of Charley Thompson, a previous pastor, whose call to preach came while he was attending Liberty. We have reached the end of the *Account Book*. However, as noted below, there are several later records scattered in various places in the *Account Book*.

The *Ledger Book* begins in 1968. At the top left of the first page is written "Rev. Harry Adams." The left column is titled "money taken in 1968-1969" and the right column is "Money pd. Out." This is by far the longest and most detailed financial entry for the church so far, four pages of entries for 1968-69. It is unclear why we suddenly have a uniquely detailed annual report, unless it was due to the new pastor Harry Adams. It may have been for audit purposes. Under "Money taken in" are such entries as, August 11 "no service (Rainy)," December 1 "no service 3 present," "Jan12 – thru Feb. no service sickness & bad weather." In all, seven days are listed as "no service" not including the Jan. 12 through February period. On Sept. 1968 a $100.00 gift is recorded from Betty Hudson (daughter of Harry and Virginia Thompson). No total is given for revenues for the year; however, the total is considerably less than one thousand dollars. Pastor Adams was typically paid ten dollars a week. The largest single expense was Dec. 16, "pd for roof 125.15," except that for "World MB," for 1968-69, a total of $210 was given in seven payments.

At the bottom of page 100 in the *Account Book* is written "no report in 1969" then adds "Bro Harry Adams – pastor"; Virginia Thompson, Superintendent "and church treasurer"; and Lillie Johnson Secretary. Pages 112 to 151 in the *Account Book* are left blank. This is Harry Adams' first of five appearances as pastor.

At the time of this writing pastor Adams is still living at eighty-six years old. He lives in Sapulpa, OK. I interviewed him on May 26, 2022, in a phone call of about thirty minutes. His wife (died May 3, 2017) and daughters attended Liberty with him. Pastor Adams said that the usual attendance in those days (not including his family) was seven or eight, and usually included "the Thompsons," as well as Hite and Lillie Johnson, and a few others he could not remember.

Church records contain a letter on Oklahoma Conference letterhead, from "Hugh Wayman, conf. Sup't," September 26, 1969, titled "Certificate of Transfer," certifying Beulah Thompson as a member in good standing of the Free Methodist Church in Woodward, and commending her to the "Liberty Free Methodist Church, in Tryon, Oklahoma, or in any other place." This was an important event in Liberty's history. Beulah of course was married to Charlie Thompson, who in 1971, following brief pastorships by Bro. King and Bill Huff, will assume the pastoral role for the church until 1979, and preside over one of the periods of greatest growth and success in its history. Hugh Waymon, now conference superintendent, was pastor of Liberty 1963-64.

In Liberty records is an 81/2x11 inch ruled sheet torn from a spiral notebook titled "Liberty Church Home Coming Nov. 2, 1969." On the front are thirty-six numbered entries, and at the bottom, continuing to the back page, another ten or so entries. Most are in blue ink, a few are in pencil, and in several different hands. This may be a sign-in sheet, or something like that. There are, roughly, two columns, the left titled "name" and the right "address." I have copied the names and the city of the address below, with OKC for Oklahoma City. Billy Ray Huff was the pastor 1969-70; Charlie Thompson replaced him in 1971. Rev. Huff and family attended the reunion, as did Beulah and Charlie Thompson, as well as several other pastors. The church is about thirty-five years old at this point.

Betty Hudson (OKC); Pam Hudson (OKC); C.L. & Arlene Herald (Tulsa); Mr. & Mrs. Herb Crawford (Perkins); Jimmy L. Bales and Jerry (Midwest City); Mr. and Mrs. Delbert Bales (Perkins); Kaye Gray (Perkins); Jina Gray (Perkins); Rev. & Mrs. Hugh Waymon (OKC); Joy, Danny, Dale Wayman (presumably OKC); Mr. & Mrs. Richard Allman (Sapulpa); Richard Lee (?); Allan Wayne (Sapulpa); Mr. & Mrs. Roy Heginbotham (Tulsa); Rev. & Mrs. Joseph T. Simpson (Enid); Billy Ray Huff & family; Mrs. Harriet (Simpson) Howerton (Wichita, KS); Mr. & Mrs. Lael Simpson (Dallas, TX); Geraldine Johnson (Tryon); AR & Mrs. Masten (Guthrie); Mrs. J. B. Rush (Tryon); Mrs. F. Chaffee (Tryon); Mr. & Mrs. Elzie Hemphill (Tulsa); Mrs. Sophia Rogers (Perkins); Mr. & Mrs. H.N. McCutchen (Wagoner); Mr. & Mrs. H.N. McCutchen, Jr. (Tryon); Chris, Kim, Bobby, Newt McCutchen (Tryon); Laura McCutchen (Tryon); Alice & Leon Hartzell & family (Midwest City); Dick Thompson (McPherson, KS); Kim Thompson (McPherson, KS); Gayle Thompson (McPherson [I think]); Mr. & Mrs. Lowell Halford (Midwest City); Verna Onile; Mr. & Mrs. Bruce Scott; Mr. & Mrs. Ben White; Mr. & Mrs. Ira Crawford (Tryon); Mr. & Mrs. Hite Johnson; Mr. & Mrs. [i.e. Virginia] Harry Thompson; Rev. & Mrs. [i.e. Beulah] C.N. Thompson; Mr. & Mrs. Raymond Farnsworth; Mr. & Mrs. Herbert Crawford [crossed out]; Mrs. Artie Grimm & four children; Mrs. Kennison Lawton & two sons; Pat & husband & son; Rev. Elmer Heginbatham; Mr. & Mrs. Don Thompson. This is eighty to ninety persons.

The reunion must have been a success because it was repeated. Also included in the Liberty records is a page apparently from the same spiral notebook, titled "Liberty Church Home Coming Nov. 8 – 1970." This is a somewhat shorter list, all on the front page, numbered but without columns and generally lacking addresses. Revs. Huff and Thompson attended and family members, as in the previous year. The list is as follows.

Mrs. Lillie Murray; Pam Hudson; Betty Hudson; Mrs (sic) & Mrs. Delbert Bales; Hite Johnson; Fern Chaffee; Billy Ray Huff; Rita Huff; Rhonda Huff; Ray Huff; Lillie Johnson; Edah Crawford; Ira Crawford; Mrs. Sophia Rogers (Perkins); Mr. & Mrs. Donald Bales; Lizzie Jones; Mrs. R.R. Farnsworth; Harry Thompson; Virginia Thompson; Geraldine Johnson; Larry Johnson; Pearl Rush; C.N. Thompson; Beulah [Thompson]; Delbert Bales [crossed out]; Orpha Bales [crossed out]; Mr. & Mrs. [unreadable]; Mr. & Mrs. [unreadable] Hagar (?) (Carney [written in another hand]); J.N. Thomas (Chandler [written in another hand]); Helen Holt (Carney); Cherie (?), Theresa, Daren, & Martie Grimm (Cushing); Johnnie Mae Grimm; Rev. Heginbatham. This is about half the number who came to the previous year's reunion.

At the top of page 101 in the *Account Book* is written 1969 and 1970, and on the next line, "liberty Church." Under "call to order by" is written "Bro Bill Huff" which is scratched out, and then "Charley Thompson Aug. 10." The Sunday School Superintendent is Charley Thompson with Virginia Thompson (his sister-in-law) as assistant. Bible teacher is "Sis Beaulah (sic)Thompson," junior teacher Sis Huff, "Beginners clas (sic) Lillie Johnson." The song leader is Ronda Huff, "church col (?) Ray Huff, secretary and treasurer Sis Lillie Johnson," "Church Treas" Virginia Thompson. Board of Trustees are Hite Johnson, Harry Thompson, and Ira Crawford. "Bleaulah (sic) Thompson taken in church by letter." "Treasure (sic) Report from camp 69 to Jan 1, 1970" follows. "Sunday Morning Offerings" are $350.67; "other offerings" $51.85; "Bro King" $50.00; "Birthday offering" $8.09, and the total $460.61. Under "money spent" is "pastor support" $232.00; "pastor retirement" $8.40; "REA & miss" $16.14; carpet $80.25; paint and supplies $43.82; and world mission budget $115.00. The total is listed as $495.61. "Money in bank" is $246.66. Finally, are signatures for "Virginia Thompson, Treasure (sic)" and "Lillie Johnson church Sec." Bill Huff was the pastor 1969-70.

The *Ledger Book* contains what appears to be the balance sheet for 1969-1970. At the top of the page is written "Rev. Bill Huff." The left column is "Money Received 1969-'70", and the right is "Money pd out." The first page has entries for 1969 from August, and the next three pages for 1970. No totals are given. For 1969, the smallest and largest Sunday offerings were $7.25 on Oct. 26, and $45.90 on Nov. 2. Some amounts given are indicated for persons. The largest expense was $80.25 for carpet. In 1970 the smallest and largest "Sunday Morning Offerings" were $6.02 March 22, and $44.25 August 2. Around a thousand dollars seems to have been collected. The pastor is paid ten to twenty dollars a week. The church continues to give to World Missions. $10.11 was given to Deaconess Hospital.

Summary of the 1960's

The late 1950's and early 1960's seem to have been a challenging time for Liberty, probably the most challenging in its history, although such an assessment is made with uncertainty. For several years there are no (extant) records, including a gap in the *Account Book*. The records for the rest of the decade are the sparsest since the church's beginning. Until 1957 Liberty had been diligent in recording the elections and good at recording finances. Collections for the church dropped to about half of what they had been in the early to mid-1950's, not including inflation. In the 1960's there seem to be no references to buildings, few to programs, and little evangelistic activity outside of contributions to World Missions. Probably a few congregants kept the church going. Pastors came and went. From 1961 to 1963 we have no record of a pastor, and the church was likely "under the superintendent," probably L.B. Vanderhofven. This probably does not mean the superintendent preached all, or even most, Sundays. Likely W.E. Heginbotham preached part of the time. It would be interesting to know if any women preached.

Oklahoma In Action shows Liberty Sunday School membership as 30 in 1960, and church membership about eleven. Sunday School drops to ten in 1963, and membership to six or seven. After slight increases, Sunday School drops again to ten in 1967 and membership to six or seven. In 1969 Sunday School is about sixteen and membership about eight. The period "under the superintendent," 1961-63, was generally the low point.

Oklahoma In Action provides the following chart for Liberty.

YEAR	TOTAL GIVING	PER CAPITA	WORLD MISSION	CAPITAL EXPENSE	PASTORAL SUPPORT	SUNDAY SCHOOL	OTHER EXPENSES
1965	752	83	113		466	69	47
1966	790	99	174		450	110	56
1967	708	101	190		440	38	30
1968	804	100	200		477	86	41
1969	617	77	207		313	94	
Last ½ of '69	516	58	115		232	122	47

A church in the 1960's with less than $1,000 a year in total giving was a poor church. It is likely that actual giving was more than the conference records indicate, but maybe not much more. As continues in the present day, when the church needs something (e.g., a part for the heating apparatus, or a windowpane, or even a door) someone in the church buys and installs it without record. Nonetheless, the church in the 1960's is clearly poor. For comparison, for the 1956-57 year, the last before 1962 for which we have financial records, "total money raised" was $1,381.83. The pastor was given $638.90. Thus, the late 1950's and 1960's were a period of decline. Even so, we see that their commitment to World Missions remained, which I think is remarkable.

Pastor Harry Adams (1968-69), who was interviewed for this history, said attendance had dwindled to six or seven when he first came to Liberty. He, like most of the Liberty pastors, was bi-vocational. This meant less time spent in the church and with church families, and proselytizing. The church, he said, was not in debt but had little income. The congregants had a history of maintaining the church physically and trying to improve it in small if not large ways. The members were attentive to each other and loving, and he had "nothing but good memories." Because Liberty was the closest FMC church to the campgrounds, some of the superintendents encouraged the congregants to be more involved in over-seeing the campground, but they generally resisted. Adam's greatest disappointment was the lack of conversions.

I asked him how he became pastor to Liberty, and he said that the superintendents, particularly Hugh Wayman, asked him to move to churches that could not find a pastor or that had suddenly lost one, and that that was typical of much of Adam's pastoral career (he was also a hospital chaplain for twenty years). When a new pastor was found for Liberty, Adams was moved to the next assignment. Adams related that it was conference policy that the churches held a vote each year on keeping the pastor. The results were forwarded to the conference for action, if any. The annual vote also served to provide feed-back to the pastor. When I began as pastor of Liberty in 2016, I was evaluated annually by the congregants. The evaluation went to the Mid America Conference and was then forwarded to me. This stopped in 2020 with the COVID pandemic.

Harry Adams was pastor for Liberty five different times. In 1968 he was thirty-two years old. He was a young pastor preaching to an older congregation.

According to the historical evidence and the testimony of living congregants, Harry Adams was well received, likeable, a good family man, an effective and loved pastor. He meets the qualification for "overseer" (some translations say "Bishop") in Paul's first letter to Timothy, chapter 3.

Oklahoma In Action shows an increase for 1969 to 1970 in Sunday School (to about twenty-two) and membership (to ten), as does the last row of the chart above ("Last ½ of '69") suggesting better times ahead. It shows average attendance in 1969 as twenty (the only year for which it provides a number). But without a doubt the 1960's was a challenging decade for the church. It likely came close to shutting its doors.

The 1970's

A half page entry at the top of page 102 of the *Account Book* is simply titled "Jan to July 31, 19.70." Then, "Treasure report." The Sunday morning offering was $476.00"; "other money received" $50.00. "Birthday Offering" $5.18. Expenses include "paid pastor" $463.00 and "preacher retirement" $10.36. The "world mission Budget" is $220.00. "... in treasure" $206.32. At the bottom is signed "Virgina Thompson" treasurer. As usual, her "treasure" reports are logically organized and clearly written. These figures indicate a great improvement in finances over the 1960's, no doubt due to increased attendance. Records from a bit later show several new names, and they represent younger generations. This is about the time when the first generation of church founders is dying, and new generations are replacing them. In the 2020's Liberty again finds itself in a time when the attending generation is getting elderly, and dwindling. It has the additional challenge of the covid pandemic of 2020-22 which negatively impacted the attendance of families with children, less so for the elders.

At the bottom of page 102 is "Liberty Society Aug 10, 1970." Then, one on each line, are listed "Pastor Bro Bill Huff"; Sunday School Superintendent Charley Thompson; Assistant Virginia Thompson; Bible Teacher Beulah Thompson; Junior Teacher Sis. Huff; Beginner Teacher Lillie Johnson; Secretary-treasurer Lillie Johnson; Song Leader Ronda Huff; "Church Collector" Ray Huff; next an unreadable word then "Charly" Thompson; Brother Huff; Beulah Thompson. This less than half-page entry is in Virginia Thompson's neat hand, in pencil (I note that her spelling is inconsistent, but this seems to have been a general characteristic of the minute takers). Pastor Billy Huff is not related to the Huff family that began attending Liberty in the mid 1970's and that continue to the present.

The report for August 1 to December 31, 1970, is a one-third page treasurer's report. Among its ten items is the pastor's salary at $480.00; "offering for Bro

Wayman" $8.61 (conference superintendent); and "money in treasure $199.38." This is Virginia Thompson's writing, but there is no signature.

As noted above, in November of 1969, and 1970, Liberty held back-to-back reunions, which attracted sizable crowds, especially the one in 1969. The one in the fall of 1970 attracted forty to fifty people, a success for a small rural church, and undoubtedly demonstrating a real affection for the church by those attending.

The *Ledger Book* begins with financial entries for 1968-69. The *Ledger Book* is hand-written, in ink, generally with "Money Received" in a column on the left, and "Money Paid Out" in a column on the right. Revenues are generally organized by "Sunday Morning Offering," "Birth Day Offering," "W.M.B" (World Missions Budget), "Other Money Received," and odds and ends. The expense column is typically arranged with "Pastor," "W.M.B." and "Other Paid Out." There are occasional exceptions to these arrangements.

The next set of entries in the *Ledger Book* is for 1969-70, in which "Money Received 1969-70" starts with August 1969. The figures for 1970 cover January through December. As mentioned above, one revenue category is "Sunday Morning Offering." Beginning 1970, the category "Other Money Received" (sometimes "Other Money In") consists of a list of persons and how much he or she gave, which in 1970 is by month, e.g., "Jan. Br. King 10.00." It is not clear why these entries are made by name, perhaps to track tithes, although I would think that these same persons gave to the Sunday Morning Offering, which is usually given as a single total for a particular Sunday. So perhaps it tracked extra-tithe giving. In 1970 five persons are listed as giving in the "Other Money In" category: Br King (Jan. $10, Feb. $10, March $10, April, $10, May $10, June $10, July $10, August $10, Sept. $10, Oct. $10, Nov. $10 and Dec. $10); Mrs. Barnard (Jan. $5, March $5, May $5, and Aug. $5); Lizzie (March "to date" $30, May $10, June $10, July $10, Aug. $10, Sept. $10, Nov. $10 and Dec. $10); "Floyd & Irva" (Oct. $20). A certain amount of fiscal discipline is required to keep such records.

The *Account Book* records a March 7, 1971, meeting called by Brother Charley Thompson (pg.103). Four items are listed, the first is "pastor voted on." Item 3 has "Supt Charley Thompson & Bro Huff" so presumably Billy Huff is still pastor (note that Charley Thompson has previously served as pastor). Some shorthand is used that is hard to read. A brief treasurer's report appears at the bottom with five items listed on five lines: "S.M.O. 1991.91" (Sunday Morning Offering); "other m.R. 512.83" (other money received); "preacher salary 1885.00"; "other money 622.97"; and "money in Tre-- 851.96." I think this report may have been transcribed into the *Account Book* from another source, perhaps from a scrap of paper used for notes. This is by far the largest sum paid to date to a pastor, and this may be the largest income reported to date.

Page 104 in the *Account Book* has at the top "Jan 1.1971 to July 1971 left 49.31." Five lines of figures and calculations are given "to July 1 1971" which are difficult to decipher. Then "From July 1 to Dec 26". "Col 138.17"; "spent 115.49"; with a difference of "$22.68." Then "left from June $15.92"; and "in treasure 38.60" followed by "for Sunday School." If the previous entry showed one of the largest incomes, this one of the smallest, and there is no reference to a pastor's salary.

In addition, the *Ledger Book* has three pages of entries for 1971, with a column for offerings and one for "paid out." As usual, the columns are not added. The smallest and largest Sunday morning offerings were $7.37 February 14 (not including days of "no service") and $107.50 October 3. The pastor was usually paid $20 a week. The largest check was for "lumber," $94.93. $265.00 was the Mission pledge. Eleven persons are listed as giving in the "Other Money Received" category. A "Building Fund" is listed under "Other Money Received" that eight persons gave to, none of which are in the "Other Money Received" category. Liberty has had a "building fund" for most, or all, the time since then. $265 went to World Missions.

In the middle of page 104 in the *Account Book* is a four-line entry, in blue ink, starting "March 1972." Then "voted on pastor"; "April 23 voted on Del to Con" (I assume "delegate to conference") and on the next line "Mrs Virgina (sic) Thompson was elected." At the bottom of the page, in pencil, is "Sunday School from Jan 1 to Jun 1 1972." Collected is $85.26; spent is $63.33; and left in "treasure" is $40.07. Finally, is "no report from church."

The "Celebrating 80 Years Pamphlet" shows that the pastor from 1972 to 1978 was Charley N. Thompson. He actually started in 1971 and ended this tenure in June 1979. He came back 1980-81, and 1997. "Charley Thompson" first shows up in the *Account Book* in minutes for January 10, 1939 (A.R. Martin was "in charge" on that date); he was one of six people who answered the roll call. On May 26, 1939, Charley or C.N. Thompson was "recommended to receive exhorter's license" (*Account Book*), and June 20, 1941, he was "recommended to the Quarterly Conference to receive local preacher's license" (*Account Book*). Perhaps more than anyone, over the years, he functioned off and on in various leadership positions at Liberty. He eventually pastored other churches and became a superintendent. There is more about him below.

The *Ledger Book* has a little over three pages of financial entries for 1972. The smallest and largest offerings were $5.00 Nov. 19 and $112.00 June 4. The pastor was typically paid $20 or $25 per week although Dec. 3 he was paid $80 (listed as "gift") and Dec. 31, $100. World Missions appear to have been $360.00. On Jan. 30, $100 was paid out for a piano. Five persons have the amounts they gave listed in "Other Moneys Received": Bro. King, Lizzie, Mrs. (sometimes "Katherine") Chaffee, Norma Trimpa, and Floyd, all of whom gave on more than one month. $20 was paid out to "Camp Meeting" June 25. World Missions were given $360.

The 1973 entry has five lines in the *Account Book*. On April 22 Virginia Thompson was elected conference delegate with her sister Beluah (sic) Thompson as "re--" (reserve). "No report from church." In the *Ledger Book* there are a little over three pages of financial entries. The smallest and largest Sunday morning offerings were $3.00 April 15 and $39 March 4. On March 25 there was no service due to "rain." Camp meeting was June 24. On Dec. 23 there was an "anniversary service at Camp." The pastor was typically paid $20 a week. The largest single expense was "lumber" at $60.38. A note shows $395.00 to "W.M.B," i.e., missions. There are no totals for revenues or expenses, and it is sometimes difficult to determine what they were. Seven persons are listed, with amounts given by month, in "Other Money Received," and they gave $627.97. The Sunday Morning Offering took in $767.02 for the year.

The April 21, 1974, report likewise has five lines in the *Account Book*. "… voted on preacher"; "Del Virgina (sic) Thompson and Beluah (sic) Thompson." "No other report." The *Ledger Book* has four pages of entries for 1974. That year four Sundays were shown as "no service." The smallest and largest Sunday morning offerings were $4 on August 18, and $56.00 on July 7. Under revenues, Sunday Morning Offering was $901.87; World Missions was $$495; Other Moneys Received was $269.03, and "Birth Day Offering" was $12.81. For expenses, $1040 was to the Pastor (about $20 a week); $495 to World Missions; and $201.80 to Other Paid Out. The difference for the year is -$58.09. The persons listed in "Other Moneys Received" were Lizzie, Bro. King, Irva, Betty, and Don and Alice.

In August or September of 1974, a young married woman, Lynda Grimes, who lived in the area, attended Liberty for the first time. With her were daughters Teresa and Lisa (who was only seven days old). She was the first of many Grimes to attend. She and her husband, Bill; and sister Danita and husband Sam Savory; sister-in-law Carolyn (married to Gene Grimes); and sister-in-law Anita (married to Bill and Gene's brother Leonard) and other family members still attend regularly in 2022 (Leonard is deceased). Lynda Grimes likes to write and has kept various memoirs relating to Liberty. One describes why she decided to attend. We rarely have first-hand accounts of why someone picks a church, and so I have transcribed it in its entirety in Appendix V "Why Lynda Grimes Decided to Attend Liberty FMC." In summary, her father-in-law had become fatally ill. While in the hospital he and the family were regularly visited by the Liberty pastor, the Rev. Charlie Thompson. Finally, her father-in-law, "With Charlie as his guide he gave what was left of his life to God." During this time Charlie "was never asking for anything and never preaching at us about the way we were living." Eleven days after the death of Lynda's father-in-law, she gave birth to a healthy, strong daughter. She "wanted to thank God for my baby," and she naturally went to Liberty, which was also close to where she lived, and which she had passed by on the road many times. She mentions that the first Sunday she attended, eight other persons were in church, and she "never felt more welcome at anyplace in my whole life." With Lynda's leadership, gradually the rest of the family began attending Liberty, and the rest, as they say, is history. How much difference some tender loving care can make at a difficult time!

The 1975 *Account Book* report says simply "March 2 voted on preacher." This was Charley Thompson. The *Ledger Book* has four pages of financial entries for 1975. The smallest and largest Sunday morning offerings were $6.60 on Jan. 12 and $152.215 on Dec. 6. A little over $2,000 was collected in Sunday morning offerings. The pastor was paid $20 or $25 a month for a total of $1,095 although a note on June 8 shows "Bro Huff," who probably was paid the $20 that would have gone to Charley Thompson. Presumably, Brother Huff preached when Charlie was away for some reason. World Missions were given $510.00. The largest single expense was $48.00 for "Jett Gas" on April 7. Persons listed as giving under "Other Money Received" are Bro. King, D.A.D., Pam H., for a total of $152.28.

Pages 106 to 109 in the *Account Book* are blank, and page 110 is titled "Liberty F.M. Proposed Assignments 2009-2010." These are the last entries.

On Sunday October 30, 2022, Linda Grimes and Anita Grimes relayed an interesting story, prompted by a discussion in church about how to strengthen faith. Quickly after starting to attend Liberty the new members were given various responsibilities, for which they did not always feel capable. Charlie Thompson told Linda and Anita that he wanted them to do programs for Easter, Mother's Day, and Christmas. They said Charlie did not consult with them about this, he simply directed them to do something. They did not have experience with such programs. They were ridding together in a pickup, heading to church, to put something together for Easter in 1975, they did not know what. They stopped at a stop sign and noticed a piece of board lying by the road. They got out and found a "piece of a hammer" also. By the time they got to church, they had found other pieces of board. They had enough to make a cross, which they did, and based on that, they came up with an Easter program. The pastor was pleased, and it worked for the kids. Anita said they thought it was God responding to their cluelessness, and they both thought it was a sign of God's interest in the church. Events like these, over many years, have strengthened their faith, and convinced them that God wants Liberty to continue.

Linda Grimes said that when she started attending Liberty Charlie Thompson had retired from farming. She, and several other members, also said that Charlie tried to retire from pastoring several times, "to go fishing." That did not happen until 1979, and even then, he came back to briefly pastor at least twice more.

I am in possession of a one sheet, two-color publication titled "Oklahoma Free Methodist." It is printed on the front and back, in two columns. It is not dated. At the bottom of the front right column is "November-December issues mailed to churches due to postage permit problems." The first column on the front page is a poem titled "Revival At Liberty," by Ruth Lillie, who is the mother of Anita Grimes. At the top of the second column, first page, is a photo with the subtitle "Van Valin Elected Free Methodist Bishop." The first paragraph states "Dr. Clyde E. Van Valin, of Wilmore, Kentucky, was elected by the Board of

Administration of the Free Methodist Church to succeed Bishop Myron F. Boyd whose retirement will become effective, October 30, 1976." Probably the issue is for November-December 1976. On the back page are reports from churches at Enid, Guthrie, Liberty, Midwest City, and Norman North. The Liberty report is as follows.

> The Bruce Scotts returned from a four week vacation in Colorado, New Mexico, Arizona and Texas.
>
> We had a great week-end of services October 8, 9 and 10 with Rev Bill Huff as our speaker. There were 11 or 12 who received salvation and the whole church a revival. The front page poem by Ruth Tilley can better explain this.
>
> On October 17, we had a Baptismal Service at the Baptist Church in Tryon. Eight of our new converts were baptized. October 24 Hite Johnson, Leonard & Anita Grimes came into the church as preparatory members. October 25 twenty-nine of our people had a skating party at Stroud.
>
> Mr. and Mrs. Leonard Grimes announced the birth of a daughter, Lora Dean on September 26.

During these times Liberty typically baptized in a pond or small lake. Probably because October was a little cool to do so, they used the baptismal fount at the Baptist church in Tryon, which still exists in 2022.

The fact that Liberty has the front column in the pamphlet, and is represented along with Enid, Guthrie, Midwest City, and Norman North, likely means that Liberty was one of the more substantial churches in the conference at that time. Bill Huff was the revival speaker (he had been pastor 1969-70) but Charlie Thompson was the pastor 1971-79. According to the 2022 members Huff was a well-liked and effective preacher. The Enid church reports, among other things, "Ina Price went to be with the Lord. Rev. Charles Thompson held the service."

A wooden plaque in the shape of Oklahoma, with a brass plate, located in a back room of Liberty church, reads "1976/ Outstanding Sunday School/ of the/ Oklahoma Conference." At least from this time to the present, Liberty has had strong children's programs, although since 2020 these have been impacted negatively by the covid pandemic, or perhaps we should say panic.

Unless otherwise indicated below, the information is from the *Ledger Book*. The 1976 entry begins with the statement "Bought Piano Mar 29—1976" and then lists thirteen people who gave for this: Leonard Grimes, Mrs. Letha Grimes, Sam Savory (still a member in 2022), C.N. Thompson, Harry Thompson, Lawrence Tilly, Bill Grimes (still a member in 2022), Hite Johnson, Gene Grimes (still a member in 2022), Bob and Gay Green, Betty Hudson, and Ira Crawford. They gave $235 and the "church budget" gave $300, for a total of $535. The pastor was paid $1,300.

Stapled to one of the three pages for 1976 is a typed piece of paper, about 3x3 inches, with "Mrs. Melvin Burson" at the top, among other things stating "Be sure to put April 15-16 on your calendars for our Spring Retreat at the campground. Mrs. Leona Fear, General Conference W.M.S. President will be our guest speaker." On the next page are stapled two pieces of paper, the top one (ragged, roughly triangle shape, about two inches wide and three long) has written "Dec.30 – 1976 – 1148.11." Six persons are listed under "Other Money Received": D.A.D., Alice and Don, Pam Hudson, Betty H ("on piano"), Pam Hudson, and Don Thompson. Also listed is "Special Offer for revival 32.60."

As per immediately above, the second piece of paper stapled, about 9x6 inches, has "Report – Treasurer 1977" and appears to be in Virginia Thompson's hand. It reads as follows. Sunday Morning Offering $4,288.85. D.A.D. $114.04. B. Day $31.06. Other money received $210.00. Extra Offering $329.65. It is not totaled, but the total is $4,973.60. Beneath is "Money pd out." Pastor's salary $1,450. U.W.M.B. $848.76. Preacher's retirement $81.75. "F.M. Papers" $36.00. "R.E.C --" (presumably "Rural Electric") $46.86. Gas $143.20. "yd work" $60.00. "... well house & plumbing" $444.46. Revival $120.00. Christmas treats $46.53. Heater $130.47. Study books $14.18. Paint $12.33. and "Miss" (miscellaneous) $19.56. It is not totaled, but the total is $3,454.10. At the bottom is written "Bal in bank Dec 29—1977 $2518.30." Two pages of detail for 1977 follow. I have not checked the balances to see if they match the stapled summary. Under "Other Money received" are listed Norma Trimpa, Donald Corell, and Merlene Heginbatham. Three special offerings are listed: in February, "compassion" $57.15; in August "for hymnals" $229.65; and Oct 30 "revival" $100.20.

1978 has four *Ledger Book* pages (numbered in the upper right-hand corner) and stapled to page one is two pages (8.5x11 inches) which appears to be a balance sheet; on page three is stapled two small notes (one cash-register style, the other lists "deposits" and "checks given," etc.); on page four is stapled another 8.5x11 in. sheet which is a letter "Dear Joy." This is the longest and most detailed financial record for Liberty to date. I have transcribed the balance sheet that follows.

1978 Liberty FMC				
	Income	Expenses	Maint & Improvements Expenses Detail	
WWMB		871.46	Septic tank	561
Penny-a-day	151.46	151.46	Paint	89.9
Birapport	27.21	27.21	Bath & maint supply	86.66
Morning Worship Offering	6174.38		Home Lumber Co	16.5
Special Offerings	520	50	Ed Aaron Lumber	700
Pastor's Salary		2120	Ed Aaron Lumber	492.6
Utilities		156.64	Sam Savory	56
Maint & Improvements		2235.12	Replace window	4.7
Publications		57.85	Replace window parsonage	2.75
Pastor's Retirement		156	Curtain for stage	65.27
Revival	173.4	100	Maint. supplies	11.45
Tryon Bank Error		90.59	Electric supplies	33.3
Miscellaneous		19.45	Yard work	60
Savings	250	3500	Piano Tuning	20
			Stove (Charlie Tarleton)	35
Totals	7296.45	9535.78		2235.13
Tryon Bank Jan. 1, 1978	2518.30			
Jan. Cash on Hand	115.55		Electricity	75.64
	9930.30		Gas	81
				156.64
Jan, 1, 1979 Ck. Acct.		391.17		
Jan. 1, 1979 cash on hand		3.35	Publ (Light & Life)	34
		9930.30	(Youth in Action)	11.25
			(Year Book)	12.6
				57.85

In Liberty's loose records are seven reports for 1978 titled "United World Mission for Christ/ Local Treasurer's Report." "Report 7" is for December 30, 1978, and it shows a total of $1050.13 for the year, which is the sum of WWMB, Penny-a-day, and Birapport above. The January report is signed by "local treasurer" Virginia Thompson. The March and subsequent reports are signed by Joy Scott. The reports are sent to Mr. Loren Martin, 6705 N. W. 30th, Bethany, OK, 73008.

$7,296 appears to be the largest income Liberty has received to date. The pastor is receiving the largest salary to date (he is still being paid week by week). $871 was sent to World Missions, also the largest said contribution to date. Quite a bit was spent on maintenance. There is no entry for insurance on the church or parsonage. And Liberty has a substantial savings account at the Tryon Bank of $2,518. Apparently, the Bank made an error of $90.59 and had to reimburse the church.

The letter stapled into the Ledger Book is as follows.

March 10, 1979

Dear Joy,

Would you please sign the enclosed letter and take it and the return envelope to the bank. When I get confirmation of the year-end balances, the audit will be completed.

Your books are at the church (if you haven't already picked them up).

I apologize again for taking so long to do the audit but several different things combined kept me behind on really everything.

Yours in Christ,
Bonnie Lou

The enclosed letter was delivered to the bank on March 14, 1979 as per instruction.

Joy Scott Treas.

The last sentence is written in a different hand, seemingly four days after the original was penned.

Camp meeting was June 26. There is a list of "Special Contributions," which seems to be the same as, or like, the previous category "Other Money Received." Listed are "Va. Thompson" (probably Virginia), "Norma," "Alice Thompson," "Johnson", and "Heginbotham," for a total of $520.

In Liberty's loose records is a letter from the Preferred Insurance Company, Oklahoma City Office 2718 N.W. 39th, Drawer 12366, Oklahoma City, OK 73157, addressed to "Liberty Free Methodist Church/ Perkins/ Oklahoma 74059" (with this address, how did the church receive the letter?), "Attention: Bruce Scott." The letter begins "On May 7, 1979 we had a telephone conversation regarding the theft of an airconditioner from the church window. At that time based on your policy of insurance there was no coverage afforded for theft." Later the letter states, "You have purchased insurance which went into effect on May 1, 1979 which does afford you the added protection for theft. Our loss report indicates the airconditioner was stolen on April 27, 1979 ...." I will address the matter of theft in greater detail below in the 1980's. In 1979 the church building was covered to $25,000 and $3,000 for contents; the auxiliary building to $11,500 with no contents coverage; and $50,000 for "Bodily Injury."

1979 is the last substantial entry in the *Ledger Book*. It has five pages. At the top is written "Savings 3329.56 Dec. 31 – 1978"; "Cash on Hand from 1978 – 3.35"; and below "checking 391.17." "1979" is written in large letters in the middle of the page, and immediately below "Bal. In Payne County Bank Jan. 1, 1979." The church seems to have closed out the Tryon Bank account and moved to Payne County Bank.

Page three has the heading "Pastor's Salary." The left column has "C.N. Thompson" at the top and the entries run from January 7 to June 10, and the total is $920. Below that is an entry "Travel Expense for Billy R. Wilson" but it is not clear what that expense was. He is the new pastor, and apparently his first check is June 17 for $40, and the same for June 24, July 1, and July 8. July 15 shows $70 and thereafter his pay is $50 a week. The column picks up on the right side of the page with Aug. 5. Immediately above is written "Billy Wilson."

According to another memoire of Lynda Grimes, during Labor Day, 1979, a 30th year reunion occurred of the "community of Sandy land" at the Free Methodist campground. Although this appears to have been a school reunion and not a religious event, the school was "a gathering place for the community," and the children and parents of Sandyland were of the same kind as the

Liberty congregants. Indeed, until 1946, the "Liberty Circuit" congregation met at Sandyland school. Many of the kids at Liberty went to Sandyland. Lynda and her family attended the reunion, and she read a prepared statement of which she kept a copy. A complete transcript of her statement is available in Appendix VI as "Lynda Grime's Prepared Statement for the 30th Re-Union of the Sandyland Community." I believe it sheds some light on the kind of people who attended Liberty in those days, and on the integration of the Free Methodist Church in the community, given the event was held at the FMC campground.

Charley Thompson has been pastor since 1971, about eight years. A new pastor has been hired, who started June 17. This was an important event for Liberty. Pastor Charley N. Thompson was present for what appears to have been the greatest period of expansion for Liberty, certainly the period of greatest tithing, and money spent on the physical church, as well as funds provided to World Missions. The next pastor does not stay long, and we will encounter Charley again.

Page 1 has two columns for "Deposits" from Jan. 12, 1979, to Dec. 31, deposited weekly. At the bottom of the second column is written the balance, $10,177.67. Page two lists "Sunday Morning Offerings" and the total at the column's end is $8,911.25. Pastor Billy Wilson was paid $2,350 and $175 was paid into the retirement fund. $1043.60 was paid to World Missions. "Insurance" was paid March 31 and was to "Preferred Risk" with a note "PD. Thru 3-20-80." Interesting items under "Miscellaneous" expenses are "altar rail Hinkle Home" $12.50; "year Books" $18.90; "yard work" Bobby Grimes with several entries at $10 a week; "Lock for Parsonage" $5.05; "Christmas Candy" $36.10; "Trophy (plate for Pulpit)" $4.70; "Pulpit (Sam Savory)" $130. Under "Special Monies" are listed contributions by Edah Crawford, Hite Johnson, Beulah Thompson "curtains," Harry Thompson, Jim Thompson "A/C," Alice Thompson, Va. Thompson, Norma Trimpa, and Wendell Sadler, for a total of $566. Under "Improvements" are listed "Bill Thompson Platform & carpet" $172; "Aaron Lmbr Co" and (I think) "Home Lmbr. Co" $578; "glass for door" $2.51; and a curious entry following June 4 but undated, "Christian Union a/c" $300. There is a Christian Union Church in Tryon, and at the time of this writing (2022) Liberty FMC, Christian Union, Tryon Assembly of God, and First Baptist Church of Tryon, participate in a church alliance of many years' duration for the benefit of all persons living in the region, and have bi-monthly community prayer meetings and an annual summer revival (more on this below). Liberty might have been helping the Christian Union church with air conditioning expenses. On Feb. 11, 1979, the church spent $25 on a "Special Speaker," Bill Huff, with a note immediately following that says, "ck. canceled" (Billy Ray Huff was pastor of Liberty in 1969-71). Rev. Huff, as previously noted, conducted a memorable revival at Liberty in 1976. Camp meeting was July 29.

"A/C" likely refers to an air-conditioning window unit. Until central heat and air was added, the church bought several window units because they were periodically stolen. The pulpit mentioned above, built by Sam Savory, is still in use in 2022. The plaque on the pulpit reads "In Memory of Edah Crawford and Family to Liberty Free Methodist Church." Edah Crawford died in 1979, a long-standing congregant, sister to Beulah and Virginia Thompson, and the family presumably paid for a new pulpit to be made in her memory. According to memories of church members in 2022, the old pulpit was taken to the campgrounds and there disappears from history.

The next two pages of the *Ledger Book* contain a few random notes, and these are the final entries. Nine blank pages are left.

"Celebrating 80 Years" shows that in 1980 Charley Thompson again took over the pastorship of Liberty, and then Harry Adams was pastor 1981-82. Following Adams is Monty Bower 1983, Harry Adams 1984-86, Irving R. Ball 1987, and Harry Adams 1988-90.

Summary of the 1970's

In the 1940's Liberty had four pastors – Walter Nelson, Milo Martin, Charley Thompson, and A.F. Dile; plus, superintendent A.R. Martin apparently was in charge 1943-45 (superintendent Ralph Butterfield may also have been in charge for a short time). In the 1950's Liberty had seven pastors – W.E. Heginbotham, Byron Wayman, C.V. McCully, W.E. Heginbotham again, Joseph Simpson, Wayne Lawton, and Kennison Lawton. In the 1960's Liberty had seven pastors – Kennison Lawton, W.E. Heginbotham, Hugh Wayman, T.F. King, Harry Adams, "Bro. King (probably T.F. King), and Bill Huff; and 1961-63 was "under the superintendent." In the 1970's Liberty had three pastors – Bill Huff, Charlie Thompson, and Billy Wilson; but Bill Huff served less than a year, and Billy Wilson only a half year in the 70's. Looking ahead, in the 1980's Liberty will have seven changes of pastors (five different pastors). In the 1990's, seven changes of pastors (six different pastors). In the first decade of the 2000's, two pastors. And in the 2,000-teens, two pastors.

In the 1930's the church was successfully established; membership consolidated; and key leaders emerged. They included four of the charter members, and others such as Charley Thompson. The superintendents were actively involved in the church, as pastors rotated, and lay leaders were key to day-to-day activities. The church remained small and relatively cash poor. It generally met at the Sandyland Schoolhouse. In the 1940's the church grew, but not a lot; the superintendents remained active; lay leadership remained essential; finally, in 1946, the congregants moved into a church building that stands in use today. In the 1950's the church grew more and prospered. It got a parsonage. Then it began to lose members late in the decade. The decline continued into the 1960's. It is not clear why. It appears that sometime in the late 1950's or early 1960's Liberty almost closed its doors. In the 1970's the church began attracting new families, the regulars were younger, and Liberty experienced its largest number of congregants and its largest revenues. Some, perhaps much, of this success is due to home-grown pastor Charley Thompson. He is the longest serving pastor in the almost ninety-year history of the church, although Edsel Hall only served a year or two less, and my calculations of time-served are estimates (a newspaper obituary states Edsel was pastor at Liberty fourteen years, which would be about what Charley served, but I believe it overstates Edsel's time). In 2022 the congregants describe the 1970's as a very lively time with typically a dozen or so kids attending. At least two summers they had a vacation Bible School that attracted several dozen kids each. If the "Oklahoma Free Methodist" is any indication, Liberty then was one of the more significant churches in the conference.

Of course, the 70's were a turbulent time in the U.S. The Vietnam war was winding down, civil rights continued to be an issue, drugs became widespread, the president resigned, the country experienced a financial crisis including inflation unprecedented in modern times, and people sat in long lines to fill their cars with the most expensive gasoline in the nation's history. There are no indications of any of these in Liberty documents, although surely, they affected the congregants.

The 1980's

Charlie Thompson appears to have left his approximately nine-year pastorship in June 1979. I have been unable to determine why, but I suspect the conference wanted to use his apparently excellent pastoral skills elsewhere, since Liberty seemed to be doing well. But he had also wanted to retire. Pastor Robin Grueser (1991-93) related in a phone interview May 26, 2022, that the conference liked to move pastors every three years or so (this tendency lasted to the twenty-first century) and this policy may have played a role in pastor Thompson's move. Billy R. Wilson was the next pastor but Charlie Thompson becomes pastor again by July 10, 1980. At that date a letter from the Preferred Risk Insurance Group was mailed to Liberty FMC "c/o Bruce Scott" which is marked through and "c/o Rev. C.N. Thompson/ P.O. Box 443/ Perkins, OK./ 74059" was added long-hand. The pastors for the rest of the decade are Harry Adams (1981-82), Monty Bower (1982-83), Harry Adams (1984-86), Irvin Ball (1986-87), and Harry Adams (1988-91). If the 1970's were a period of pastoral stability, the 1980's were the opposite. Nonetheless, according to current members of the church, this decade continued to be an exciting and lively time for them. Once again, the congregation was a more stabilizing factor than the pastor.

Harry Adams is the third longest serving Liberty pastor at about eleven years of service, from the 1960's to the 1990's. He noted, in his interview, that the church was remarkably self-sufficient. The congregation conducted the Sunday School, took care of the facilities, and basically ran the church except for the preaching and conference related duties. The records show that this was generally the case since the beginning, and indeed this remains true to the present (2022). Therefore, the lack of a steady pastor was not as debilitating as it might have been at another church.

In May 1979, an air conditioner window unit was stolen from the church. The church had insurance, but not for theft, so they added it. A letter from the Preferred Insurance Group, on "7-10-80," addressed to "Rev. C.N. Thompson," indicates that insurance is added for theft, and mentioned is "CP8331 is $560.00 to cover the following items: RCA Whirpool (sic), 24,000BTU Air Conditioner, Ser. #E91812357, Model no. AGF25040, Cost $560.00." Prior to the theft coverage the insurance cost was $380.00, and afterwards $386.00. The "effective date of endorsement" was "6-27-80."

Liberty suddenly began to experience vandalism and theft. The church was broken-into on several occasions. In the loose records of the church is a xerox copy of "Personal Property Loss Itemization." It is signed by "Charlie Thompson – Treas" and dated "3 Mar 82." In 1982 Harry Adams (early in the year) and Monty Bower (late in the year) were pastors. What was Charlie doing as Liberty's treasurer if he was not the pastor? Without this evidence, I would have assumed that he had moved away and was serving either the conference or another church. Four items are listed: piano, purchased May 1976, replacement cost $11,000, depreciation $200; sweeper, purchased 1997, replacement cost $88, depreciation $20; clock, purchased 1975, replacement $20, depreciation $5; and "16 small chairs," "gifts," replacement cost $32, depreciation $6. A note is added, "chairs were given by Okla. Free Methodist Conference." Preferred Risk Insurance Companies sent a letter March 23, 1982, to "Liberty Free Methodist Church/ P.O. Box 443/Perkins, OK 74059." "We have received the personal property loss itemization listing stolen items. We have depreciated items for a minimum amount making total net items of $1009.00 after depreciation. There is a $100 deductible to apply leaving a net amount due of $909.00."

There appears to have been a gap between pastor Monty Bower (1982-83) and Harry Adams (1984-86). Probably the church was then under superintendent Elza Boldman. There also appears to be a gap between Irvin Ball (1986-87) and Harry Adams (1988-91), and again Liberty was probably under the supervision of Elza Boldman. In any case, the 2022 members of Liberty remember Elza well. Unlike most superintendents, they said he was relatively quiet, to the point of appearing timid. At conference events he was sometimes referred to as "timid-man," a play on his last name, one which somewhat embarrassed him. They thought he was pretty good as far as superintendents go. When asked what he emphasized in his meetings with Liberty, they said the business side of church -- planning, expanding the church, and in general "what most superintendents do."

The thefts mentioned above continued, and in 1988 Liberty member Lynda Grimes wrote an article published in the local newspaper as follows.

Dear Friends,

As Easter grows near and the time for rejoicing our Savior's Resurrection we at Liberty would like for you to remember the one, or ones in prayer who have been stealing from our church.

Liberty is located four miles south and 3 miles east of Perkins. We average around 40 in our services and we have a close, loving church family.

Just because we are few in number does not mean we're weak in spirit, but over the past couple of years we have been tested several times by someone stealing things from our church.

We have lost three air-conditioners, a piano, chairs, Sunday School supplies, 2 American flags, 1 Christian flag, cleaning and restroom supplies, stuffed animals from the nursery, a film projector, vacuum cleaner, plus numerous other small things.

We have taken each loss and break-in in stride and carried on, but each time we wonder if the person that is doing this is needy, and needs our help, or if it's just a sinful nature. We do know they need our prayers.

Sometime during the week of March 14-19 the subject of our prayers came out cut the electric wires from the church to the parsonage. The cost to replace the wire will be $550. The cost the person who cut the wire will receive will be a whole lot less than this. They will probably melt it down and sell the copper or sell the wire to someone who can use it and sell it cheap just to get rid of it.

Please join us at Liberty Church in praying for this party during the Easter services and hopefully they will fall under conviction and ask for forgiveness of their sins.

God Bless Each of You

Lynda Grimes member of Liberty F.M. Church

One hallmark of Liberty was a large "liberty" bell and clapper that was located outside the entrance to the church. It weighs about two hundred pounds (it is still there). It was stolen too but was recovered from a local creek where it had been dumped, perhaps because the thieves were afraid of being caught with it. At one point the vandals began to disconnect the well-water pump.

Two members of Liberty, Sam Savory and Leonard Grimes, plus the previous pastor, Charlie Thompson, decided to try to catch the thieves. Charlie had a "big pistol" (as Sam tells it). They hid where they could see the well house and stayed up all night. Unfortunately, or fortunately as the case may be, the thieves did not return. Sam and several members of the church in 2022 tell the story as a humorous episode. Harry Adams, who was pastor during some of the vandalism, also relayed the story when I interviewed him. As the church entered the 1990's the vandalism ceased, except that occasionally someone would drive through the yard and make ruts, or perhaps break a window. This continues, albeit rarely. The last ruts and broken window occurred in 2019.

Linda Grimes mentions "around forty in our services" and "a close, loving church family." An average of forty members is probably about the most Liberty has ever averaged. As best I can tell from the evidence, Liberty has typically been a close and loving family oriented church – certainly there is no overt evidence of division.

The Tryon Ministerial Alliance

According to Rev. Harry Adams, the Tryon Ministerial Alliance began functioning sometime in the 1980's. This corresponds with an article in The Oklahoman, June 7, 1997, by Pat Gilliland, titled "Revival Helps Tryon Keep Faith Churches Bring Hope as Town Loses Businesses."[17] "For a week each summer, preachers and members from the Christian Union, Baptist, Free Methodist, Assembly of God and Christian churches share fellowship, praise and prayers under a tent in Tryon." "The town's pastors formed the Tryon Ministerial Alliance nine years ago," that is, in 1988, when Harry Adams was pastor. Originally the main event of the Alliance was a multi-day revival that was held in June. Its primary purpose was spiritual, "to get people saved," as Pat Starling was quoted in the article, wife of Lorn Starling, the pastor of the First Assembly of God. However, the Tryon bank had closed, then the grocery store, and then the elementary school of the Perkins-Tryon District (in the fall of 1997). The Alliance must also have attempted to hold the community together, which in 1997 consisted of "about 500 residents." Today it has about half that.

---

17. This article is in the collection of Karen Grotheer, wife of the 2022 pastor of the Christian Union Church of Tryon.

Four churches started the Alliance: the First Assembly of God, the Baptist Church, the Christian Union Church, and Liberty Free Methodist Church. These continue to constitute the Alliance in the present day. The 1997 Oklahoman article also mentions the Church of the First Born, and current members of the Alliance remember a few other Tryon churches that joined the Alliance over the years, exiting when they closed doors. Harry Adams, who last pastored in 1994, remembers the Alliance revival as a high point of the year, and generally thought highly of the Alliance. I add, that in 2022 the Alliance is thirty-four years old. None of the present-day pastors or members remember any significant divisions or controversies in the history of the Alliance. This is despite differences in church doctrine and the usual human tendencies towards parochialism. The Alliance importantly illustrates the fact that uniformity is not necessary to unity. It also illustrates how different churches can come together to effectively meet the needs of a community in distress. At least, humble churches can. At some point the Alliance began collecting donations during its meetings and used the donations to provide help to the needy people of the community. The practice continues to the present. In August 2022, the Alliance had about $1,400 in the bank, which is more than usual. The Alliance has made important contributions to the community of Tryon and surrounding areas and continues to do so today.

The 1997 article mentions a "30-by-60-foot tent" which was used for the revival. It was set up in the open area in front of the Christian Union church and Baptist Church (these two churches are located next to each other). All of the churches except Liberty are located in Tryon. The tent was used into the twenty-first century. It was laborious to put up, according to current members of the Alliance. Eventually it was replaced by open air "pavilion," essentially a metal frame structure covered with sheet metal. The Alliance functions to the present with additional purposes beyond revival and community preservation, as will be discussed in later sections. The Pandemic of 2020-2022 is the only time in the memory of present-day Alliance members that the June (sometimes late May) revival was not held.

The Free Methodist Church *Year Book 1989* lists seventeen churches for the Oklahoma Conference, one of which is Liberty. The Liberty Sunday School enrollment is a total of fifty-seven with six classes. Only five churches in Oklahoma have higher SS enrollment, and one of those (Claremore) is fifty-eight. The other four are metropolitan churches. Average Weekly Attendance for Liberty Morning worship is listed as forty-five, and for Sunday School forty. Adult "Membership" is thirty-one, about five per cent of the total Conference Membership which is six hundred and three. In this year were three "professions of faith." Finances are as follows. World Missions, $397; Home Missions $203; Conference $1585; Pastor's Salary $3,900; Program and Promotion $173; Physical Plant Operation $1120; Miscellaneous $92; and the Grand Total for the year is $7470. Harry Adams of course is the pastor.

Summary of the 1980's

The key event of the 1980's appears to be the creation and functioning of the Tryon Ministerial Alliance. Heretofore mention of interactions with other churches or groups is rare (except Sandyland School). From 1988 to the present Liberty pastors and at least some congregants met several times during the year with members of at least three other churches to pray, preach, eat, and coordinate for the benefit of the local needy. When the occasion arises, they use each other's churches, for example for funerals and revivals. Whoever had the idea for the Alliance, it was a good one.

Whereas conference superintendent Hugh Wayman had shown considerable involvement in Liberty events and affairs until his retirement in 1978, the next one, Elza Boldman (superintendent 1977 to 1991, co-superintendent in 1977) appears less involved, although Liberty was probably directly under his supervision 1983-84 and 1987-88. I have heard superintendents say that 90% of their time is consumed by 10% of their pastors and/or churches. The case may be that Liberty was a stable church with no serious problems and that the superintendent's time was best used elsewhere. However, a long-term trend seems to continue in the 1980's, that the superintendents are slowly less involved in the normal affairs of most churches in their jurisdiction. The trend is also fewer superintendents, with more complex jobs, for more churches, in which the congregants are culturally and ethnically less uniform than previously.

According to the 2022 members of Liberty, the 80's were "good times," with nothing remarkable. The kids were growing up, the parents were working, and a few leaders from the three or four largest families made sure the "regulars" came to church. Sometimes these leaders were grandparents, but roughly half were in mid-life.

The *Year Book 1989* shows very strong children and youth programs. Only five churches in Oklahoma show more enrolled in Sunday School, and those are all metropolitan schools except Claremore. Interestingly, Liberty's total giving for the year of $7,470, is the lowest of the seventeen churches in Oklahoma by far except for two churches "under superintendent," one with $0 and the other with $250. Every other church's giving was in five figures.

Also noteworthy is that Liberty continued the building fund started in the late 1970's. According to the current congregants, the main purpose of the fund was to save enough to build a new church. I have been unable to locate any minutes or related financial records from the 1980's. In the 1980's the congregants were optimistic about the future of Liberty and were planning for the needs of the next generations.

During the 1980's President Ronald Reagan and Pope John Paul II survived assassination attempts, but the President of Egypt, Anwar Sadat, and Prime Minister of India, Indira Gandhi, did not. In 1981 the U.S. Center for Disease Control issued the first warning about AIDS. In 1983 the internet was born. Soon thereafter the first personal computers are sold. In 1986 the space shuttle Columbia explodes, and the Chernobyl Nuclear Power Plant fails with disastrous radiation leaks. In 1987, on Wallstreet, the DOW falls 22.6% on "Black Monday." In 1989 protests erupt in Tiananmen square, Beijing. And in 1989 the Berlin Wall falls, marking the end of the Soviet Union.

The 1990's

Harry Adams was pastor 1988-91. Robin Grueser took over about June of 1991 and served until 1993 when Adams again resumed the pastoral role. According to a phone interview of May 25, 2022, Rev. Grueser had previously been associate pastor at the Midwest City FMC, a church he said he grew up in. He was about thirty-three when he became Liberty's pastor. He also had responsibilities for taking care of the conference campground in Perkins. He had started preaching, he said, in 1974 when he was about seventeen. The superintendent asked him to go to Liberty because he had need of Rev. Adams elsewhere. For a year pastor Grueser commuted from Midwest City, and the next year he lived at the campgrounds near Perkins, about a half-hour drive. Average attendance was twenty-five to thirty adults and children. Liberty, he said, was not wealthy, but had no debt. Finances were helped because someone had left about sixteen thousand dollars, and these had been put into savings. The main families were the Grimes, the Huffs, and the Savorys, "folks along the river out there" (the Cimarron River). The congregants were very self-sufficient (as we have heard before) and Liberty was "run like a congregationalist church." The strengths of the church were "the strong family ties" and "the legacy of Charlie Thompson." Pastors Grueser and Adams knew each other and had a good relationship. Robin said that the conference required an annual vote on the pastor (a requirement that goes back to Liberty's earliest days). Robin said he was very happy at Liberty, but in 1992 superintendent Robert Andrews wanted him to pastor the Guthrie church (where he remains as pastor in 2022, a remarkable thirty years later). Pastor Grueser indicated that he joined and left Liberty around conference time, in June, and this was typically when the conference made pastoral changes, barring any unforeseen circumstances. This was true going back to Liberty's beginnings.

The current Liberty congregants have fond memories of pastor Grueser. They said that the superintendent persuaded them to vote to let Robin move to Guthrie, and these many years later they still have regrets at doing so.

There seems to have been a gap between Harry Adams (1993-94) and Lonnie Hill (1995-96) when the church was likely under superintendent Kirby Bertholf. Unlike Elza Boldman, the 2022 members of Liberty thought Bertholf was too aggressive. He wanted them to close Liberty and move to the church at Guthrie.

A plaque on the west side of the sanctuary reads "This addition dedicated to the memory of Beulah Rush Thompson and Virginia Rush Thompson Charter Members of Liberty Free Methodist Church June 9, 1991." The addition in question consists of a room used primarily for Sunday School and two bathrooms. It is located on the west side of the sanctuary. During this addition, that is in 1991, central air and heat was also added to the church, which put an end to the temptation to steal window units.

Beulah Thompson, charter member of Liberty (at the age of thirty-one), was born September 11, 1904, and died May 16, 1990, at the age of eighty-five. She was married to Charlie Thompson, who as we have discussed became Liberty's longest serving pastor, and one of its most effective. She served the church through good times and bad, and left this world while Liberty was in a period of stability. Her funeral services were at the First Methodist Church of Perkins, probably because the Liberty sanctuary, which can comfortably accommodate eighty or so, was too small for the crowd. Officiating were Bill Huff, Harry Adams, and conference superintendent Elza Boldman.

Beulah's sister Virginia Cora Rush Thompson, also a charter member of Liberty (at about age twenty-seven) followed her sister to the next life less than a year later, on January 1, 1991. She was born November 7, 1908. Beulah was her older sister by about four years. Virginia's services were at the Christian Union Church, Tryon, OK. Again, this was presumably to accommodate the crowds. Harry Adams and Beulah's husband, the Rev. Charlie Thompson, officiated. Her mortal remains rest in the Tryon cemetery. Her newspaper obituary (preserved by Linda Grimes) reads: "The daughter of Taylor and Mary (Daniels) Rush, she was born Nov. 7, 1908, in Trenton, Mo. She grew up around Tryon and Carney, Agra and graduated from Tryon school. She married Harry Thompson on Dec. 24, 1929, in Chandler. After their marriage, the couple lived in Tryon except nine years in Oklahoma City. In addition to being a homemaker, she worked as a saleslady at John A. Brown's. She was a member of the First Free Methodist Church. Survivors include her husband, Harry, of the home; one daughter, Betty Hudson of the home; one grandchild; and two great-grandchildren. She was predeceased by four sisters, Beulah Thompson, Verna Patton, Lizzie Hones, Eda Crawford, and four brothers, Jack, Rex, Lloyd and Floyd Rush. Pallbearers will be Wallace McLaury, Marion Wright, Bob Green, Don Thompson, Dick Thompson, and Harley Thompson." "First Free Methodist Church" is probably a misunderstanding for "Liberty," which, as we have noted, was the first FMC in the region.

Virginia's husband Harry Abner Thompson outlived her by a couple years. He was born September 6, 1902, and died November 4, 1993. Services were at the Christian Union Church of Tryon. Officiating was pastor Harry Adams. Harry is buried in the Tryon cemetery.

In 1996 the Oklahoma Conference changed its name to the Mid-American conference, after mergers with Arkansas and SW Missouri churches of the dissolved Ozark conference. This roughly marks the beginning of administrative consolidations and geographic expansion of the conference that continues to the present. The conference was managed differently in mid-century than fifty years later.

In the section above on the 1980's, I referenced an article of The Oklahoman, June 7, 1997, by Pat Gilliland, about a tent revival held in June, conducted by the Tryon Alliance of Churches. The article mentions that Tryon has lost its bank, grocery story, other businesses; the primary school is to close in the fall of 1997; and the town is down to around 500 residents. However, attendees come to the Tryon revival from Agra, Carney, Ripley, and Perkins. It also states that the oldest attending pastor is Charlie Thompson, age 92. The article states "The Rev. Thompson of Perkins, pastor of the Free Methodist Church four miles north of Tryon, says he has retired three times but agreed to close out this year's revival, preaching at 7:30 p.m. Sunday." According to memories of present-day congregants, Larry Popovitch only pastored Liberty a few months of 1996. Edsel Hall became pastor in 1997, but apparently after the June revival. Present-day memory is that several potential pastors visited Liberty during 1996-97, with Charlie Thompson filling in the gaps and serving as the main pastor. The article clearly states that Charlie is the pastor of Liberty, although he does not show up on any other records I know of. The other Tryon Alliance pastors mentioned are, in order, "lay minister Gary Percell of Drumright," Church of the First Born; Lorn Starling, "a bi-vocational pastor [who] manages an auto parts store in Cushing," First Assembly of God; Ted Gibson, "pastor of the Christian Union Church who came to Tryon in the 1970's"; and "Rev. Marvin Skinner, Tryon Baptist Church pastor." Probably Charlie's statement that he has "retired three times" refers to Liberty.

The 1997 revival was in a 30-by-60-foot tent, and "one night about 120 people listened." This was the night that lay minister Gary Percell gave the sermon, and presumably when the author of the article was present. 120 represents about a quarter of the population of Tryon at that time, although people are mentioned as coming from several surrounding communities. It seems like a large number for a Tryon revival. Present-day congregants of Liberty remember that Charlie was "the closer" at the revival, that he was very good, and that in general it was a successful revival. Several of them thought this year, 1997, was the first year the tent was used.

In 1999 the conference periodical was "In Touch," edited by Rev. Eric J. Snyder, 5014 E. Newman Road, Joplin, MO 64801. It was published six times a year. The three Numbers I have, for February, April, and June, are six pages each, single fold with a loose page, in two colors (blue and black). The lead article in Vol. 7, Number 1, February 1999, is by Superintendent Kirby Bertholf titled "A Gift Worth Fighting For." He concludes by reviewing the conference's "battle plan" which "is still a good one: (1) Intercessory prayer by all the people, (2) Godly leaders equipped to preach the word, mature the faithful, and reach the lost, (3) Church growth and revitalization through persistent effort, (4) Church planting through demonstration of faith and commitment. And how do we interpret the battle results for the Mid-American Conference in 1998? "As the Lord God of your fathers has spoken to you: do not fear or be discouraged"!!"

Two short articles are by two persons who will pastor Liberty, Rev. Jeff Johnson who wrote "Journey with the Saints: Fannie Crosby (1980-1915)," and Denise Abston, who wrote "Prayer Focus." A third article is also by Rev. Johnson, titled "May God Continue to Pour Out His Spirit." A quarter page section is titled "In Touch with the Mid America Conference." It contains three items: "Teen Retreat" (at the Perkins campground), Special Thanks (from Superintendent Bertholf), and "Homecoming," which read as follows.

Well done, good and faithful servant. Charles Nathan Thompson has heard those coveted words from our Heavenly Father. At age 94, on November 16, 1998, Charlie Thompson is finally "home." He was born September 29, 1904. He married his childhood friend, Beulah Bush, to whom were later born three children: James, Gayla, and Donald. In 1942 he was called into the ministry and spent 41 years ministering on the then Oklahoma Conference. The last poem he wrote read, "Oh, God, we rest our case, At the throne of grace. And there we leave our soul, Completely under God's control."

The text is accompanied by a small photo of the Reverend, apparently in a hospital bed. Beulah's last name was Rush, not Bush. We know that Charlie pastored Liberty as late as 1997 (at the age of ninety-two) and closed a memorable revival in Tryon that June, probably to over a hundred people. He was a vigorous man. He began his career in ministry at Liberty, and most likely ended it there as well, after many adventures. And we remember that while his wife in 1936 was starting a new church (Liberty) with a sister and brother, he fought against the Lord's call, until one day while farming he fell to his knees at a stump and agreed to live God's way.

On page six of "In Touch" is an "Attendance Report from the Mid-American Conference for 1998" (1997 is also listed). Liberty's attendance is 35 in 1997, and 31 in 1998. This is surprisingly low, based on other materials described herein. However it corresponds with pastor Grueser's estimate of attendance in 1990-91 at twenty-five to thirty. The following churches are listed with 1998 data: Edmond (attendance 65), Enid (56), Geary (22), Green Valley (?), Guthrie (36), Joplin (35), Liberty (31); Midwest City (123), Miller (40), Mt. Vernon (19), OKC First (52), MacArthur (88), Stillwater (16), Siloam Springs (43), Tulsa (25), and Woodward (8). The average is 42 but this includes Oklahoma City and Tulsa churches. If we just consider rural churches, then Liberty's attendance was about average.

In 1999 John Huff was Liberty delegate to "Claiming the New Millennium for Jesus!/ 101st Annual Session of the/ Mid-America Conference/ Free Methodist Church of North America." His delegate book, a blue three-ring binder, is in Liberty's possession. There are twenty pastoral appointments for 1999-2000 including J. Edsel Hall for Liberty and Jeffrey Johnson for Midwest City. Three churches are shown as "Under the Superintendent." Billy Ray Huff is evangelist. Larry Popovich is transferred to the Great Plains Conference. Elza Boldman is a hospice chaplain in Oklahoma City. Denise Abston (who will pastor Liberty in the future) is a delegate for Midwest City. The Board of Ministerial Education and Guidance recommended that Jeffrey P. Johnson, who in a few years will have Liberty "under supervision," "be received by transfer" from "Faith Christian Fellowship, International."

A section of the conference binder covers the "state of the work" for seventeen churches. Liberty's report is two pages, but the data is limited. It shows "0" for conversions and "New Christians enrolled in discipleship classes." For 1997 and 1998, respectively, morning Sunday School is 29 and 27, and membership is 34 and 33. The 1998 membership is twenty-two adults, two "preparatory," and nine youth. "Total funds raised in 1998: $12,826" and for 1997 "$11,464." Liberty's "Conf. Budget" was $1,713; "Harvest "2,000 $150"; "Home Missions" $316; and "World Missions" $550. "Goals Projected: Try to get more cooperation in our conference project" and "Strategy Planned: A fund to send some of our youth and children to our campground activities and see if this will help." Edsel gave the following report: "The church is a challenge to me to reach others in the community. Out (sic) visitation of our membership and others in the area is good. I believe the Lord is helping me in the messages each Sunday and see some good response and some conviction, also. The college course I believe has helped me in my sermon preparation and more time spend with Bible Study."

Interestingly, the calculation for church apportionments was changed in 2000 to 10% with the footnote "The goal of 10% is to provide predictability and fairness to Conf. Apportionments." Liberty's "1999 Receipts" are $12,500 (this is an estimate since the conference was mid-June) and its apportionment for 2000 is $1,250. At some point the Conference changed the calculation back from a percentage, because the calculation was moved, once again, to 10% in 2020, essentially for the same reason it was in 1999. Liberty's giving goals in 1999 for World Missions was $625 and Home Missions $250.

The Historical Committee reported that "The Oklahoma Conference kicked off it's hundredth year with a celebration at the Mid America Conference/Camp, June 9-14, 1998 at the Perkins Campground." Among those presenting "historical vignettes" was Hugh Wayman, a Liberty pastor and superintendent.

In John Huff's conference book is a copy of the "Liberty Free Methodist Church Directory." It is not dated but is among papers for 2000. It lists fifty-eight people including Edsel and Juanita Hall. Also in John's conference book is a list of Liberty "Proposed Assignments for 2000." It lists "Superintendent—Leonard Grimes," "Assistant—Amanda Grimes," "Sunday School Song Leader—Danita Savory & Lisa Baker," "Church Song Leader—Louise Dodrill," "Treasurer—Sam Savory," "Finance Committee—Sam Savory, John Huff, Leonard Grimes, Earl McDaniel," "Adult Class—Anita Grimes," "Assistant—John Huff," "Young Adult & Teens—Lynda Grimes," "Middler (sic) Class—Almeda Gambill & Sondra Ford," "Primary Class—Mary Huff & Janet McDaniel," "Childrens (sic) Church—Lynda Grimes, Lisa Baker & Amanda Grimes," "Ushers—Mary Huff & Eddie Ford," "Assistants—Dustin Ford, Tony Gambill," "Church Secretary—Carolyn Grimes," "Dime-A-Day—Lora Allender," "Program Committee—Janet McDaniel, Almeda Gambill, Lynda Grimes," "Trustees—Sam Savory 2000, Gene Grimes 2001, Eddie Ford," "Sunday School Secretary—Danita Savory," "Stewards—Mary Huff, Betty Hudson, Louise Dodrill," "Nominating Committee—(Supt.) Leonard Grimes, Greg Savory 2001, Bill Grimes 2001, Mark Gambill," and "Piano Player—Teresa Dees." A comparison of this list, with that in Appendix VII for 2017-2022, shows that many of these congregants are still serving in elected positions over twenty years later. In 2022, John and his wife Mary are elderly and mostly confined to their homes.

In the 1990's the pioneers passed away, after half a century of service to the church they founded. These included two charter members (Beulah and Virginia) (their brother Floyd, also a charter member, had previously died), a sister who was also a long-time member (Edah Crawford), Liberty's longest and probably most outwardly successful pastor (Charlie Thompson) and Virginia's husband and long-time congregant Harry Thompson (who never became a formal member). Of necessity a new generation must take hold, or the church will fail. In reflecting on those days, members of these families said, laughingly, that almost as soon as they started attending, they were given important tasks for which they were not necessarily well prepared, such as Sunday School teachers and leaders (like Lynda Grimes), treasurer (Sam Savory is still treasurer in 2022), Bible Study leaders (Anita Grimes), etc. The pioneers were ready for some relief. Like the pioneer generations, these next families have now been serving the church close to half a century. They too are hoping for an infusion of new blood.

The pastors of the 1990's, in order, were Harry Adams, Robin Grueser, Harry Adams, Lonnie Hill, Larry Popovitch, Charlie Thompson, and Edsel Hall.

None served more than two years consecutively except that in 1997 Edsel Hall began his long period of service.

Summary of the 1990's

If a previous estimation is correct that average attendance in 1988 was "around 40," the attendance in the early 1990's has dropped "25 to 30," then to 35 in 1997, and 31 in 1998. This latter level of attendance, with minor increases and decreases, continues to the covid pandemic of early 2020. That is, from 1980 to 2020, for a period of roughly forty years, average attendance was the most consistent in the history of the church.

The 1980's had seven changes of pastors, same for the 1990's. During these two decades Harry Adams served four times, and Charlie Thompson twice as pastor. These two decades are marked by the search for a steady pastor. Looking back from 2022, the congregants felt that the conference sent them some young potential pastors who, naturally, were ambitious for larger, more urban assignments, and who were not really committed to Liberty. Even so, as we have seen previously, the come-and-go of pastors did not seem to affect the overall functioning of the church. The Sunday Schools, the commitment to missions, taking care of the facilities, funerals and weddings, community meals in the auxiliary building, the Tryon Alliance meetings, all proceeded unabated. During the 1980's and continuing in the 1990's, and indeed into the present, the two events of the year that generally produced a full church house (about 90 adults and children) were the children's Christmas play and the Easter service.

Until about 1980, the church kept decent records of finances, votes, assignments, and official membership. Fairly suddenly this stops. From about 1980 to 2016 no records of minutes were kept at the church as far as I have been able to determine, and it may simply be that no one kept minutes. The treasurer, Sam Savory, kept a personal record of finances. The congregants did what needed to be done to keep the church and its various programs running, with little documentation thereof. Most people do not particularly like to keep records. In the early years, Liberty may have been fortunate to have Virginia Thompson and a few others who were diligent and skilled at record-keeping. Probably the gradual distancing of the superintendents from the daily affairs of individual churches also contributed to the decrease in record keeping. This was related to fewer superintendents with more duties. I do not know whether the greater church's de-emphasis on administration and supervision was deliberate or not. Nor is it clear if it was good or not; this remains to be seen. The larger trend in the U.S. from the late twentieth century is fewer people in church, therefore reduced church income, and this was and is probably a factor in the type of administration the church has, not just Free Methodists. At the same time, the church grew exponenetially outside the U.S. (not just the Free Methodists).

The 1990's was a relatively prosperous decade in the U.S. In 1990 the Hubble Space Telescope became operational. Also, in 1990 Iraq invaded Kuwait. The Soviet Union failed on Christmas Day, 1991. The U.S. went to war against Iraq to liberate Kuwait and the war ended after about a month in 1991 when Iraq withdrew its forces. In 1994 the North American Free Trade Agreement went into effect. In 1995 the World Trade Organization was created. Also, in 1995 the Murrah Federal Building in Oklahoma City was bombed, killing 168 children and adults. In 1996 the first animal was cloned. And in 1999 the Euro currency was created to offset the power of the U.S. dollar. During the 1990's the globalization movement started, sometimes referred to as the "New World Order." At the end of the decade large demonstrations against globalization began to occur.

The perception of the congregants is that the 1990's were very similar to the 1980's. They were good times and the church seemed to be doing well.

The 2000's

Charley Thompson is the longest serving pastor. Edsel Hall is close behind but his approximately twelve years of consecutive service is the record for unbroken pastorship. Charley Thompson has the second-most years of consecutive service – approximately eight years (1971-79). The contemporary pastor, Ron Faulk, is third with six and a half years of consecutive service and counting (2016 to present). Harry Adams served about eleven years but over five different times. These estimates could be off a year or so.

Edsel Hall became Liberty's pastor in 1997 and retired in 2009. He was born in 1922 in Stillwater, OK. He was thirteen years old when Liberty was founded. He died Sunday, July 14, 2013, in Claremore, OK, at the age of ninety-one. He married Juanita Chloe Austin in 1939. They both graduated from Stillwater High School in 1940. They had three sons and a daughter and grandchildren. According to his newspaper obituary, "After graduation, they moved to Wichita, Kansas where Edsel worked for Cessna Aircraft for two years. He was drafted into the Marine Corp in 1942, and dutifully served his country until he was honorably discharged in 1946 having obtained the rank of Corporal. After being discharged, he returned to Stillwater and took up farming on the family farm. In 1951, Edsel entered the ministry in the Free Methodist Church [at the age of twenty-nine] and was appointed minister of several churches around Oklahoma. After retiring from ministry, he served the Liberty Free Methodist Church for 14 years. After the death of his beloved wife, Edsel met and married Pauline Brown in 2003. He enjoyed woodworking, traveling with Good Sam Club and family, and nature. The most important mission in his life was teaching and exemplifying God's love and grace." The record as I know it shows he was Liberty's pastor about twelve years. We can safely assume he was pastor twelve to fourteen years.

Edsel and Juanita were married for sixty-two years. She ministered with him at Liberty for four years, until 2001, when she died. His second wife, Pauline, ministered with him until they were divorced. He became pastor of Liberty when he was seventy-five, which is somewhat remarkable, and served until he was eighty-seven, which is more remarkable. According to the obituary quoted above, he went to Liberty "after retiring from ministry." The pastor with the longest years of consecutive service did so as semi-retired. Edsel Hall was blue-eyed, long-faced, typically had short hair, and wore glasses. From what I can tell, he was the kind of pastor who kept himself neat and trim and wore a tie and jacket when on church duties.

The church members described Edsel as a "a wonderful man"; he spent hours with families when a loved one died; he was "very involved with kids"; and he routinely visited with families just to visit. He seemed to particularly like Psalms and the Book of Acts. He preached about both sin and love. One of the grandchildren he brought to church still occasionally attends in 2022. Edsel was a bit extroverted. For example, when he was seventy-six years old, he bought a new truck. The dealer had a marketing ploy that anyone who bought a vehicle could do a bungee jump. At his age, Edsel did the bungee jump – twice. He was also a long-term and active member of Good Sam.

The Free Methodist Church *Yearbook 2007* lists thirty-four churches and church-planting projects for the Mid-America Conference, twenty-eight in Oklahoma. One is listed for Istanbul, Turkey, and one for the Dominican Republic. Each conference has a summary page titled "Statistics for calendar year ending 12/31/2006" which focuses on membership, and another page focused on "Giving Streams." For membership, each church is asked for seventeen sets of data (not including "totals"). I have not added up the data given, but my estimation is that about 60% is missing for all churches. For Liberty, under "Members," seven is given for youth, and the other categories – "Prep" and "Adult" are missing. There is no data for "Converts" or "Baptisms." Under "Church Profile," twenty is given for "Adults" and six for "Senior Adults," and no data is given for "children" or "Youth." "AVG Attendance" is forty for worship, and thirty-five for Sunday School. This generally suggests that about half the congregants on any Sunday were members, and half non-members. It also suggests a strong Sunday School program. Income for Liberty is $25,841. The only other data is that $400 went to World Missions. Of the thirty-five churches and planting projects, seventeen provided data on income, eighteen did not. Interestingly, information on the pastor's salary is not requested.

This data suggests that Edsel had increased tithing; adult attendance is good compared to what we know about previous years; and Sunday School is strong. However, it is difficult to draw valid conclusions from such sparse statistics. In a backroom of Liberty Church is a framed "Certificate of Excellence" which reads as follows. "This certificate is awarded to Liberty Free Methodist Church for five year average/ 15% growth in worship/ 195.5% growth in Mission Giving/ 60% growth in membership/ 23.3% growth in general giving." I have not indicated capitalization or all line divisions. It is signed "Dr. Jeffrey Johnson, Superintendent" and "Dr. David W. Kendall, Bishop." It is dated May 31, 2009. This is presumably the five years covered is 2003-2008. As to why most of the data for Liberty is missing from the *Yearbook 2007* is unknown; perhaps Edsel was not fond of paperwork as, apparently, quite a few other pastors were not. Or the conference did not have a good way of getting the data. It certainly seems that Edsel, and the Liberty Congregants, would have been pleased to report the positive numbers for their church.

On page 110 of the *Account Book* is a list titled "Liberty F.M. Proposed Assignments" and under that "2009-2010." The list is: "Superintendent – Leonard Grimes"; "Assistant --- Amanda Grimes"; "S.S. Secretary – Danita Savory"; "Song Leader – Lisa Baker"; "Church Secretary – Carolyn Grimes"; "Treasurer – Sam Savory"; "Finance Committee – Sam Savory, John Huff, Gene Grimes"; "Adult Class – Anita Grimes Assistant – John Huff"; "Jr. High Class – Lynda Grimes"; "Assistant – Teresa Dees"; "Preschool class – Mary Huff"; "Assistant – Almeda Sumpter"; "Children's Church – Lynda Grimes; Assistant – Amanda Grimes & Lisa Baker"; "Trustees – Bill Grimes, Eddie Ford, Gene Morris"; "Dime-A-Day – Joshua Simmons (Two Guns)"; "Nominating Committee – Mary Huff, Saundra Ford, Bill Grimes"; "Piano Player –Teresa Dees Assistant – Lynette Morris"; "Church Decorator – Teresa Dees"; "Stewards – Rachel Savory, Lora Allender, Leona Burton"; "Program Committee – Lynda Grimes, Almeda Sumpter, Saundra (sic) Ford."

Immediately below, and filling out page 110, is a statement titled "August 21, 2009" that "Edsel Hall performed the marriage ceremony for Steve Sumpter & Almeda Gambil a reception was held in the parsonage following the wedding. May God bless this union!"

At the top of the next page (111) is the statement "Pastor Edsel Hall had a busy Sunday. This was his last Sunday to preach at Liberty Free Methodist Church after serving for [blank] years. On this day Edsel had a dedication for Tony & Ashley Gambil's children, Brooklyn and Emma. Also on this day, Calvin & Charlene Jordan were accepted in membership. They were a welcome addition to our church." As it turned out, Edsel was called to fill the pulpit a few more times after this.

Towards the end of his tenure at Liberty, Edsel developed some form of dementia. His personality changed somewhat, becoming more assertive, and he repeated himself more, and his stories and memories seem to focus on his early marriage and family. But his commitment to ministry remained strong and is remarkable.

One of the unusual events of 1999 was the "Y2K" scare. Supposedly many of the computers around the world were going to crash at the millennium and usher in a period of greater or lesser apocalypse. A considerable number of people in the US, as well as other countries, stocked up on supplies and survival equipment (generators, ammunition, etc.). The members of Liberty were unperturbed, as usual. The turn of the century and second millennium was just another day.

Dr. Jeff Johnson became superintendent in 2001, while Edsel Hall was pastor of Liberty, and served until 2020 (19 years, none with other superintendents). Since 1935 he is the longest serving superintendent. Elza Boldman was superintendent 17 years (1974-1991, four years with other superintendents). Hugh Wayman served 15 years (1963-1978, four years with other superintendents). After Edsel retired in 2009, Liberty was supervised by superintendent Johnson about a year. During this time several persons filled the pulpit besides Dr. Johnson.

Dr. Johnson occasionally filled the pulpit while Edsel was pastor. During a phone interview of October 4, 2022, Dr. Johnson related that he once took Bishop Leslie Kober to Liberty. He thinks that is the only time a bishop attended Liberty. The bishop preached, and while he was preaching mice ran along the platform in front of the pulpit, to the amusement of the congregation, if not the bishop. One of the reasons superintendent Johnson took Bishop Kober to Liberty was because the greater church was considering closing the smaller churches. Dr. Johnson wanted the bishop to see how vibrant and active Liberty was, and how important to the members, young and old. Perhaps he wanted the bishop to see the vibrant Sunday School programs. In addition, small churches like Liberty produced a disproportional share of church leaders, such as "exhorters" Floyd Rush, Elzie and Marvel Hemphill, and James Thompson, as well as pastors W.E. Heginbotham, Charlie Thompson, Jeff Grimes and no doubt others. The closure of small churches has mostly been avoided as a matter of policy in the history of the Free Methodist Church. A different cost-saving effort has been the merging of conferences, which has happened several times. Dr. Johnson noted that merged conferences have never produced a healthier conference.

Dr. Johnson relayed that during Edsel's tenure Liberty became more involved in conference business and activities than it had historically. For example, Leonard Grimes served on the conference Board of Administration. He was one of three brothers who regularly attended Liberty with their families. Leonard died suddenly October 11, 2010, at the age of seventy. His funeral was held at the campground in Perkins to accommodate the large crowd which Dr. Johnson estimated to be several hundred. In 1968 Leonard married Anita Tilla, who still attends Liberty and in 2022 functions as Director of Missions and Sunday School Superintendent. Dr. Johnson said that Leonard's death was a sad and substantial loss for the conference as well. However, Liberty members continued to be active in the conference, for example Jeffery Grimes (a nephew to Leonard) has served on several conference Boards many years and is on the Board of Administration in 2022.

Dr. Johnson said that Edsel had asked at least a couple times to retire, but no immediate replacement could be found – a situation not unusual in Liberty's history. The main problem was that the funds raised by the church were not enough to support a pastor full-time, and it was typically a long drive to a job for a bi-vocational pastor. The churches that paid $400 a week or more normally did not have a problem finding a pastor. One husband-wife team went to Liberty from Oklahoma City, but they were "not a good match for Liberty." After Edsel's retirement Dr. Johnson preached and had various others preach, including sometimes Edsel when no one else was available.

While Dr. Johnson was at Liberty, he said the average attendance was thirty or so. He thought the strengths of the church were its strong sense of community, the fact that they were always willing to help each other out, strong children's programs, kindness, and local ministries. Their weakness was being "a rural church in the twenty-first century." Dr. Johnson said that Liberty was a typical small, rural, Free Methodist church. There were few transient persons or families in the area, and this made it hard to attract new people. However, the church was a boon and a blessing to the families who attended and to the local communities, including the public schools, that it ministered to. The forced separation of church and school, particularly in rural areas, has not benefited the schools. It has deprived them of needed resources, both material and human.

Late in 2010, just after Leonard Grime's funeral, Denise Abston became pastor of Liberty. Her tenure will be addressed in the 2010's section.

Summary of the 2000's

No decade in Liberty's history was so dominated by one pastor, Edsel Hall, although Charlie Thompson is close for the 1970's. Otherwise, what was said of the 1990's generally applies to the 2000's. Church business, the Sunday School, the Tryon Alliance, weddings and funerals, dedications and baptisms, went on as usual. Liberty was somewhat more involved in the conference. Attendance was about the same. The members were mostly the same, just getting older, and the kids were growing up. Charlie Thompson and Edsel Hall shine through the fog of history to reveal two exceptional, committed pastors who did a great deal for their church. Both had outstanding Sunday School programs. Both were countrymen with strong, able wives with whom they ministered side-by-side.

Superintendent Johnson supervised Liberty about a year. Modern superintendents are no less worked than those of decades ago. From the data I have, my reading of the duties of superintendents is that twentieth-century superintendents spent more time in fewer churches in a more limited geographical area, visited those churches several times a year, and were more involved in day-to-day affairs of the church, whereas in the twenty-first century they spend time with more diverse churches in a wider area and may not visit many churches at all during a year. And they generally know less about the routine affairs of individual churches. Certainly, the amount of territory of modern superintendents is greatly enlarged, but of course transportation is better. The Mid America Conference in 2022 has churches in Missouri, Oklahoma, and Texas, though the preponderance is in Oklahoma (twenty-one of twenty-seven).

Whereas the 1990's were a time of relative stability and prosperity in the U.S., the 2000's were not. On Sept. 11, 2001, terrorists attached and destroyed the two towers of the World Trade Center in New York, killing about 3,000 people. The U.S. and allies launched Operation Enduring Freedom in Afghanistan October 2001, quickly driving the Taliban out of the capital, in what would become one of the longest wars in U.S. History. When the U.S. and its allies withdrew suddenly and unceremoniously in August of 2022, the Taliban regained control of the country in a few short months. Iraq was invaded March 2003. Hurricane Katrina devastated New Orleans August 23, 2005. Apple began selling I-Phones in 2007. The I-Phone may be the most influential invention of the twenty-first century so far. 2008 experienced a global economic turn-down and the largest financial crisis since the depression. The cause was the failure of the "sub-prime" mortgage market due to the greed of some of the world's largest banks, many of whom subsequently came under administrative control. As usual, Liberty continued to hold services and support ministries regardless of these world disturbing events.

The 2010's

Denise Abston was pastor from late 2010 to the fall of 2015. Ron Faulk, Ph.D.; Dwight Gregory, Ph.D.; Steve Smith; and perhaps others preached from November 2015 to the end of May 2016. Ron Faulk became pastor at that point, continuing to the present. Dwight Gregory and Jeff Johnson continue to preach occasionally, as well as Liberty members Jeff Grimes and Eddie Ware (in 2022 Jeff is ordained and pastor of the Enid Free Methodist Church).

Denise Abston is the first female regular pastor for Liberty although I am reasonably sure she is not the first female to preach there. For example, Liberty granted Elzie Hemphill an exhorter's license in October 1945. Superintendent Jeff Johnson introduced Denise to me in my University Hall office at St. Gregory's University, around 2007. She was on her way to turn in a syllabus to the Adult Continuing Education Program for a course she was teaching. From that time, we have interacted regularly at conferences and by phone calls and other means, pray for each other and our families, and know each other well. I interviewed her several times about her tenure at Liberty. She went there from the Mid-West City church where she had been an assistant to the pastor. Liberty needed a pastor, and superintendent Johnson asked her to go. She said that she prayed about it and felt that her move to Liberty was what the Lord wanted. As the first regular female pastor of any duration, and initially perceived as a "city-girl," she and the congregation went through a period of adjustment, but it was short.

The church's children and youth programs were strong when she got to Liberty, and she continued to develop them. The church members were also involved in ministry programs in the nearby city of Ripley, helping with school and community events, providing Thanksgiving baskets for needy persons, and ministering as they could. Denise did not mention Tryon, but similar ministries were going on there, although the school had long closed. She thought the strength of Liberty was its kids and strong sense of family, but in a sense, this was also a weakness. The church members were by-and-large loving, gave freely of their time, and were good at serving others. The church had an on-going building campaign, and they were looking forward to constructing a new sanctuary, although tithing had declined from Edsel's years. Unfortunately, when kids graduated from high school, they generally did not return to Liberty. The Life Church in Stillwater particularly drew a lot of youth and adults away not just from Liberty, but from other small churches in the area, which is a good illustration of the modern problem of churches cannibalizing others instead of bringing in new Christians.

Denise attempted to create a list of all the formal members of Liberty Church, but the list was never finalized, I think for several reasons, perhaps the main being that the records were not available to do so. My impression is that Edsel Hall was not fond of paperwork. But as I discovered later, the congregants were ambiguous about creating such a list. Generally, the concept of formal church membership has changed over the decades. A concept that was once important and functional, is much less so in the twenty-first century. I think this marks an important social change. Whether it is good or bad, progressive or regressive, remains to be seen. A progressive argument might be that the de-emphasis on formal membership reflects a diminishing emphasis between insiders and outsiders. A regressive argument might be that such an effacement represents a failure of standards and identity, that the church is seen less as a kingdom apart from the world and more of an institution within it. More practically, the de-emphasis of formal membership might simply represent the desire to be more attractive to a population that is significantly less rigorously Christian than it used to be.

I add that the language of the rules for discipleship tends to be foreign to the broad present culture. Many moderns in the West do not have a consistent language to talk about spiritual phenomena, and indeed my observation is that they simply do not have the width and depth of spiritual experiences that previous generations did. For some reason they have become spiritually shallow (perhaps because they have abandoned God's commandments). Spiritual experience comes from seeking God. And you cannot seek God effectively until you make a heart-felt effort to follow His commandments. Increasing numbers of modern youth are not taught to seek God, much less to love Him. And if they wanted to seek God, they have not been taught how to do so. It is difficult to earnestly subscribe to rules one may not understand very well. On the other hand, in much of the world outside of the West, increasing numbers of people are seeking and experiencing God, and the body of Christ there is growing exponentially. As the Jews contemporary to Jesus rejected him as the Messiah, and the good news passed on to the "gentiles," so now Western culture increasingly rejects the Messiah, and the good news is passing on to the "new gentiles." Or such is the appearance.

My own view of formal church membership is that of my godfather, a Jew, whose parents (his father was a rabbi in Berlin) were murdered in the holocaust. His name was Leo Keiles and he died at the age of ninety-nine due to a fall at a hospital in Dallas where he was a practicing chaplain (yes, ninety-nine years old is correct). He belonged to both a Reformed and an Orthodox synagogue. I asked him why. His first answer was that he was "hedging his bets" (he had a good sense of humor). His second was instructive. He said that his sympathies were with the reformed movement, but that the orthodox, though usually the minority, were the foundation of any church. They represented and maintained the highest, uncompromising standards, closest to the historical ideals, and without them the church would fade into worldliness. The orthodox are the connection to the past, and a church without a past is built on sand. He convinced me. Therefore, I believe in formal membership for church, with the highest standards of faith and behavior. Members should hold each other accountable to the highest standards, with vigilance, as scripture calls for. The challenge is to avoid elitism. After faith, humility is the chief spiritual virtue. Elites lack humility. Loss of humility should be cause for loss of formal membership status. Easier said than done.

Denise commuted from the Oklahoma City area (I commute from Shawnee, about the same distance). She, like Harry Adams and Robin Grueser, very much enjoyed her time of service at Liberty, and remains in contact with many of the congregants, young and old. In 2022 she is Assistant to the Superintendent (Bruce Cromwell), serves on the Board of Administration, and lives in the Oklahoma City area.

The author is the current pastor of Liberty. In 2015 I was Academic Dean at St. Gregory's University in Shawnee. Dr. Johnson, and later Denise Abston, were faculty members, and thus we knew each other well. In September or October Dr. Johnson asked me if I would pastor Liberty. I prayed about it and agreed to at least start the process, since the church should also have a say.

I had two main concerns. The first was that it needed to be in God's will. I have enough experience to know that any other course beside God's is likely to lead to disaster. My second concern was time. I had multiple duties with the university, and I was directing Restoration Chaplaincy, Inc., a jail and prison ministry with about two dozen chaplains serving three to four hundred offenders and staff. I told the Lord that if He wanted me at Liberty, then He was going to have to enable me to preach without long preparations. Interestingly, He did just that. For a couple years the Lord gave me whole sermons with little preparation except to look up passages of scripture.

In December 2017 the University closed its doors. I also resigned from some volunteer work, and so had more time to spend on church matters. I then had to spend more time on sermon preparation, and the Lord quit short cutting the sermon preparations. This says something interesting about how the Lord works. He works, but He also wants us to work, and not just receive marvelous gifts we can use effortlessly. What is important is our constant and hard-fought effort to listen and pay attention to the God within us and around us and to obey Him. God demands effort to stay constantly engaged with Him. Without that effort we drift away.

An essential partner to that effort is patience. As the psalmists often tell us, God wants us to wait patiently for Him. God has all the time in the world, and it is important that His plan to build the Kingdom of Heaven on Earth is fulfilled completely in each and all its details. God does not short cut His plans. Furthermore, the patience of the saints is often the means of drawing attention to God and bringing the lost to Jesus. Patient endurance often produces more fruit than the great sudden victories we typically hope for. Those sudden victories can also easily lead to pride. "But what does the Lord require of you? … to walk humbly with your God" (Mica 6:8).

When I say, above, that the Lord quit short cutting my sermon preparations, I do not mean that His anointing left me, which includes a strong conviction of the truth that I am preaching. I have had a few occasions, less than a dozen in thirty years, in my servant life when I preached and the Lord's anointing was not with me. I know it immediately. It is not fun. I fumble like a blind man. Perhaps on those occasions, that too was God's will; or perhaps not. I have been greatly blessed with the Lord's presence. But sometimes I am more heavily "anointed" than others, we might say. Sometimes the anointing is more extraverted. When the power and the conviction are on me, even unbelievers feel it. Oh, how I love that inspired, self-confident, energy-filled preaching! How I like to project it to the crowd! However, in my later years, I have begun to suspect that that might be "early" rain, and not the "latter" rain. It might not be the best, most mature, most sustainable preaching, the kind that bears the most fruit. Always I think the Lord requires patience and endurance, and humility. It is easy for pride to creep in when you can wow the crowds. It is easy to feel certain of yourself when they admire you. But it doesn't make people more friendly to you. Not only is it intoxicating for me, but it is also for them, to some extent. In his life, Jesus did not often intoxicate the crowds.

As a matter of fact, I am not all that certain about myself, although I am certain about Jesus Christ. He is the master, not me. Projecting personal certainty to the crowds is not entirely truthful, at least not for me. That great, extraverted, powerful public anointing is not necessarily bad, I think, and I confess I still love to have it, and do sometimes. But it may not bear the most fruit. And at the end of all we do, He is the vine, and we are the branches. And he demands that we bear much fruit and prunes us to do so. There is another kind of preaching, more quiet, less emotional, more direct, clearer, more cutting, "sharper than any two-edged sword, piercing until it divides soul from spirit, joints from marrow; it is able to judge the thoughts and intentions of the heart" (Heb. 4:12). The crowds love emotion, but in my spiritual experiences, which include quite a bit of what might be called "warfare," I observe that God does not ordinarily use emotion to get people to change. But it is not unusual for the enemy to do so. Emotion is close kin to the primitive. And it is egoic. I think God speaks more clearly through us when there is less of "us" there. This preaching is more subtle, harder to come by, but I think its effects are longer-lasting. It is also harder to do. It requires even greater effort, and even more patience and humility.

Although I was saved in my twenties, I did not hear from the Lord until my early forties (mid 1990's) and it was then that I was called. My first ministry call was as a jail chaplain – something that had never occurred to me. Nonetheless the proof is in the pudding, and I was, to my own surprise, an effective jail and prison chaplain from the start (spring 1997), not "I" of course, but the Lord working within me.

I was ordained in the Church of the Nazarene in 2011 by General Superintendent Eugenio Duarte. The process for becoming ordained in the Church of the Nazarene is very similar to that in the Free Methodists. Like many of the men and women who preached at Liberty, I began with a local license ("exhorters" license in early FMC language) and began preaching in my home church, Twin Lakes Church of the Nazarene, McLoud, OK. I then received a conference license and began filling the pulpit at various churches in what was then the Southeast District of the Oklahoma Conference (now the Oklahoma District) of the Church of the Nazarene, while I continued to be a chaplain assigned by the Nazarene Church. I was bi-vocational, a professor and dean at St. Gregory's University. My call to be a jail and prison chaplain has never been retired. At one time I had a certificate to minister in Oklahoma Department of Correction and did so about fifteen years, mostly at John Lillie Correctional Facility in Boley. But a couple years after pastoring at Liberty I dropped my DOC ministry.

I am a chaplain-evangelist who became a pastor. In some ways I am more evangelist than pastor. Restoration Chaplaincy, Inc., of which I and the current director, is recognized by the Pottawatomie County Safety Center as the chaplaincy privileged to provide ministerial services to offenders. We minister Sundays starting at one o'clock, and the same for Thursdays. We also baptize, deliver death messages, counsel, train, and provide other services. Between late 2010, when we bought a portable baptistry, and 2020 (when covid shut down a lot of things) we baptized about 400 men and women.

Liberty church is located about forty-five miles north of the Safety Center. To be at the Safety Center by one o'clock, I must leave Liberty by about twelve-ten p.m. Until pastoring Liberty, I had not had a strict schedule for preaching. The Liberty congregants have said that they like knowing when they are going to leave church on Sundays, so the strict schedule has worked out for all. The "strict schedule" still allows me to preach about forty-five minutes, which is long enough. When we have special events at the church, I skip going to jail. This is facilitated because usually a half dozen chaplains are present at the Center on any Sunday.

Because I am both a jail chaplain and a church pastor, I will add some background information about the differences between the two. One of the surprising truths I learned about jail ministry is that men and women who were not very supportive of, or contributing to, their families, almost always cry about being separated from them when they find themselves in jail. Hardened men will tear-up when talking about their families, although they might have abused their partners and neglected their kids. Ninety per cent or more of men and women in jail and prison, whether they designate themselves as Christian or not, want someone to pray for their families, and that they be unified with them. This is an important door to engagement. Outside of salvation, family is probably our most valuable resource. It is no secret why the "world" is attacking the natural family. The great majority of men and women in jail have children, most by two or more partners. Preaching about family, children, and relationships is usually effective.

When men and women are separated from their natural families, they will tend to form new ones. My experience with several thousand incarcerated men and women over a quarter century, is that nothing can take the place of, first, the original mother and father, and second, the extended family. Probably the most shocking fact I learned from jail and prison ministry, is that *there are very few men and women in jail who had a mom and dad at home* – less than five per cent in over three thousand cases I have known. Maybe less than two per cent. There are lots of offenders raised by women, and men, and relatives, and others – but not a mother and father in a stable home. Those without a mom and dad, consciously or unconsciously, long for the family they never knew, and the great majority want to provide something better for their kids, even when they have not, or cannot (e.g., if you have kids by three different mates). The answer to the problem of overflowing prisons (and drugs, homelessness, rootlessness, drop-outs, abuse, anomie, depression, suicide) is clear and simple. Ensure children are raised by a mother and father in a stable home. Sometimes circumstances are such that a child cannot have both, as in the case of the death of a parent. But to deliberately and premeditatively deny a child a mother and father is to deny them the opportunity to be all they could be. Nothing can effectively replace the natural, biological family.

Small, rural churches tend to be very family oriented, and no wonder. However, this makes it difficult for those who were not raised in a normal, biological family to feel comfortable there. Over twenty-five years I have invited many men and women who have served time in jail or prison, and their loved ones, to come to church. Sometimes they come, but the intimate, familial atmosphere of the typical small church, where there is no place to hide, is foreign to them. The small number of the ex-incarcerated who develop zeal and a sense of calling, can fit in almost anywhere, but they are a small number of the ones who profess faith. And those who are not comfortable, do not return. Sometimes they find larger, usually urban churches to attend, probably because of the relative anonymity. Another chaplain and I once tried to start a "downtown" church for ex-offenders and the homeless. We kept it open for two years at a homeless mission in Shawnee, but we could never get more than a few people to come, so we closed it. Since I have been pastor at Liberty, we have had one prior inmate who attends more or less regularly. He says it is because of the love that he feels there. It might also be because I give him a ride.

It is notorious that people get "jail house religion." Some offenders who appear genuinely saved, and even have zeal, revert to a lost lifestyle when released. But some do not. The difference is often relatively simple. Those who quickly find a prayer group to pray with, tend to stay the course of salvation. Those who do not, backslide. There is power in prayer, and more power in group prayer. People ask me if the enemy is real. I know many stories of offenders who, the day they get out of prison, and are walking down the street, get tempted through their greatest weakness. If it is drugs, someone will offer free drugs. If its lust, someone will offer to party. If it is money, a shady deal with come along. I counsel offenders to know their weakness, because the enemy does, and that is exactly where they will be attacked, and quickly. We are rarely attacked where we are strong. Hence Paul's instruction in Ephesians Chapter six for believers to "put on the whole armor of God so that you may be able to stand against the wiles of the devil." Of those who profess salvation, it is impossible in my experience to predict who will stay the course and who will backslide. I have been surprised many times, both ways. But to have a chance to stay the course, an offender must participate regularly in a prayer group.

Ordination in the Church of the Nazarene and the Free Methodists recognizes a call to preach. But there are various kinds of preaching. It depends on the population. Jail offenders are newly traumatized, in a strange place, unfamiliar with the routines, and (mostly) recently separated from their families. They tend to be open to change. In prison for a year, men and women become accustomed to routines. They have usually found a group to belong to, out of necessity (possibly gangs but also Christian or other religious groups) because it is difficult to survive in prison by yourself. You need someone to watch your back, and to stand with you when someone tries to take your food or clothing or commissary, or just tries to establish power over you. Prison populations are harder to preach to and require a different approach than those in jail. This is just a sketch. Even in jail there are different groups that require different approaches, for example sex offenders and child abusers, violent offenders, and the addicted.

A stable, long standing rural church, with stable membership, has a very different population and requires different preaching than an urban church with many transients. Some cultures require different approaches than others. A small, stable rural church tends to have congregants who are experienced Bible readers, and perhaps more importantly, have a prayer life that extends for many years. A sermon meaningful to them would be meaningless in an urban church with many transients, much less a jail or prison population. It is amazing how little most offenders know about God or Jesus, and unfortunately this is true for most Americans. The unchurched have heard of God and Jesus, but tend to have very erroneous conceptions about God, the Son of God, faith, sin, grace, mercy, love, righteousness. They tend to think prayer depends on language rather than faith, and that baptism works miracles whether they have repented or not. They tend to over-emphasize the miraculous and under-emphasize the work that leads to keeping and maintaining faith. They over-emphasize the technical, and do not understand "love the Lord your God with all your heart" (Deut 30:6). They know very little about patient endurance or walking humbly with God. They know little about humility and have little self-discipline. They are easily carried away. The waves and billows easily sweep over them. They do not understand the communal nature of faith. Preaching to them must be founded on the basics and is in some ways more like counseling and small group work than preaching to an established congregation.

It is not possible to evangelize the unchurched and unknowing by correcting even egregious misunderstandings. The truth must be preached rather than errors corrected. The spirit of truth will slowly lead them away from misunderstanding. When I preach to offenders, I usually let them interrupt with questions (which they do in any case). I do not generally correct misunderstandings in public. Instead, I emphasize the truth of the subject at hand. And the subject at hand is usually what God has done in my life – which is so easy to testify to. I am generalizing of course. Preaching must be according to the situation and audience. But all preaching must tell the truth to be effective. And one of the greatest truths we know, is how God has acted in our life. When people hear us, in our own words, witness about what God has done in us and for us and with us, they know it is the truth. They are convicted by the truth. That is how the spirit of truth works. Whether they accept or deny the truth is up to them. But many who most vehemently deny our witness, are the ones in whom the seed of truth will eventually bear fruit. That is God's business, not ours.

I also discovered that the ones I am preaching to are not always the ones who get saved. Many times I have had someone tell me, years after the fact, that I did not know they were listening, but they got saved by my testimony. I have also had times when I felt the Lord wanted me to preach or witness to something in particular, that did not seem suitable or appropriate to the moment and the listeners (or those who I thought were listening). I once had a dream, and the next Sunday when I was in jail, it suddenly came to me to go around the corner and tell the dream, and what I thought it meant, to a group of men there, who were being taught by another chaplain. I have learned to be obedient. I went around the corner and did what I thought the Lord wanted. I got no response. I left. Afterwards, one of the men told the other chaplain, that he had had the same dream and did not know what it meant until I spoke!

A church like Liberty allows for a relatively deep exploration of spiritual truth and experience. On one hand, what everyone needs is to experience God. On the other, where "two or three are gathered in his name," there is an opportunity to understand God in new ways, based on the experiences we have had, as well as to make greater sense of those experiences. Experiences with God are *always* purposeful. The question is, what is the purpose? What is God calling us to do? These are good questions for a mature church. Furthermore, preparation to make oneself available to God and meet God, and then doing what it is that God calls us to do, facilitates further experiences with God. Few people in jail or prison can recognized God's call. They are oblivious to the Spirit and how it works. This unfortunately is also true for many church members. Therefor preaching at Liberty has been enjoyable because I am able to discuss mature matters of the spirit with experienced Christians. We all grow together and look forward to an eternal acquaintance.

The small church is not to be idealized. There are plenty of small churches, rural and urban, that are not in God's will, and the kingdom they are building is not a heavenly one. However, the family and community orientation of many small churches, the long prayer experiences of the congregants, their regular study of scripture, and the necessity of faith to keep the church going, make many small churches the best place to experience and understand God and His Word.

I became the regular pastor starting June of 2016. I concentrated on preaching and getting to know the congregants. We have communion the first Sunday of the month and on special occasions. In 2016 we left the elected positions as they had been, except that we added a Board of Administration as this was recommended by the *2015 Book of Discipline* (p. 34). The members of the Board of Administration are the pastor as ex officio (does not vote), the Secretary to the Board (at that time Carolyn Grimes), the Chair of the Finance Committee (Sam Savory), the Finance Committee members (Gene Grimes, John Huff), the Sunday School Superintendent (Almeda Sumpter), and the delegate (Jeff Grimes). We also created a Membership Care Committee, also recommended by the *Book of Discipline* (p.136, 139), with the same membership as the Administrative Board. The *Book of Discipline* has the task of prescribing spirit and order across a depth and width of churches that is almost unbridgeably wide. It *would* be unbridgeable, except for the unifying power of the Spirit. So far, in six years, the Board of Administration and the Membership Care Committee, have not had to function formally. Probably a small church does not need them. Nonetheless, it is good to abide by the church's discipline.

In 2016, in addition to the above-mentioned Boards, there were twenty-one elected positions, seven associated with Sunday School. These positions are the same in 2017 which can be seen in Appendix VIII. Many of the positions are filled by the same people. I began keeping minutes for our formal meetings. These are kept in a white three-ring binder titled *Liberty FMC 2016* ... along with divisions for Business, Programs and Events, Conference Related Materials, the Tryon Ministerial Alliance, Liturgies and Religious materials, Historical Material, and the church Directory. The permanent location of the binder is at the church, but I take it home to work on. Unless otherwise indicated, the quotes below are from *Liberty FMC 2016* ....

In 2015 Liberty had an income of $19,320 with similar expenses (I am not aware of detailed financial records for 2015). In 2016, income was $23,327, with similar expenses. I was paid $600 per month. In late 2015 and 2016 average attendance was about what it had been for thirty years, that is, about thirty adults and children, perhaps a few more. We probably averaged eight or nine children and youth per Sunday. However, for the Christmas program and Easter, the church was full. For many years one of the members from the 1970's, Sam Savory, who had also been Treasurer since the 1970's, had a fall picnic at his house. It also drew a large crowd, of eighty to a hundred people.

In 2016 the Tryon Ministerial Alliance consisted of Bob and Coleen Fowler with the First Baptist Church; Lorn and Dolores Starling with the Tryon Assembly of God; Steve and Karen Grotheer with the Christian Union Church; and I and my wife Susan with Liberty. Prayer meetings were held at rotating churches bi-monthly. They started at 7:00 p.m. and ended about an hour later with finger food and deserts. As might be expected, the "finger food" was more often like a regular meal. We had an ice cream social August 20. The pastors and wives met occasionally on Saturdays for planning. Bob Fowler took the lead in those meetings, whether by election or consensus I did not know. The highlight of the year was a week-long revival held in the metal pavilion in the park in front of the Christian Union and Baptist Church. Each of the pastors took turns preaching. No records were kept for the revival except for brief notices in minutes. It was hot in June which did not appear to deter the local folk from attending. My memory is that fifty or so attended nightly in 2016.

Life at Liberty continued smoothly through 1917. A pastor who lives fifty miles away has a challenge visiting congregants, making hospital visits, getting to know the community, and otherwise becoming integrated into the life of the church. This is more challenging if he or she is an introvert, as I am. This is less of a problem when the congregation is self-reliant, as Liberty has been and is.

A board and society meeting were held Sunday May 21, 2017. The usual elections were conducted. At my request, the pastor's salary was designated for housing, which helps with taxes. We discussed up-dating the church directory (which we did), having a workday at the church, and writing job descriptions for the elected positions. The annual meeting of the Mid-America Conference was Sunday June 4 (starting in the evening) through Monday June 5, at the United Methodist Church in Shawnee. About a month later we had a workday at the church, about twenty people showing up on Saturday. We scraped, painted, cleaned, repaired, gardened, and otherwise maintained and improved the church.

The next Society and Board meeting was Sunday August 12, 2018. Eddie Ware (wife Teresa) was recommended to the conference as an ordination candidate. A nominating committee submitted recommendations for the elected positions which was to be voted on August 26. A Society and Board meeting was held August 26 at which the various positions were elected, and Eddie Ware was approved as an ordination candidate. The treasurer, Sam Savory, noted that the previous year the church was about $7,500 short in income and the difference was taken out of savings. Savings stood at about $70,000 the primary purpose of which is to build a new sanctuary. However, the savings account (sometimes also referred to as the building account) has not had an increase "in the last couple of years" (Board minutes).

The minutes also note that "Last week we baptized Logan Ford, in the rain, on the north side of the church. Logan had requested this himself and (in the rain as well as in church) gave a testimony to his belief in Jesus Christ the Son of God. ... We had a crowd good of fifty or so. Many gathered around with umbrellas (if they had them). We had lunch afterwards." Logan was baptized in a horse trough which had been brought to the church for that purpose. The crowd was undiminished by the light but persistent rain. Some had umbrellas, few had raincoats, and many just got wet. The minutes note that several other youths had requested baptism.

On Sunday September 2, the following were baptized: Brooklyn Gambill (DOB 5-17-2007), Emma Gambill (DOB 05-23-2008), Braden Mayfield (07-28-2011), Fischer Savory (DOB 09-10-2007), Devin Ford (03-30-2011), and Amy Weaver (07-01-2008). "We had a large crowd of around sixty, the weather was great, and we had a communal meal afterwards." The meals are held in the auxiliary building, whose maximum capacity is about fifty. The children and some adults rotated in and out of the building. Amy Weaver is my granddaughter.

A Society and Board meeting was held Sunday September 16, 2018. Minutes were approved and minor administrative changes were made, such as increasing the size of the Board of Administration. This was the last Society and Board meeting of 2018.

The Tryon Ministerial and Church Alliance meetings for 2018 were a prayer meeting March 21 (at Liberty); on May 5 Liberty hosted a ministers and spouses' breakfast; a prayer meeting May 16 (Baptist); and the revival was May 30 through June 3. The theme of the revival was "Who Are We?" The time was 7:00 p.m. Wednesday night Steve Grotheer preached, Thursday Ron Faulk, Friday Mark Chase, Saturday Mark Skinner (a guest speaker) and Sunday Gene Herndon. The remaining meetings for the year were a ministers and spouses' breakfast July 7 (location uncertain); prayer meeting July 18 (Christian Union); a ministers and spouses' breakfast September 8 (Christian Union); prayer meeting September 19 (Assembly of God); a breakfast November 3 (Assembly of God); and a prayer meeting November 14 at Liberty. During the November 3 meeting the financial report showed the Alliance had $1,020.32 in the Payne County Bank.

On September 2, Betty Marie Hudson died. She was the daughter of Virginia and Harry Thompson. Virginia or course was a 1936 charter member of Liberty Church. Betty attended Liberty almost all her eighty-seven years, longer than her mother did. From her obituary, "Betty was born on January 14, 1932, to Harry and Virginia Thompson in the Tryon rural area. She was a graduate of Sandy Land Grade School and Tryon High School. Betty loved her family, church, shopping for bargains, biscuits and gravy, coffee and most of all, her Lord. She was a dedicated Christian, kind, faithful, classy and a role model for others. She was a retired Physical Therapy Assistant…." She was soft spoken but confident and "classy" is a good description. She took care of her appearance and always seemed ready for whatever might happen. In the short time I knew her, she was always pleasant, with at least a slight smile on her face. She wore glasses and my guess is that, like her mother, she was careful and efficient in the things that she did. Her funeral was at the Christian Union Church of Tryon, and she is buried in the Tryon cemetery.

In 2019 a Society and Board meeting was held Sunday September 29. Annual reports were made as follows. The Sunday School Superintendent (Almeda Sumpter) was not present. However, Liberty had a very strong children's program, the foundation for which had been laid by Linda Grimes, and built on by Almeda Sumpter, with multiple classes for different ages through adult Bible class. Ten or so children attended on a typical Sunday. The Christmas and Easter programs were also very strong. Everyone enjoyed watching the kids learn and perform. On some Sundays about as many teachers and youth were in Sunday School as were in the sanctuary for the sermon. This was not unique in the history of Liberty. The Worship Team (Lisa Baker, Teresa Ware) noted that when Lisa is not in church, Danita Savory leads worship as she has for many years. Teresa, the piano player, "needs prayer against arthritis."

The Mission Chair (Anita Grimes) reports on missions once a month. "This year we made donations to the Mission of Hope in Stillwater, three times. We also made donations for water filters for Guatemala. We conduct food donations and dispersals in the fall and donate regularly to the Tryon Church and Ministerial Alliance that maintains a fund (through donations) for needy persons. Blinds and curtains were replaced in the sanctuary. We have new flower boxes outside." The Trustees (Dustin Ford, Bill Grimes, Sam Savory) reported "Bill mows and takes care of the yard. Sam keeps the lights burning and the AC/Heat working with help from various. Considerable work was done on the church this past year and is on-going. LED lights were installed in the sanctuary, the railing in the front of the sanctuary was replaced, and the floor was replaced in the sanctuary – the old carpet (which had started to smell) was replaced with a quality composite hard floor …." The Stewards (Anita Grimes, Carolyn Grimes, Lavonna Welch) recorded that they help prepare for communion once a month, "Covers on the tables are changed to match the seasons," "blinds and curtains were replaced" (Betty Hudson left $1,000 for this in her will).

The Program Committee (Sondra Ford, Lynda Grimes, Almeda Sumpter) said that last year's Christmas program drew about a hundred with "standing room only." About fifteen children and youth participated. "This year will be the 45th Church Family Christmas" led by Linda Grimes. Other programs were "Mother and Father Day gifts for all mothers and fathers; holiday decorations; Sunday School decorations, e.g., as the seasons change; decorating and preparing luncheons. The baptism and child/youth dedication luncheon had eighty or ninety people, more than the auxiliary building could comfortably hold. The Easter luncheon had a similar number." The committee members also help host the Tryon Ministerial Alliance community prayer meetings and the summer revival. "This year we helped host the funeral for Betty Hudson, a long-time member of Liberty."

The annual report from the conference delegates noted that Jeff Grimes and Eddie Ware were progressing in their ordination work; "The annual Mid-America conference was excellent, and the ordination service was particularly enjoyable. We have a new bishop Keith Cowart, who previously served as Superintendent of the Southeast Region. He replaces Bishop David Kendall who retired." "A Superintendent Search Committee has been formed with the Bishop as Chair" (this is for a replacement for superintendent Dr. Jeff Johnson).

Elections were held. Under new business, the recommendation was made to create a "Church Renovation Plan with Budget," and "Pastor Ron to put it on paper, Sam to assist with cost estimates."

For the Finance Committee, Sam Savory reported that there was $6,080 in checking and $70,070 in savings. "$1,500 had been approved by a vote in September for renovations .... This has been spent already. Sam noted that in 2015 about $19,320 was collected; 2016 $23,327; 2017 $16,900; 2018 $15,780. The Conference dues last year were about $3,200 and insurance about $1,700 every six months." "Pastor Ron noted that revenue is barely enough to keep the church operating. Discussions ensued about this issue. One reason for the renovation plan is to attract new members." For a complete financial report for 2019, see Appendix VIII, Liberty Balance Sheet 2019-2021.

Under New Business "Jeff Grimes noted that he had got a sample chair which has been in the back of the church for several weeks. Various have sat in it and it is more comfortable that (sic) the existing pews (which are hardwood). Jeff recommends that we replace the old pews with new chairs. This chair is about $45 and includes a rack underneath for Bibles and music books." Jeff moved that we buy the chairs, for a total cost of about $5,000. After discussion, a modified motion was passes: "The Board of Trustees will make the decision about what exact chair to buy and will report back to the church on this decision (for discussion) by October 13."

"Reports and Information Items" included the following. "1. Infant and toddler dedications were held Sunday Sept. 1. The following children and youth were dedicated: Renlee Nicole Muller dob 07/24/2019 (parents present Mason and Kelsi Muller): Brayden Cole Allender dob 06/07/2019 (parents present Kaimon and Lydia Allender); Hadley Grace Grimes dob 08/30/2018 (parent present Ryan and Amanda Grimes); Chevy and Lincoln Weaver dob's 12/15/2013 and 03/05/2017 (parent present Bobby Weaver) [these are the pastor's grandchildren]; Vivian Nadine Faulk dob 01/03/2014 (parents present Mathew and Merill Faulk) [also the pastor's grandchild]." "2. Youth baptisms were also held Sunday Sept. 1. Baptized were Hayden, Ethan and Megan Grimes (parents Jeff and Niki Grimes present). On this Sunday services primarily consisted of a short sermon, communion, dedications, and baptisms in which the youth were immersed outside. About one hundred church and family members were present on a pleasant, clear, late summer day. A feast was held in the auxiliary building, starting about 1:15 p.m."

During 2019 the Tryon Ministerial and Church Alliance met Wednesday evenings on January 16 (Baptist Church); March 13 (Christian Union); May 15 (Assembly of God); and revival was May 29—June 2 at the pavilion in Tryon. The next regular prayer meetings were July 17 (Liberty); September 18 (Baptist); and November 13 (Christian Union). The theme of the revival was "The Ascension of Jesus." Pastor Gene Herndon preached Wednesday night of the revival, Ron Faulk on Thursday, Steve Grotheer on Friday, Saturday evening was a time of testimony and music, and Rev. Mark Chase preached Sunday evening. Attendance averaged about forty. A large floor fan was kept running to cool off the hot June evenings. Several coolers with drinks were distributed around the pavilion. The preachers used a microphone and speaker system and made liberal use of handkerchiefs to keep their faces free of sweat.

Before the regular community prayer services, pastors and wives usually met at 6:00 p.m. and the regular prayer services were at 7:00 p.m. A typical prayer service consisted of several songs, a report on finances (disbursements, income, and balance of the Alliance's fund at the Payne County Bank), an introduction by the home pastor, and then perhaps a half an hour or prayer which took the combined congregations to about 8:00 p.m. Sometime in the evening a collection was taken. The host church provided snacks and drinks or a meal for afterwards, and these usually lasted a half hour or so. The other churches have kitchens included in the main church building and this is where the meals occurred. Liberty provides the food in the back of the sanctuary, instead of moving everyone to the auxiliary building, which involves a walk in the grass without much light. An average Wednesday evening prayer service had about two dozen people, sometimes more, sometimes less. They were often the same people as in previous prayer meetings.

Summary of the 2010's

Church leadership was unusually stable during this decade, with two pastors serving five years each. Both pastors, Denise Abston and Ron Faulk, commuted to Liberty, Denise from the Oklahoma City area, Ron Faulk from Shawnee. Both are bi-vocational. Strong lay leadership produced a healthy, vigorous Sunday School program. A dozen or more child dedications and youth baptisms were celebrated 2015-19. Average attendance in 2019 was around 35, about what it had been since 1980. However, many more people than that consider Liberty to be "their" church, although they may only come Christmas and/or Easter. The sanctuary was improved with hard floors, LED lights, new blinds, and improved bathrooms. New chairs are soon to arrive. The Tryon Ministerial Alliance continues to be strong. The church continues to support ministries at home and abroad.

Liberty has kept attendance relatively strong. Its child and youth programs are the envy of many other small, rural churches. The congregants continue to be relatively self-sufficient and help each other out routinely. During the 2010's Liberty had no "church troubles"; unity was strong and disputes rare or non-existent. It is a family church with relatively strong families. Ministries are strong, as they typically have been at Liberty. It is a solid member of the Tryon Alliance. The sanctuary has been noticeably physically improved in the interior. The church is over a third the way to have enough savings to build a new sanctuary. Perhaps most importantly, the faith of the congregants is strong, and the spirit is present in services.

In terms of liabilities, Liberty generally lacks people in the middle age group. It has youth, and grandparents, but several high schoolers, who have been strong members, will soon graduate. If history is any precedent, they will not return. No new families have joined Liberty in recent years. Several of the elders are in poor health. The tithe has fallen below break-even; expenses in 2019 were greater than income. The building, though improved, is still a century-and-a-quarter-old frame building without insulation and the usual amenities of newer sanctuaries.

In 2020 the balance seems in favor of the strengths, and the problems manageable. However, life seldom proceeds smoothly for long. In its eighty plus year history, Liberty has been remarkably immune to outside events, but that immunity will soon be tested.

Some of the outstanding events of the decade are as follows. In 2010 the worst oil spill in the history of the U.S. occurred at the Deepwater Horizon oil rig in the Gulf of Mexico. In 2011 Representative Gabrielle Gifford is wounded and several killed in an assassination attempt. This roughly marks a period of increasing unrest and violence in the U.S. and across the world. In 2011 Osama bin Laden, mastermind of the September 11 attacks on the Twin Towers in New York, is located in Pakistan and killed by the U.S. military. Also, in 2011 world population exceeded seven billion. It did not reach one billion until the mid-1800's, and two billion in the mid-twentieth century. It reached eight billion in 2022. In 2013 a terrible tornado devastated the Oklahoma City area, killing many and causing great damage. In 2015 the federal government mandates same-sex marriage across the fifty states. In 2017 hurricane Harvey strikes Texas and Louisiana, causing one of the costliest natural disasters in U.S. history. In 2019 the longest federal government shutdown in American history occurs, thirty-five days, ending January 25. During this decade the Black Lives Matter movement begins. Climate change is debated in America and across the world. The 2010's was a period of stability for Liberty but beyond the church is increased violence, unrest, and instability.

The 2020's

Discussion of the mission of the greater church, the "body of Christ," is a routine part of Sunday services. We are all called to spread the gospel and work to establish the Kingdom of Heaven on earth. In the last few months of 2019 and into 2020 Liberty had been discussing the specific mission of Liberty and the ways this body can witness and testify to what God is doing. The first Society and Board meeting of 2020 was February 2. "After discussion the previous two weeks, the following statement in italics was approved by the congregation as the Mission statement. *The Mission of Liberty Free Methodist Church is "to proclaim liberty throughout the land" (Lev. 25:10) and "the good news of the kingdom of God" (Luke 4:43; NRSV). Fulfilling the Mission requires us to live an exemplary Christian life; to discern and act on God's call to labor in His harvest; and daily prayer and thanksgiving.* The vote to approve was unanimous. The congregation committed itself to live by the Mission Statement. The following week, the Mission Statement was printed and posted in the foyer to the sanctuary.

The information items were as follows. "1. Update on Renovation Plan. A new steeple has been installed on the roof. 85 new chairs have been purchased and installed and of the approximately eighteen wood pews all but six have been sold for $100 each (Bill Grimes remembers the pews from the 1950's and probably they are considerably older than that. Two of the nine-foot pews remain in the back of the church). Two new toilets, with wall supports, have been installed. Roof shingles have been replaced. A new composite wood floor has been installed in the sanctuary, replacing the old carpet. LED lights have been installed in the sanctuary. New blinds have been installed in the sanctuary. The renovation is in good progress. Thanks to all who contributed many hours, and funds, for these renovations, especially the Trustees and Stewards, but many others helped as well." "2. Update on Christmas program. We had another very successful Christmas program, with a full church, about a hundred present. All children participated who wanted to. We had a dinner together afterwards. The Christmas program is one of the highlights of the year. Thanks especially to the Stewards and Lynda Grimes." "3. Update on Tryon Ministerial and Church Alliance. Our last community prayer meeting was in January and about thirty-five were there. We have them every other month. We have started have a supper for the pastors and wives immediately before the prayer meeting, instead of having a breakfast on Saturday morning. The Alliance presently has about $600 remaining in its funds for the disadvantaged. We started the fall with about $1,500. Funds are primarily given for propane, other utilities, and food. Members consist of the Tryon Assembly of God, Tryon Christian Union, Tryon Baptist Church, and Liberty FMC."

The steeple, white, about twelve feet tall, was the idea of Sam Savory, who also built it and put it up. It was a nice addition to the church, shinning in the sunlight, and visible for miles.

Sometime in February rumors and early reports began circulating in the various media, and among congregants and friends, about a new virus that had appeared in China and was starting to spread around the world. The first reports of infections in the U.S. were on the east and west coasts, especially New York and San Francisco. Across the many media, formal and informal, were contradictions, uncertainties, and confusions. Conspiracy theories and political slants were also numerous, signs of the volatility, anger, and dysfunction of the times. As usual, the congregants of Liberty took in the reports with a grain of salt. By March national and state public authorities were declaring a major public health crisis and cases began showing up in Oklahoma. The church Bishops, and superintendent Johnson, gave advice and directives to the Mid America Conference. For the first time in its history Liberty was impelled to close its doors for an extended time.

A Society and Board meeting was held in June. The specific Sunday has not been preserved. As usual the meeting began about 11:10 a.m. The first item was on Liberty staffing changes resulting from the covid pandemic. The Society and Board minutest indicate that "Quickly after the bishops indicated closure of church assemblies, we started thinking of ways to continue functioning as a church community. After consulting with various church members, I recommended to superintendent Johnson that we make Jeff Grimes Associate Pastor, Eddie Ware Assistant Pastor, Almeda Sumpter and Sondra Ford deacons, all with the privilege to administer the sacraments, including communion. Dr. Johnson, in a phone call Wednesday March 25, approved. Following procedures as outlined in the *Manual of Discipline*, I contacted each of the members of the Liberty Administrative Board (Lisa Baker, Sam Savory, Eddie Ford, Eddie Ware, Almeda Sumpter, and Jeff Grimes), who unanimously approved these positions. I wrote letters outlining the appointments and with job descriptions, to each of the new staff. These letters are attached to this report, and copies were sent to the Mid America Conference staff at 6500 W. Reno, Midwest City, OK. On Easter, four home based communion services were held (and one at the church with five attending)." Easter was April 12. We had a regular Easter service in church, which five people attended. I had recommended that anyone with any health problems, or who had any reason to worry, should not come.

Following the above was an "Update on the corono-virus ("covid19") pandemic. On Sunday March 22, at the request of the bishops and with confirmation by superintendent Rev. Dr. Jeff Johnson, Liberty FMC temporarily ceased to assemble on Sundays [with exceptions noted above and below], as did 99% of all other churches in Oklahoma and across the U.S. This unique event (in modern times anyway) was to stop the spread of the virus. The pastor texted short Wednesday and Sunday Bible studies and sermonettes, but due to technical difficulties not all people received them all the time. Within days of the temporary closure, work began on creating a web site for the church (now Libertyfmc.com), most of the work being done by Dustin Ford (thanks!)" About forty people were on the list to receive services by text and email. This list continues to be used to the present.

Next was an update on the renovation plan. "Of the approximately eighteen wood pews all but two have been sold for $100 each (Two of the nine-foot pews remain in the back of the church). The renovation is mostly complete, and the remaining work was put on hold by the coronavirus pandemic and associated temporary closure of services. Remaining tasks include replacing a broken window, hopefully a new roof on the church, painting. Thanks to all who contributed many hours, and funds, for these renovations, especially the Trustees and Stewards, but many others helped as well."

And finally, was an update on the Tryon Alliance. "Our last community prayer meeting, scheduled at Liberty for Wed. March 18, was cancelled due to the corono-virus. The Alliance presently has about $..... [no figure was given] remaining in its funds for the disadvantaged. We started the fall with about $1,500. Funds are primarily given for propane, other utilities, and food. Alliance members consist of the Tryon Assembly of God, Tryon Christian Union, Tryon Baptist Church, and Liberty FMC."

Liberty did not hold services in church from March 22 to June 6, except for an Easter Service on April 12 and a communion service the first Sunday in May and June. I did send out brief Bible Studies and sermonettes on Wednesdays and Sundays, respectively. For several months the messages were sent via the church web site, but when it became disabled and we could not get it functioning, I sent them out by text message. Interestingly, the text messages seemed more popular than the web site. From the input I received, the roughly forty people who received the messages appreciated and enjoyed them. Once we began Sunday Services again, I continued the text messages for almost a year. Until the present, we text the group regarding special events.

The pandemic unfortunately cut attendance at least in half. We went from thirty-five-ish, to fifteen, or less. Particularly affected were children and youth, who to date (this is being written in the fall of 2022) have mostly not returned. We have a few children eight and under who come occasionally, but the older children come every other month or so. About half of Sundays we have no children. Similar trends are reported by the other churches in the Mid America Conference, and indeed by the small churches in other denominations.

A Society and Board meeting was scheduled for December 13, 2020. However, a cold front rolled through, bringing bad weather and enough snow to make travelling unadvisable. The meeting was held the next Sunday. As usual, this was the time for reports on the various church functions. There was no report from the Sunday School Superintendent Almeda Sumpter who was not present. She was a nurse and, like many in the health care system, was overworked because of covid virus infections. According to the minutes I noted that "Several home communion services were held, and some services to children continued during closure. At this time, Sunday School attendance is running about two-thirds of what it was pre-pandemic." There was no report from the Worship Team, who were also absent. I noted that "worship continues normally, with Teresa on the piano and Danita conducting singing when Lisa is absent." The Missions Chair (Anita Grimes) reported ".... The first Sunday of each month, I give some report on what is being done around us or in other places that is helping people. We have been very limited on funds this year, so we have not been able to take things to the Mission of Hope in Stillwater, OK. We bought gift cards for groceries for six families for Thanksgiving and Christmas. We are sending a donation for an animal to Heifer International this Dec. This animal or animals will go to another church to help improve their poverty, by providing food and income. (Pastor notes that the church provided $100 to him (the pastor) in December to buy food for a man that comes occasionally to church)."

The Trustees (Dustin Ford, Gene Grimes, Sam Savory) reported "Quite a bit was done last year on the renovation plan. This year we mostly did the usual maintenance and repairs. Bill continues to take care of the lawn. Dustin helped put together a website for the church. Sam and Eddie Ford kept the H/AC system running. Sam replaced the front door, which was on the renovation plan. Many others (including the stewards) did the things that needed to be done." For the Stewards (Anita Grimes, Carolyn Grimes, Lavonna Welch) Anita reported "The stewards are responsible for setting up for communion on the first Sunday of each month. We decorate the church for different seasons and holidays. We make sure the church has supplies such as a paper goods and soap. We help with anything that needs to be done in the church. (Pastor notes that the Stewards recently decorated the church for Christmas)."

The Program Committee (deacon Sondra Ford, Lynda Grimes, Almeda Sumpter) had no report. I noted that "the Christmas program is usually the biggest event for the PC. This year we had a smaller Christmas program during the regular time for church on Dec. 20 (today). About a dozen children, youth and young adults participated. About two dozen persons beside those were present. Linda and Almeda noted that it was very sad that we could not do our normal program, but an abbreviated one is much better than none. This year was the 46th consecutive Church Family Christmas. Other programs: Mother and Father Day gifts for all mothers and fathers; holiday decorations; Sunday School decorations, e.g. as the seasons change; decorating and preparing luncheons. Many of the church events are made to work by many members across various committees, the people pitch in and do the work as needed." I also reported "we normally help host the Tryon Ministerial Alliance bi-monthly prayer meetings about twice a year, and breakfast meetings for the same about twice a year, but we did not host any this year because of the pandemic. We also help host the annual Tryon revival, usually held in June, but again this was canceled this year."

"Pastor notes that a Mid America FMC conference was held May 31 at 6500 E Reno, Midwest City (Midwest City FMC Church), 3 to 5 p.m. Our new conference superintendent was introduced, Rev. Dr. Bruce Cromwell, although he had not assumed office at that time. About half of the thirty or so in attendance wore face masks. On June 28, at New Start Family Church 5910 S. Douglas Ave., Midwest City, the new superintendent Rev. Dr. Bruce Cromwell was introduced. On September 27, at 6500 E. Reno, in the evening, a Mid America Conference meeting was held, with two main events: the ordination service, at which our own Jeff Grimes was ordained by the Bishop, and a recognition and thank you for our now ex-superintendent Rev. Dr. Jeff Johnson, who has served as Super for nineteen years and overseen a great increase in churches, church membership, and a great increase in Hispanic membership. Our appreciation and thanks to Dr. Jeff. We note that Dr. Jeff was elected co-pastor of Liberty this past year." That is, the Conference held meetings May 31, June 28, and September 27.

The Nominating Committee presented a slate of nominees, which were duly elected. Reports and Information were as follows. "1. Pastor Ron: this is the year of the viral pandemic, which is ongoing. The number of cases nationally is hitting new highs currently, after previous highs in late March, early April. The Chinese/covid virus began affecting the US around the first of the year, and Oklahoma by February. Both nationally and locally there was a lot of conflicting information about the virus, how virulent it was, and what to do about it. We received notifications from the bishops and Superintendent Johnson to follow state and/or recommendations of the national Center for Disease Control, and to use common sense. After considerable discussion, considerable misgiving, and discussions with Dr. Johnson and Dean Denise Abston, we suspended physical services March 22. Lynda Grimes and Sam Savory helped me communicate with members, and vice versa, building prayer lists, communicating by phone, etc. We received a letter from Dr. Johnson dated March 26, 2020, summarizing the situation and notifying us that the regularly scheduled annual conference would be on-line. We had a regular church communion in church on Sunday April 12, and again on May 3. We re-started regular services Sunday June 6. …. Donations and tithes were down considerably but have increased recently. However, services and ministries seem to be proceeding about as usual if not better. .... During the pandemic these deacons and assistants have provided valuable and needed services, whether conducting communion, or filling in for me during the two times I have been in "quarantine," etc. So, during the pandemic, the ministers of the church have been more active than usual. I note that our various communities, as well as the nation, are experiencing a much higher level of stress than usual, with the various social and individual disorders that result in such times. One sad fact is that the Tryon Alliance of Churches has suspended all physical community activities, and we haven't met during the pandemic (e.g. our communal prayer meetings and our summer revival)."

During the Board meeting's Finance Committee Report, "Pastor Ron noted that revenue in 2015 was $19,320; 2016 $23,327; 2017 $16,900; 2018 $15,780; and 2019 $13,961. Eddie Ware asked how much expenses were this year, and about what is our average monthly expense. Sam said that this year we have spent about $16,660 and still need to send out contribution to the greater church. Our monthly expenses run about $1,600. The largest expenses are the pastor's salary at about $8,000; insurance at about $4,000. Pastor notes that the formula and procedure for support for the conference was changed by the new superintended to 10% of church revenue; and they would like that at the end of each month. Pastor notes that we have been taking funds out of savings to make ends meet, and this obviously can continue only so long. It is essential for tithing to increase." Liberty previously sent in its apportionment to the Conference once a year. The treasurer, Sam Savory, requested that we be able to send the apportionment in quarterly instead of monthly. This was granted by Superintendent Cromwell.

The final part of the Board meeting had to do with confirming the deacons and addressing changes in appointing and maintaining deacons as recently made by the greater church. The old terminology was "consecrated deacon," the new is "conference deacon." "The Conference Deacon's particular ministry role is defined by his or her gifts, passion and calling from God" (*2019 Manual of Discipline*, paragraph 6610, p. 141). Note that Conference Deacons are an issue of the local church." "On an annual basis the local Board of Administration shall review and approve conference deacons within their care as to their character and performance in ministry (*Manual*, 6600, p. 140)." They were so approved.

Almeda Louise Sumpter, Sunday School Superintendent, Deacon, and an important member and leader of the congregation, died of the covid virus September 25, 2021. She was sixty years old. She, and her sister Sondra (also a Deacon), were born to John and Mary Huff, who had been attending Liberty since the 1980's. Nursing was her life work and she no doubt contracted covid in the hospital where she was employed. Her funeral was at the Mehan Union Church since Liberty was too small for the crowd. Ex Liberty pastor Denise Abston read the obituary, and I gave the homily. Two or three hundred people attended. Almeida had made sure that children, grandchildren, and other family members made it to church. Her loss was a significant loss to Liberty, and a great loss to her family.

Another sad loss occurred June 29, 2021, when Harley Dean Holman died after a long illness. He was the husband of Carol Holman, a long-time member of Liberty. The funeral was at the Tryon Baptist Church, due to the size of the crowd, and because one of Harley's close kin was a minister in the Baptist church. He, Corey Woods, and I officiated at the funeral. Harley was in the last graduating class of Tryon in 1968. He and Carol were married in 1979. He worked in construction and farming. He is buried at Tron Cemetery.

A year went by until the next Society and Board meeting, November 28, 2021. The annual reports from the Sunday School Superintendent, the Worship Team, and The Missions Chair, were similar to the previous year. The Trustees reported "we repaired the hot water heater, installed a new thermostat in the auxiliary building, and we obtained thirty padded chairs for the auxiliary building which we received from a church in Harrah who no longer needed theirs. We also replaced the front door to the church." The Stewards "assisted with two funerals this year, one for Harley Holman, one for Almeida Sumpter." For the Program Committee I reported "On Sunday Dec. 19, starting 7:00 p.m., we had a Christmas play and singing, led by Lynda Grimes. Approximately 100 adults and children attended, i.e., there was standing room only. About twenty children participated, and ten or so adults. We had food afterwards in the auxiliary. We were surprised by the numbers attending. It was a great success, and all had a good time." I also reported that "Jeff [Grimes] has started pastoring a church in Enid, and is enjoying everything but the drive. He still attends Liberty as he and the family can. We have a new Superintendent, Bruce Cromwell, who is certainly busy and seems to be doing an excellent job. The previous Super, Dr. Jeff Johnson, preached for us once this year, and is in MOL regular contact with Pastor Ron." Annual elections were conducted, and the results can be seen in Appendix VII.

For the Pastor's Annual Report I wrote "This is the second year of the viral pandemic, which is ongoing. The covid virus became generally noticeable around the first of the year 2020. The number of cases nationally and internationally varies considerably by season. Both nationally and internationally there continues to be a lot of conflicting information about the virus, how virulent it was, and what to do about it. However, besides the relatively brief time we suspended services from March 22, 2020, to May 31 (during which time we did have two communion services), we have had continuous services. The Tryon Church Alliance began holding its regularly scheduled prayer meetings the third Wednesday July 2021, and Liberty hosted one of those the third Wednesday this September. Sunday attendance this past year has been from about twelve to twenty-four, occasionally more or less. I continue sending out Wednesday Bible Studies by text message. Donations and tithes are down. Services and ministries seem to be proceeding about as usual. ..... Rev. Jeff Grimes is pastoring an FMC church in Enid, and is enjoying his new position. Elder Candidate Eddie Ware continues to do an excellent job with Adult Sunday School and is a great help to me in filling when I need to be absent. Dr. Jeff Johnson, co-pastor, has preached once this past year."

"With fewer members attending, each person becomes more essential than usual. Thanks to all who have been faithful during these difficult times. The future depends on what we all do today."

The Treasurer told the Society and Board that "We have about $1,300 in checking and $60,000 in the building fund." For a complete financial report see Appendix VIII, Liberty Balance Sheet 2019-2021.

The next Society and Board Meeting was February 13, 2022. I gave the Society a brief on Rev. Thom Cahill and his wife Sherry, who are missionaries to Asia. "As per information in a phone call Ron had with the Cahills, the goal is to train 10,000 national leaders, and reach one million Asians, through "Gethsemane Leadership Team." Rev. Thom is responsible for scheduling, recruiting, etc. Trainings to be by Zoom, videos, on-site seminars, and college courses as needed. There are twelve basic courses on video. The program will take about three years to complete." The Society voted to "Provide financial and spiritual support for the Cahills and the FMC Mission in Asia. Provide at least $600 annually …."

I gave a progress report on the "history of Liberty" that I am writing. "It is looking more like a book. There are significant records up to 1979, and little after that, but several of the current members starting (sic) coming in the mid 1970's. Would anyone like to write their own memoire or history? Ron passed out "Sample Questions" to prompt members about the kind of information that would be especially valuable to Ron (copy attached). Several members said they would write something. Ron would like to be done in about a year. He is getting materials from the conference too. Generally, church history materials are scarce."

Relevant sections of my pastor's report for the year were as follows. "… the Christmas program this year drew a church full of people, around a hundred. About twenty children participated, perhaps more. Donations and tithes are up a bit (see the Board meeting). Services and ministries seem to be proceeding about as usual."

"The jail ministry (Pot Co Safety Center) continues about as usual, with a half dozen chaplains ministering on Sunday and Thursday afternoons, as usual. Men and women regularly accept the gospel and are saved. Much of the work is discipleship. The facility is planning to add a wing, to expand the population of inmates from 300 to close to 400."

During the Board meeting the 2020 financials were formally presented and accepted by the members. 2019 and 2020 expenses were included for purposes of comparison. Sam Savory and I reported that "2020 income was $17,705, and 2021 was $18,276. 2021 expenses were $20,794. The pastor's salary at $8,200 is the largest expense (he thanked the congregation for a $200 a month raise back in the fall); the next largest is insurance at $4,788, which seems excessively large but we have been unable to find something cheaper. Contributions to ministry were third at $1,930 and the conference apportionment was fourth at $1,820. We have about $73,000 in reserves and the building fund. We spent very little on the church itself. In 2022 we will also give about $600 to the Cahills for Asia World Missions." As previously noted, a copy of the financials may be seen in Appendix VIII, 2019-2021 Liberty FMC Balance Sheet.

Easter was April 17. Unfortunately, my family was exposed to covid. My wife, Susan, and I have two grandchildren who live with us, Chevy age seven, and Lincoln age five. We also have a ninety-one-year-old uncle. Lincoln came down with a fever of 104 F the Monday before Easter, which continued to Tuesday, but was down thereafter. His pediatrician said she did not know what he had and took blood tests. They came back Thursday, and he had covid, although by then his symptoms were normal. No one else had symptoms, but obviously safety cautioned quarantine. This was the third time I missed a Sunday service because of quarantine. I was especially disappointed because we had two infant dedications scheduled. I called Dr. Jeff Johnson on very short notice, and he did the Easter service. The Society and Board minutes of October 9, 2022, report that "On Easter Sunday we had two infant dedications: Kaylyn and Greg Dodd dedicated Berkleigh (DOB February 11, 2022) and Ryan and Amanda Grimes dedicated Newt (DOB March 3, 2021). Since pastor Ron Faulk was in quarantine due to covid, Rev. Jeff Johnson, Superintendent Emeritus, conducted services." Interestingly, none of the other four people in our house contracted covid from Lincoln. Many other members of the church reported covid infections during this time but Almeda Sumpter is the only one who died from it.

A 2022 Society and Board meeting was held Sunday May 29. The main purpose was to discuss and choose an insurance policy. Excerpts from the Society meeting minutes are as follows. "Sam Savory, recently received renewal of our church's insurance for next year from Church Mutual Ins. Co. and the cost is $5,416." "In 2021 our insurance with Church Mutual was $4,788; in 2020 $3,914; and in 2019 $3,700. Last year's church income was $18,276, and $5,416 is 29.6% of last year's budget. The primary reason for the cost is coverage for sexual misconduct." "In 2020 we had a quote for insurance not including sexual misconduct, from Graham-Rogers, and it was $2,315."

I emailed Denise Abston, one of our liaisons with the conference, about whether the sexual misconduct insurance is required, and she sent me an email on May 10, 2022, in which she states, "I would recommend that they talk with Brotherhood Mutual to see if they can get a significantly reduced policy and invoice." "Here is the relevant section that she sent: "Insurance Requirements: * Property Insurance *Liability Insurance * Conference and FMCUSA must be listed as additional insured** This protects the church, the conference, and the denomination. We also strongly encourage every church to obtain sexual misconduct liability insurance. For many years, this has been the number 1 or number 2 reason why churches and pastors are sued."

Anita Grimes made a motion to "Pay one month of current policy while continuing search for another policy …." Some of the discussion is as follows. "We do not [now] have any regular children's programs, and when we do have kids, one of the parents or grandparents teaches them. We do not transport kids, or do sleep-overs, although we have in the past and hope to have kids so we can have regular programs in the future. The renewal rate of $5,416 seems more than we can afford, although we could take it out of our building savings, but that is not a good precedent to take. …. There are probably lots of small churches who cannot afford the coverage and who do not take it." Anita's motion was accepted unanimously.

New business was "we agree to host a Tryon Church Alliance community prayer meeting on the third Wednesday in June, pastors' meeting at 6:00 p.m., and church meeting at 7:00 p.m. with beverages and snacks afterwards. We hope the Alliance can resume regular bi-monthly prayer meetings."

I reported that "I have had a chance to talk with previous pastors Robin Grueser and Harry Adams. Harry is now 85 and his wife is deceased, but he seems otherwise to be doing well. Some of you are still in contact with Robin, who reports that numbers are down at his church in Guthrie, as ours are here. Both have fond memories of their time at Liberty. I will be incorporating some of their observations in the history of Liberty."

On Sunday July 3, the Society and Board met again. I reported that "On June 20 we received a quote from Seth Valentine with "Church Insurance Specialists" with an office in Shawnee, the total was $4,129. The quote is attached. However it only allows $105,000 for the church and $25,000 for the auxiliary, although it has one million in coverage for "Sexual Acts Coverage." We discussed this in church last week. We thought the coverage for the church too little. It would cost us at least $200,000 to replace the church. I ask Seth for another quote. It came June 28, and is also attached. Coverage for the church is $150,000 but the Sexual Acts Coverage has been reduced to $50,000, which he said is the smallest amount they offer. The total is $3,825."

"Anita Grimes moves that we accept the $3,825 quote which has $150,000 coverage for the church." This was seconded by Carol Grimes. Some of the discussion was "If we lost the church, with $150k plus what we have in the bank, we could just build a new church. We would like to have more than $25k for the auxiliary, but overall this seems the best deal we have found." The Society voted unanimously to accept the quote.

I then reported "We hosted a Tryon Ministerial Alliance Community prayer meeting Wednesday June 15. All the pastors were present: Rev. Mark Chase (Baptist); Gene and Beth Herndon (Assembly of God); Steve and Karen Grotheer (Christian Union); and me. Pastors met before-hand and came up with a schedule for 2022-23. Pastor Ron was voted to take over the scheduling and logistics for the Alliance, and Steve will continue to hold the checkbook and write checks. The Alliance has about $1,400 in the bank, very good for this time of year. We took up a collection that Wednesday. Attendance was about thirty, and the crowd seemed very pleased to be there and to be resuming the prayer meetings. I was encouraged. We had finger food and drinks afterwards, and people stayed for half an hour or so to re-connect and visit. It was a good prayer meeting."

Finally, I reminded the group that "the Mid America FMC conference is the last week of July. Also, the Cahills, the missionaries to Asia we are supporting, will be at Liberty the last Sunday in July, July 31. Let's try and have as many people here as possible."

Another 2022 Society and Board meeting was held Sunday October 09, beginning a few minutes before 10:00 a.m. This is the last Society and Board meeting of this history. As this was a typical Sunday service – except for the Society and Board meeting -- I will describe it in some detail.

Present were Sam and Danita Savory; Anita Grimes; Lavonna Welch; Gene and Carolyn Grimes; Bill and Lynda Grimes; Eddie and Teresa Ware; Max Knowlton; Lora Allendar and granddaughter Renlee Muller; Michael Hutchinson; and pastor Ron Faulk. As usual, we began with a devotional by Anita Grimes. She read a selection from "Our Daily Bread" then we sang a song. We noted the birthdays and anniversaries and sang for them.

We normally have adult Bible study about 10:15 a.m., led by Eddie Ware. Since before I was pastor, Liberty has used the *Faith Connections* journal for study, published quarterly by The Foundry Publishing of Kansas City, MO. The journal is written by Wesleyan scholars, theologians, and pastors, and is part of the Nazarene Publishing House. It is an excellent Bible study guide. On this Sunday we called to order a Society and Board meeting during the time normally scheduled for Adult Bible Study. Since this is probably the last meeting before the new year, we began with reports from the various committees. The Sunday School Superintendent, Anita Grimes, with a few additions from the group, reported that "students who left during the pandemic mostly have not come back. We have enough kids for Sunday School about every other Sunday. There are many secular activities now on Sundays, like ball practice and games. Several of our kids go to programs on Wednesday at the Mehan church, where many of their friends go. Some of the kids went to Life Church, but when asked, said they did not learn anything about God or Bible, it was a lot of entertainment." The Worship Team had nothing new to report.

The Missions Chair, also Anita Grimes, told the group that "Last year we continued our support of the Mission of Hope in Stillwater; we hosted the Cahills (missionaries in Asia) and gave them about $1,000; we renewed contact with the Vincents (who are in restricted access region in Asia) and hope to support them financially next year as well; and we give gift cards to needy families for Thanksgiving and Christmas." I note here that the Vincents had once been supported by Liberty, but lost touch several years previously, apparently because they started communicating through email. When I met the Cahills at the Mid America Conference, I ask them if they knew the Vincents, and they said no. Through an apparent serendipity, or God at work, the Vincents happened to be back in Oklahoma, and happened to meet Liberty member Carol Grimes. We have since established regular contact.

The Trustees reported "Not much was done on the church this year, except for improvements in handicap access. Thanks to Bill for mowing!" The Stewards "assisted with the Tryon Ministerial Alliance prayer meetings, and with communion." The Program Committee noted the Christmas play. The Society discussed the problems having one this year, and how many kids might be involved. They decided to have one, which will be the 48th year that Linda Grimes has directed a Christmas play.

The conference delegates reported that "The conference was July 24-25 at Generation del Espiritu Santo FMC, Oklahoma City. This was first time at an Hispanic church. Bishop Keith Cowart gave a wonderful sermon and Superintendent Cromwell gave a good charge to the conference. Grace

Community church of Buffalo, MO, previously a Methodist Church, was added to the conference. We are seeing quite a bit of interest from Methodist churches in joining the FMC, due to the split in the UMC primarily over Gay marriage and the authority of the Bible."

"At the conference we learned that Hugh Wayman died in the last year. He pastored Liberty in 1963-64 and was Superintendent of the Conference for many years and filled the pulpit at Liberty many times besides when he was pastor. His brother Byron was pastor of Liberty in 1951-52. His son Danny Wayman was received into the FMC by transfer from the United Methodist Church during conference. [The pastor] visited with Danny during conference."

The Nominating Committee motioned to keep the electors the same as last year and this was accepted. During the discussion several noted that when they first joined in the 1970's they were quickly elected to positions because the older generation had served for so many years, and now they were in the same situation, but with no new members to elect.

The minutes record that "The Tryon Ministerial Alliance is operating normally. We meet the first Wednesday of the month. Pastor Ron Faulk oversees scheduling, and Pastor Steve Grotheer oversees funds finances. On the third Wednesday of the month, pastors and wives (and any other interested persons) meet at 6:30 p.m. and the prayer meeting is at 7:00 p.m., after which we usually have snacks or a light supper and drinks together. The August meeting was at the Christian Union Church, and about two dozen persons were there. The next meeting is October 19 at the Baptist Church. The Schedule for 2022-23 is posted on the church bulletin board."

The minutes record that "we talked ten or fifteen minutes about the state of Liberty, and the fact that many members have not returned since covid struck. The members present said they would continue to contact family members to remind them that the church cannot continue without them. How can we get the kids back? Not easy to do. Liberty will never be able to entertain kids the way larger, urban churches can, and we are not sure that we would want to. All agreed to continue praying and listening to the Lord for what we need to do for Liberty FMC, which is now 86 years old."

Finally, during the Society meeting, I noted that "On June 25 I electronically filed our Annual Church Report with the greater church." Usually the report is required around February. "Covid is still around but seems less deadly and life seems to be getting back MOL to usual. With fewer members attending, each person becomes more essential than usual. Finances continue to be challenging. Thanks to all who have been faithful during these difficult times. The future depends on what we all do today."

"Please remember in your prayers Restoration Chaplaincy and its work, mostly at the Pot Co Public Safety Center. The lives of men and women are being changed for the better every week."

The Society meeting was closed, and the Board meeting began with the Treasurer, Sam Savory, reporting that "on the seventh day of the eighth month we were down to about $10 in the checking account, so we transferred $5,000 to it from savings/building. As of this past week, the checking account had $6,302, and $65,000 remained in savings/building. As usual, a full report on the year's finances will be given after the first of the year. We will likely run a deficit this year, and obviously we are in trouble if this continues."

The next and final item was a motion from Teresa Ware to "put $50,000 into a 9-month CD at the Payne County Bank, which is now paying 2.5 %." The motion was approved. The Society and Board meeting adjourned at 10:55 a.m.

After a few minutes, we began regular services as we normally do, by singing three songs, led by Danita Savory at the pulpit and Teresa Ware on piano. What songs we sang are not recorded, but we often sing "Count Your Blessings," "More About Jesus," "What A Friend We Have in Jesus," "Nothing But the Blood," "The Old Rugged Cross," "Amazing Grace," "When We All Get to Heaven," "Victory In Jesus," with songs appropriate to the seasons. After the music, we completed our prayer list. After prayer we took up a collection. If any children are present, we let them carry the collection plate. None old enough being there, Sam Savory, the Treasurer, passed the plate, and received the funds.

At this time, around eleven o'clock, children normally proceed to Sunday School, and I preach. In my quarter century of preaching, I have rarely if ever used a lectionary. However, in the spring of 2020 (as it happened, when covid first hit), in consultation with the congregation, we decided to more or less systematically cover all the major sections of every book in the Old and New Testaments, in three to four years. Like most preachers, my habit is to circle around Biblical texts that are most meaningful or useful to me, or maybe that I know best. The congregants and I wanted to deepen our knowledge of scripture by reading the whole Bible. Thus, in the spring of 2020 I started using a lectionary most Sundays (even though the cycle of readings normally starts the first Sunday of Advent).

A note on lectionaries: most Christian church services are modeled on Jewish ones, which should not be surprising since the first Christians were Jews and God rules over all. During Jesus' time the synagogues were using standardized schedules of scripture readings, which may well date to the Babylonian captivity, about five hundred years before Jesus. Both Jews and Christians continued to develop these standardized schedules into modern times. Pause to consider that the normal form of worship services for Jews and Christians has been recognizably similar for 2,500 years.

The western or Roman (Catholic) Church schedule of readings, or lectionary, is the basis for many if not most Protestant churches (I prefer the term Reformed churches). It consists of a three-year schedule of readings that starts with the first Sunday of Advent. The Eastern (Greek) churches typically use a one-year lectionary. Hence, the Roman Catholic and Reformed churches mostly use the same three-year cycle of Scripture readings.

Following a lectionary ensures that most scripture is covered in one to three years. It also means that someone can walk into very disparate Christian churches around the world and hear readings and exposition on the same scriptures (only, of course, if they use a lectionary). The disadvantage of lectionaries is that, perhaps God wants a particular church to reflect on a particular Sunday on different scripture and exposition than is scheduled years in advance. As I mentioned above, the great majority of my preaching life I have not used a lectionary, preferring to use whatever scripture comes to me in the process of praying about a sermon. And even today I do not use a lectionary when in jail or prison. However, in the past two years, reading almost all scripture through the lectionary, has given me (and I hope the congregation) a new appreciation for the great unity of scripture, and developed my understanding of certain key scripture by cross references to passages I do not normally read.

October 16 we covered Psalm 19, Jeremiah 31:27-34, 2 Tim 3:14-4:5, and Luke 18:1-8. For several years I have been emphasizing that God created humans according to an age-old plan and for specific purposes. In this sense, humans are important to God's plans, and therefore each human life is intrinsically meaningful. Furthermore, God equips us for our purpose. He equips us with his commandments and his ancient Word. And He equips us with "the promise of the Father" that Jesus told us about, and that Jeremiah and others prophesied about, that is the Holy Spirit. As Jesus said, *we* are the temples of the Spirit. God does not live in material buildings. Our immediate spirit-driven purpose is to build the Kingdom of Heaven on earth, which, again, is first a spiritual kingdom, within us and among us. Beyond that, our purposes are largely unrevealed. Jesus tells us we can hardly imagine them. God is future focused. To work effectively, we need to be forgiven of our sins and really accept that forgiveness, so that our guilt does not impair us from what God calls us to do. We need to also remember, as Jesus tells us in the parable of the widow and the unjust judge, that good wears down evil. Good is more powerful than evil, love is more powerful than hate, and evil is often astonished at the power of God's good and good people. The power is in persistence. Good naturally persists better than evil. Jesus tells us directly, "pray always, and never lose heart." Prayer, as always, is one of our greatest and most effective tools, along with humbleness. Humbleness can be lowly and self-effacing, and yet be persistent and overcome evil. The lowly widow overcomes the powerful, prideful judge "who neither feared God nor respected man."

Services concluded about 12:10 p.m., and I drove to the Potawatomie County Safety Center, getting there about one o'clock (I leave the jail sometime between two-thirty and four o'clock). Five men and two women chaplains were there. Staff patted us down and conducted into the facility. We had a short prayer together then dispersed. The other chaplains went to be locked into individual pods, each pod has five cells which hold two or three people each. All offenders who want ministry exit their cells into the holding area. I went first to the medical unit, and then to "Booking" where new arrivals, suicide risks, the mentally ill, and offenders dangerous to themselves or others are kept. Medical and booking usually takes half an hour to an hour to cover. Most of my ministry to these offenders is one-on-one. Much of the time is mundane, inquiring about family and health, but sometimes God works in awe-inspiring ways.

One of my more interesting recent cases was a thirty-six-year-old man who had been in a shoot-out with police after a traffic stop. The police officer was killed but not before shooting the man five times. I will call him Bill (not his real name). He hung between life and death several days. I originally met him in the medical unit. He was in a cell by himself and would not turn from facing the wall when I asked, through the door-window, if he needed anything. The man in the cell next to Bill's, however, always had questions about God. I talk with a loud voice, so the others can hear if they want (or not). After a couple of months Bill started responding to me by saying "no." Eventually we had short conversations. I usually start by listening to prospects. I often do not know what to say at first, that is, I do not have anything from God to say. But as I listen, God reveals things to me, for them. I have also learned not to get in a hurry when evangelizing. I never push people to any commitment they are not certain they want to make. If anything, I slow them down. They need to be sure of this, the most important commitment they will ever make.

Bill eventually began telling me about his life and the things he had done. I mostly listened. I was non-judgmental. I too have sinned. Later, he asked questions about God, partly based on what I had discussed with his neighbors. Then he asked about my life. This is a crucial moment – when we have a chance to witness to others what God has done for us. That is key because this is the truth. What God has done for us comes first in evangelizing. Theology comes later. Bill eventually began looking forward to my Sunday visits, which were the only contact he had with anyone outside of law enforcement and medicine. I typically spent a half hour or so with him. I will add that for three years he never went outside his cell (about eight feet by ten) except to go to court, and that only happened a few times.

We became acquainted and talked about each other's lives and especially families. He had several grandchildren. We began praying together. After about a year he was moved from medical to maximum security. He told me he had been using drugs since he was sixteen, and this was the first time he had been free of drugs in twenty years. His appearance began to change, and he began to gain some peace. He worried about his family. He never expressed much worry about himself. He also routinely asked me to pray for the family of the officer he had killed, and he expressed deep regret for killing him. There was no dramatic moment of conversion, but he came to believe and have faith in Jesus, the Son of God. He came to Jesus his own way, accompanied by me, his friend. A couple of years had gone by, and he was in the middle of his trial. I was struck by the great change in his appearance. When I first saw him, his face was rigid, his expression guarded, his eyes small, his color ashen. Two years later his face was relaxed and expressive, open, with much more color, and his whole attitude had changed. He was soft spoken and even humble. He did not look like the same person. He did not argue. We had talked about the possibility of the death penalty, but he was given life in prison which he calmly accepted. After about three years he was transferred out to the Department of Corrections. We continue to exchange occasional letters. So far, his great change in outlook and demeanor remains, as does his commitment to follow Jesus, to sin no more, and to be about the business of building the Kingdom of God on earth where-ever he is.

Every conversion is different. If you go into a pod of men or women, under the trauma of a recent arrest, most of whom are also drying out from drugs (90% of people in jail were on drugs) get loud with them about sin and changing their lives, and ask who wants to get "saved," half of them will raise their hands. But they are grasping at straws. They do not know who Jesus is. Their repentance and commitment to not sin is not valid – they do not really know what sin is or what they are committing to. That is not real salvation. It will not stick or change their life. Salvation is from God, not us. God works in His own time. On the one hand Jesus is urgent about laboring in the harvest. On the other we are cautioned to wait patiently for the Lord to act. We need to labor diligently, always "staying awake" and "paying attention." But our labor is nonetheless patient, waiting for God to act. We scatter seed, He brings the fruit to ripeness.

Wednesday October 19 the Tryon Ministerial Alliance had a regular prayer meeting at the First Baptist Church in Tryon. Pastor Mark Chase, pastor Steve Grotheer and his wife Karen, and I met about 6:30 p.m. to discuss the evening's program, the future schedule, and what the Alliance might want to do in the next year. Not for the first time, we discussed having a joint ministry in lieu of a prayer meeting, but without conclusion. Pastor Gene Herndon and his wife Beth, who are normally present, were in Florida. The meeting began at 7:00 p.m. with several songs, including "Victory in Jesus," all accompanied by piano. Twenty persons were present, most or all over forty years old, about even divided between men and women. Four were from Liberty. The meeting adjourned a little before 8:00 p.m. for a community dinner.

Appendix IX. shows the revenues and expenses for the Tryon Alliance from 2020 to October 2022. These figures are from the Payne County Bank. These are not representative years, due to the covid pandemic which began in early 2020. January 2020 is probably representative. It shows $733.20 given out by the Alliance to the needy. By March the Alliance had ceased meeting due to covid. Late 2022 will probably be the next time that resembles historical revenues and disbursements. Even so, in 2020 the TMA gave out $1,574 to needy persons; in 2021 $955; and in the first nine months of 2022, $1,051.

Services at Liberty continue, as they have for eighty-six years. Linda Grimes is preparing a simple program for Christmas, which we are all looking forward to.

Conclusion

In the spring of 1935 a lay couple, "Brother and Sister Will Ridens," journeyed about fifty miles east from their Free Methodist Church at Guthrie to the Sandyland School at Tryon, "to preach the old time holiness gospel." They were evangelists. A local couple, Brother and Sister J.W. Jones, provided them a place to stay through the summer. "A few hungry souls" kept coming to hear the good news, and in August 1936 the conference sent G.J. Eikermann and his wife to be the first pastor of the new congregation. A Free Methodist Society was formally established in August of 1937. Four local persons including a brother and two sisters – Floyd Rush, Flossie Rush, Beulah Thompson and Virginia Thompson – answered "the seven rules for full membership." Mrs. Lucia Eikermann, probably the pastor's wife, "presented her letter from Wisby society" (quotes are from the *Account Book*, p.1). Thus, with five charter members, the Liberty Chapel Free Methodist Society came into being.

They met in the Sandyland School house until 1946. That year they purchased an acre, and the Oklahoma conference gave the Liberty Society what had previously been a congregationalist church in Perkins. Someones, it is not recorded who, disassembled the church, minus its square steeple, and moved it in wagons about eight miles to the present location at the corner of Union and Worthy roads in far north Lincoln County, roughly equidistant between Tryon and Perkins.

In the 1950's a building for a parsonage was purchased from elsewhere (from who and where is not now known) and moved to the acre, about fifty feet north of the church. Also, in the 50's electricity and plumbing were added. In 1988 Liberty was one of the four organizing churches of the Tryon Ministerial Alliance, that functions to the present. In the 1990'2 new bathrooms and two rooms for Sunday School were added to the sanctuary. Around this time the parsonage was remodeled into an auxiliary building which since has been used for Sunday School classes and for meals (it retains a kitchen). By the mid

1990's the Liberty facilities were much as they are at the present, except that the old clear-pine nine-foot pews, probably original to 1946 if not before, were replaced with cushioned chairs in 2019; a composite floor replaced the old carpet; and a small steeple was added.

From 1935 to 2020 few if any outside events had a noticeable effect on Liberty. However, the covid pandemic of 2020 caused the first extended (about two month) closure of the church, except for the Easter service and the communion service of the first Sunday of May. In addition, several home services were conducted. The pastor began sending short, weekly messages by text. The Tryon Ministerial Alliance also suspended services. Starting June 6 normal meetings and services resumed. For the Tryon Alliance, this was about a year later. Liberty's Sunday School Superintendent, Almeda Sumpter, died from Covid. She was the only regular attending member to die from the pandemic. Covid reduced adult attendance by half, and child and youth attendance by about two-thirds.

In the present, eighty-seven years after the Ridens' went out to sow the seed of the gospel, Liberty Church continues to evangelize the good news, study the Bible, minister to the needy, Baptize and bury, wed and welcome, and participate in what is now the Mid America Conference of the Free Methodist Church. The Liberty Society has weathered great changes since its humble beginnings: World War II and many other wars, the fall of the Soviet Union, tremendous advances in technology (nuclear energy, the jet, computers, the internet, cell phones, electric vehicles) the addition of roughly six billion people to the world, the covid pandemic of 2020 which continues, and so on. Through all, Liberty has kept up the work of building the Kingdom of God on earth. Probably church services today are not that different than 1935. Many of the songs are the same. Passages of scripture have not changed, nor the church's commitment to the authority of the Bible. Its commitment to support missions is the same. During most of its history its children's programs have been strong and are probably one of the keys to its longevity. It continues to be a self-reliant church, relatively unphased by quick turnover in pastors. It is family oriented and mutually supportive. It has been remarkably free from internal divisions.

Starting in the 1970's the pastors' lengths of service have been longer. Liberty's maximum average attendance in its eighty-six years was probably around fifty, and that not for very long. From 1935 attendance grew slowly to a peak in the early 1950's. It experienced a relatively quick decline and reached its lowest numbers in the late 1950's and early 1960's. At this point its existence was threatened. The faith and perseverance of a few key persons kept the church going. In 1968 pastor Harry Adams said attendance averaged seven or eight. At this time the church had become elderly and seemed to be declining again, but then a few young families reinvigorated the church. From the late 1970's to 2020 attendance was remarkably stable, in the 30 to 40 range. However, for the Christmas program and Easter the church was often at a maximum capacity of close to a hundred.

The men and women who started Liberty in 1935 were in their twenties and had young families. They were still the foundation for the church in the 1970's. Then another group of men and women in their twenties, with young children, joined the church and, for another forty years, were its foundation. Now, as Liberty approaches its centenary, it stands at its third new start. In the last six months a few younger members have started attending, and the future may belong to them.

Appendices

Appendix I. Liberty Leadership

The Pastors and Leaders of Liberty Free Methodist Church, Tryon, Oklahoma, 1935-2022

Several sources exist for identifying the pastors in the 1935-1922 history of Liberty Free Methodist Church. No sources are complete, none are in full agreement, and sometimes they disagree significantly. The two most important are the minutes and records of the Society and Board meetings as found in the *Account Book* and *Ledger*, which go from 1935 to 1975, and 1968 to 1979, respectively, though with significant gaps. Second is the *History of the Oklahoma Conference* which mostly covers District Superintendents to 1949 but mentions Liberty. Next is *The Free Methodist Church/ Oklahoma In Action/ Past Present and Future*, covering the conference 1955 to 1970 but with a list of Liberty Pastors 1940 to 1969. The greater church at some point produced annual *Yearbooks*, with data on individual conferences and churches, including who the pastor was. Finally, we have the memories of current church members which include stories told by elders of the past. Once in the 1980's, though minutes are few, memories are more numerous and reliable.

Disagreements among sources arise for several reasons. The *Account Book* minutes to 1975, which we would expect to be the most accurate, emphasize elections and finance, and abound in references to the pastor's and superintendent's reimbursement (usually on a weekly basis) but often do not mention the pastor's name. They do however frequently reference titles, such as chairman, person in-charge, and/or person presiding. These may refer to a conference superintendent, person other than pastor, previous pastor attending the church, or pastor. There are several examples of previous pastors attending church because they were pastors chosen from the church membership in the first place, no other preacher presumably being available. In a sense they were lay pastors as opposed to professional ones. They served out of necessity, after meeting the first-level requirements for preaching, and went back to being "just" members or churchgoers[18] as they could.

Another source of conflict is indirectly reference by *Oklahoma In Action* when it states, "The material for this book was gathered during December, 1969; and January, 1970; in meetings by the Conference Superintendent with the Official Boards of the local churches" (front of the first page, not paginated). That is, it's records date from decades after Liberty was established, and apparently relies heavily on memories of ten or twenty years past. The *History of the Oklahoma Conference* suffers from the same problem. I have only been able to find copies of four *Yearbooks,* the earliest being 1989. No doubt others could be found with effort and time, but it is not clear that they would add much to what I have. Having provided annual data to conferences for many years (Nazarene and Free Methodist) and knowing other pastors and chaplains who fill out the forms, I conclude they reasonably well present the overall health of the churches, and trends in the conference, but most of the numbers are estimates, and individual figures and records are not always as accurate as they might appear.

The problems are compounded because Liberty's means for paying pastors have been limited. The pastor would have needed to be bi-vocational or retired. This is a typical problem for a small, rural church, in a sparsely populated, sometimes economically challenged area. Therefore pastors come and go, and the conference superintendent (or other conference authority, such as a designated elder) provides the presumably necessary consistent oversight. Laypersons step in to do what needs to be done, and this not unusually leads to their interest in more formally serving the church, including learning to preach and serve the flock under supervision of a "superintendent." A few advance to ordination.

---

18. See below for more detail. "Members" were those who had formally acceded to the "general rules of the Discipline" as the *Account Book* puts it (p.1). Membership could be, and sometimes was, retracted. The rest of the congregation consisted of what I term "church-goers" or "attendees" or "congregants," and may have attended Liberty for many years. I cannot determine whether, typically, more "members" were in attendance on any particular Sunday, although the record shows that on at least some occasions, the "members" were a minority. "Memberships" was not typically required to serve in elected positions, of which there were, and are, many.

For example, the minutes indicate that Floyd Rush, one of the charter members, received his "exhorter's" license in the 1937 meeting which organized the society, a license which was periodically renewed. Charley Thompson, one of the early members, became "exhorter" in 1939 (the first step in the ordination process) and was recommended by the church to receive his "preacher's license" (the next step) in June 1941. He eventually became the formally designated, ordained pastor for Liberty (more than once) and pastored other churches. Almost certainly he had preached many times at Liberty before becoming pastor, but there is no record of this. This lack of notice is unsurprising because such service was normal to the times. To some extent this remains true today. When the current (2022) Liberty pastor is sick or otherwise unavailable, usually one of the members who has a local license (roughly equivalent to "exhorter") fills the pulpit, and this is not usually shown in the minutes, which come from official meetings typically held twice a year or so.

The early minutes contain quite a few references to men and women seeking, and receiving, an "exhorter's license." I have listed all the references to licenses in the minutes in the chart below titled "Record of Liberty Members Seeking Exhorter's License, Local License, and Ordination." For example, Elzie Hemphill received an exhorter's license July 25, 1945. This is also the date that Charley Thompson is first referred to as "Rev." though probably he had been ordained some time before this. Floyd, Charley, and many others including some women, undoubtedly filled the pulpit on some occasions, and perhaps regularly, and perhaps for months in-between pastors, without being ordained, or being mentioned in the minutes. Given all the variables mentioned above, what and who constituted the "pastor" is not as clear as we might expect.

In addition to this, occasionally months passed between "regular" pastors. This is clear from the *Account Book* and *Ledger*. In more contemporary times, when Edsel Hall retired in 2009, Dr. Jeff Johnson did not take over full time until March 7, 2010. In between, several different persons preached. When Denise Abston left in the fall of 2015, Dr. Ron Faulk did not start full-time until June 2015. In between, Dr. Faulk, Dr. Gregory and Steve Smith took turns preaching, and possibly others. In a half dozen cases or so the names of the temporary or trial pastors are known. However, for the sake of consistency, I have not listed them below.

In a small, not wealthy church, necessity often forces leadership roles on laity. Such roles are neither less effective nor less legitimate for being necessary. Indeed, in its roughly 2,000-year history, the leaders of Christianity have typically come from just such situations. The history of Liberty is a testament to the perseverance of a faithful laity, with strong local leadership, supported by overworked conference superintendents. The natural emphasis, then, in Liberty's records, tends to be on the familial, rather than on the star; on the prosaic, rather than the poetic. Pastors come and go, but the faithful members and regulars remain, including the exhorters, as do also to some extent the superintendents. The Liberty minutes tend to skimp on who the pastor is, although the person "in charge" is often noted, but it is difficult to know how often the person in-charge (e.g., a superintendent) filled the pulpit. I assume that this is often until the 1970's.

Of course, a pastor would naturally be present when the superintendent was in the building, and the fact that a superintendent was "in charge" of a meeting does not mean no pastor was present or did not preach. It is also natural for a minute-taker to assume readers would know who the pastor was. Minute-taking, that un-glamorous and not usually wanted job, is often the primary if not unique source for reconstructing the history of a not-for-profit organization. Over time the minute-takers are the ones who most influence "history." An adage says, "the victors write history." For organizations, "the minute-takers write history." Minute-takers, of course, have their own perspective on events, and emphasize certain things at the expense of others, as we all do.

Through the 1950's the superintendent (or equivalent) is mentioned frequently. Thereafter, rarely, although the minutes are also less comprehensive in the 1960's and after. But clearly around 1960 there was a change in the function and relationship of the superintendents to Liberty. According to Dr. Dwight Gregory, who in 2022 is on staff with the Mid America Conference at the Midwest City church (OK), this was generally true across the denomination. Through the mid 1960's the superintendents were routinely present and involved in the affairs of Liberty, normally including quarterly meetings. Up until 2,000 or so, the superintendents were typically at Liberty at least once a year. The superintendents in the early days seemed to have been more involved than their later peers in training members for service in the local church and the conference, including preaching and ordination (relying less, for example, on seminaries, as we tend to do today. Of course, there was less higher education then than today). The result is that they had significantly more influence on the day-to-day affairs of churches than today.

The superintendents and church members then were also probably more interested in, and attentive to, doctrine, than we are today, at least at the local level. The Liberty minutes show they took steps to ensure that "members," per se, knew and were formally committed to the "rules of the discipline" (e.g., *Account Book*, p.1), and lived by them. There are periodic assertions in the minutes that members are living in accord with the rules of discipline, or at least, more skeptically, were not known not to. Such assertions are never or very rarely found in minutes today. An emphasis on the rules of the discipline would be facilitated by the fact that there were fewer people in those days, living in closer community, who knew what their neighbors were doing, and vice versa. The world had less than two billion people in the 1940's. Population is surpassing eight billion as this is being written, an astonishing increase since Liberty's founding. Generally, the early members of Liberty knew, and relied on, their neighbors more than we do, although they had fewer of them. And churchgoers held each other more accountable than we do. Furthermore, the "individualism" and encouragement to "self-assertion" of twenty-first century neo-liberal culture was unknown to them. They were a more communal people.

The minutes to the 1960's also reflect a clearer distinction, than we do today, between formal "members," and other persons who attended church. Despite the distinction, those who were not formal members were elected, as far as I can tell, to all positions in the church, and served equally with "members." The minutes sometimes note that certain elected positions (like trustees) require so many "members," and that too many non-members are currently on the job. The minutes also note several times when members request to vacate their "member" status (and are allowed to do so), although they still attend church and function in elected positions. The relationship between "members" and attending "non-members" is an interesting one, that probably indicates something about the religious attitudes of churchgoers in those days. It might indicate something about the higher doctrinal rigor and spiritual experiences required of "members," and/or a greater concern with individual sin and what constitutes sin, and how that might affect the church or their own spiritual status. I do not think it is controversial to say that church goers (FMC and others) today are less concerned with sin than eighty years ago. Furthermore, as mentioned in the main body above, the *History of the Oklahoma Conference* observes "A perplexing problem through the years has been the unsystematic methods of collecting funds ..." (p.23). At the 1947 conference the "Rev. E.M. Olsteen submitted a plan" which was adopted to the effect that "the funds to be raised were apportioned to the various circuits on the basis of $12.25 per member..." (ibid). That is, official church members were expected to submit their donations or tithes more "systematically," and to give a minimum amount. This placed higher expectations and probably higher financial burdens on "members," as opposed to the regular congregants. It seems likely this was also a constraint on the number of "members" of a church. This policy is an echo of the pew-renting that occurred in the nineteenth century.

Virginia Thompson was a charter member of Liberty who attended most Sundays for roughly a half century. Her husband, Harry, attended regularly from the late 1930's until his death in 1993 (according to the records and memories of 2022 regulars). He seemed to have participated fully in church activities and helped the church out as he could. But he never became an official member. No one in 2022 knew why.

Above I mentioned that references to the superintendents vanish for long periods of time after roughly the 1960's. The same is true for references to licenses. From 1935 to 1951 there are references every year but one (1938) to persons seeking to be exhorters, primarily, but also for local licenses and ordination. There is one reference in 1957, and none thereafter until the twenty-first century, not in the *Account Book* to 1975, nor the *Ledger* to 1979, although for the latter this is not so surprising given its emphasis on finance. Nonetheless the omission is striking, and probably indicates a change taking place not just in Liberty, but in the greater church as well. It might mean the pastors and churches needed less oversight, for example that the pastors were more "professional" and there was less of a tendency to fill the pulpit from within the congregation. It might also speak to increased ease of transportation, so that the pastors could live further away, increasing the availability of better pastors. Or it might mean there was less money for supervision. Or it might mean a philosophy change. Probably there were several causes.

On the other hand, Liberty today continues to occasionally, but regularly, produce members who seek a local license, conference license, and ordination.

Member Jeff Grimes was ordained in 2020 after preaching and serving several years with a local license. Due to the covid pandemic, Jeff's normally scheduled ordination ceremony could not be held, but he was granted the privileges of ordination because another church in the conference needed a pastor – another example of the church adapting to necessity. Months later the bishop formally laid hands on Jeff. In another example, Eddie Ware currently (2022) has a local license and is pursuing ordination, and fills-in for the current pastor several times a year. Almeda Sumpter and Sondra Ford (another pair of sisters attending Liberty) became deacons during the pandemic, with privileges for administering communion (Almeda, who was also Superintendent of Schools, died in 2021 due to covid infection). And, it should be pointed out, our superintendent emeritus, Dr. Jeff Johnson, preaches at Liberty once or twice a year.

Some things have changed – compared to Liberty's early years, there is much less oversight and influence by the current superintendent (who lives in another state), the conference is much larger and the superintendents fewer; formal "membership" is less emphasized than it used to be; there is less emphasis on doctrinal purity at the local level; modern pastors tend to be more academically prepared; and in the last twenty-five years the average pastor at Liberty has served about five years (a period that includes one-year under superintendent Dr. Jeff Johnson) whereas in the first sixty-two years of Liberty the average pastor served about three years. On the other hand, Liberty meets its challenges much as it always has. It continues to produce both local and conference leaders; a few faithful members serve many elected positions, and generally keep the church going; as elsewhere noted it continues to emphasize both local missions and World Missions; and it continues to be financially challenged.

Based on all the sources I have access to, and generally giving preference to the minutes, I believe the following list of the leadership of Liberty FMC is reasonably accurate. I believe it is more accurate than any list I have found. I use the term "Leadership" instead of "Pastors," because many persons filling the pulpit, especially in the early years, were not ordained, as we tend to think of "pastors" today, and because some of them were superintendents.

Liberty FMC Leadership 1935-2022

Pastor, chairman, person in-charge, etc.[19]	Superintendent or equivalent, presiding, in-charge, etc.	Historical markers
1935 spring—summer, Bro. and Sister Will Ridens		They were the first to preach "the old time gospel" at Sandyland School, Tryon, OK.
Aug. 1936-1938, G.J. Eikermann[20]		G.K. Eikermann was "our first pastor." Aug. 18, 1937, Liberty Society organized with five members, in a meeting called to order by G.K. Eikermann.[21]
	1938-1939, A.R. Martin	
1939- July or August 1940, Walter Nelson		
	1940-41, W.H. Maddox	
1941-1942, E. Milo Martin		
	1942-43 Ralph Butterfield?	
	1943-1945, A.R. Martin	
1945-1948, Charley N. Thompson[22]		June 30, 1946, was the first meeting in the new church at Worthy and Union roads, NW of Tryon. 1946 was also the first-year musical instruments were allowed.
Sept. 1948-1949, A.F. Dile		
	1949-1950, R.E. Butterfield or F.M. Shipley	
June 1950-April 1951, W.E. Heginbotham		In 1951 Liberty gets electricity.

19. "Pastor" does not necessarily mean ordained. And many services were by men and women who were not the pastor.
20. Name spelling in the sources vary considerably. I generally use the most common spelling.
21. Floyd Rush, Flossie Rush, Beulah Thompson, Virginia Thompson, and Lucia Eikermann.
22. C.N. Thompson was recommended for his "exhorter's" license by Liberty Jan. 1939, and "preacher's license" June 1941.

Pastor, chairman, person in-charge, etc.[23]	Superintendent or equivalent, presiding, in-charge, etc.	Historical markers
1951, May 1952, Byron L. Wayman		May 1952, "a building has been bought for $200" as parsonage.
July 1952-1953, C.V. McCully		
July 1953-1954, W.E. Heginbotham	1953-1954, A.R. Martin	
1954-1956, Joseph Simpson		
Aug. 1956-Aug. 1958, Wayne Lawton	1956, L.B. Vanderhoofven	
	1958-1959, L.B. Vanderhoofven	
1959-1960, Kennison Lawton		
	1960-1963, "under the superintendent," probably L.B. Vanderhoofven.[24]	
Aug. 1962-1963, W.E. Heginbotham		
Oct. 1963-1964, Hugh Wayman[25]		
1964-1968, T.F. King		
July-Dec.1968-1969, Harry Adams		
Jan.-June 1969, Bro. King		
Aug. 1969-1970, Bill Huff		
	1970-1971, Hugh Wayman possibly	
1971-June 1979, Charlie N. Thompson		
June 1979-1980, Billy R. Wilson		

23. "Pastor" does not necessarily mean ordained. And many services were by men and women who were not the pastor.
24. 1963 is the last reference in the minutes, in the 20th century records, to a superintendent.
25. Byron and Hugh Wayman were brothers. Hugh Wayman became superintendent in 1963 according to records, which also show he was pastor of Liberty 1963-64.

Pastor, chairman, person in-charge, etc.[26]	Superintendent or equivalent, presiding, in-charge, etc.	Historical markers
1980-1981, Charley N. Thompson		
1981-1982, Harry Adams		
1982-83, Monty Bower		
	1983-84, probably under superintendent Elza Boldman	
1984-1986, Harry Adams		
1986-87, Irvin R. Ball		
	1987-88, probably under superintendent Elza Boldman	
1988-1991, Harry Adams		Liberty and three other churches form the Tryon Ministerial Alliance that continues today.
1991-1993, Robin Grueser		
1993-1994, Harry Adams		
	1994-95, possibly under superintendent Kirby Bertholf	
1995-96, Lonnie Hill		
1996-97, Larry Popovich		Name change to Mid-American conference after merger with Arkansas and SW Missouri churches of dissolved Ozark conference.
1997, Charlie Thompson		At age 92. He dies two years later.
1997-2009, Edsel Hall		In 2009 Edsel is 87. He dies 2013.

---

26. "Pastor" does not necessarily mean ordained. And many services were by men and women who were not the pastor.

Pastor, chairman, person in-charge, etc.[27]	Superintendent or equivalent, presiding, in-charge, etc.	Historical markers
	2009-10, Jeff Johnson, Ph.D.	Since 1935 the longest serving superintendent (19 years).
2010- Nov. 2015, Denise J. Abston		Liberty's first female regular pastor.
Nov. 2015-May 2016, Ron Faulk, Ph.D., Dwight Gregory, Ph.D., Steve Smith		
June 2016 to present (fall 2022), Ron Faulk, Ph.D.		March 22 to May 31, 2020, church services were not held due to the covid pandemic except two communion services. Jeff Grimes ordained Sept. 27, 2020. In 2020 Dr. Jeff Johnson, superintendent 19 years, was replaced by Dr. Bruce Cromwell

Record of Liberty Members Seeking Exhorter's License, Local License, and Ordination ("Preacher's License")[28]

August 18, 1937. "Floyd Rush was recommended to the official board for exhorters (sic) license." This is the meeting at which the Liberty Society was organized.

Nov. 16, 1937. "Floyd Rush was granted exhorters (sic[29]) license."

May 26, 1939. "Charlie Thompson was recommended by the society to receive exhorters license."

July 16, 1940. "motion … to renew Bro. F.M. Rush and C.N. Thompson exhorters license."

June 20, 1941. "Charlie Thompson was recommended to the quarterly conf to receive local preachers license."

27. "Pastor" does not necessarily mean ordained. And many services were by men and women who were not the pastor.
28. All records are from minutes in the *Account Book*. There are no such references in the *Ledger*.
29. In the minutes, apostrophes are frequently left out.

Nov. 21, 1941. "any exhorters license to renew? None. / Any exhorters to be recommended for local preachers license. None."

May 15, 1942. "No recommendation for exhorters license."

Oct. 3, 1942. "It was voted to renew Floyd Rushes exhorters license."

March 26, 1943. "4. recommendation for exhorters license." Apparently, there were none.

July 16, 1943. "4. no recommendation for exhorters license."

July 7, 1944. "on motion Floyd R. renewed exhorters license."

July 13, 1945. "it was moved and second to renew Floyd Rush's exhorters license."

July 25, 1945. "The name of Elzie Hemphill was recommended for exhorter's license."

Oct. 26, 1945. "The name of Elzie Hemphill was recommended by the society as a suitable person to receive exhorters license. On motion the license was granted."

July 2, 1946. "James Thompson was recommended by the society as a suitable person to receive exhorters license."

July 11, 1946. "Motion moved & second to grant exhorters license (to James Thompson)./ Motion made and second to grant Floyd Rush exhorters license."

Aug. 27, 1946. "Motion made & second to renew the exhorters license of Elzie Hemphill's."

May 31, 1947. "Bro. Hemphill & Bro. Rush exhorters license to be renewed." I note that "Bro. Hemphill" may be an error for "Sis. Hemphill" or it could be "Marvel Hemphill" (see below). "James Russell Thompson is recommended … to receive local preachers license."

June 4, 1948. "…Elzie Hemphill and Floyd Rush were called as suitable persons to have their exhorters license renewed. On motion they were renewed."

July 12, 1949. "Were there any recommendations for exhorters license? no."

June 28, 1950. "Marvel Hemphill was recommended for exhorters license." "Floyd Rush & Elzie Hemphill exhorters license are to be renewed."

April 3, 1951. "Donald Thompson was recommended for exhorters license." "Elzie Hemphill's exhorter license is to be renewed."

July 31, 1957. "Wayne Lawton was recommended at the last quarterly conference by the Conf. Supt. & therefore needs no recommendation at this time from the society for Local Preach."

This last remark reminds us that the "local preacher's" license was normally recommended by the church but approved by the conference, and that possibly other Liberty member were granted conference, or local, license, without the fact showing up in Liberty minutes.

From August 28, 1957, to August 22, 1962, there are no Liberty minutes in the *Account Book* (or anywhere else that I know of), and the minutes thereafter (ending in 1975 in the *Account Book*) are generally briefer and less organized and contain no references to local licenses. The records in the *Ledger*, which go from 1968 to 1979, are almost exclusively financial – matters of funds "paid in," funds "paid out," and balances, and also do not contain references to licenses.

Length of Pastor Service 1936-2022[30]

Years Served	Number of Pastors Serving	
1 or less	14	
1 to 2	7	
3 to 4	3	
4 to 5	1	T.F. King, 1964-68, Jan.-June 1969
5 to 6	1	Denise Abston, 2010-2015
6 to 7	1	Ron Faulk, 2016-2022 & continuing

---

30. As noted in the introduction, lengths of service are approximate, and several include more than one term (e.g., Harry Adams served 11 years across five different terms). "Pastor" here may mean a superintendent, or non-ordained person.

11 to 12	1	Harry Adams, 1968-69, 1981-82, 1984-86, 1989-91, 1993-94
12 to 13	1	Edsel Hall, 1997-2009
13 to 14	1	Charlie Thompson, 1945-48, 1971-79, 1980-81, 1997
	Total= 30	This includes five superintendents

From 1936 to 2022 (86 years) 30 non-duplicated pastors served an average of about 3 years each.

From 1936 to 1997 (61 years) 26 pastors served an average of 2.3 years each.

From 1998 to 2022 (24 years) 4 pastors served an average of 6 years each.

Appendix II. Church Membership Requirements

Church membership requirements are listed in the *History of the Oklahoma Conference,* by Walter O. Nelson, published in 1949, pp. 8-9. The *History* references the establishment of Liberty FMC on p. 20. The statement of requirements is as follows.

I. Reception on Probation

> None shall be admitted on probation until they give evidence of a desire to flee from the wrath to come, by bringing forth fruits meet for repentance, and give affirmative answers to the following questions:
>
> 1. Have you the assurance of sins forgiven?
> 2. Do you consent to be governed by our general rules?

II. Admission into Full Membership

> None shall be received into full membership unless they give evidence of a renewed heart by living up to the requirements of the general rules, and have met in class six months on probation, have been baptized, have wherever practicable been recommended by the official members of the society, and give satisfactory answers to the following questions, which shall be proposed to them before the society or public meeting of the church.

1. Have you the witness of the Spirit that you are a child of God?

2. Have you that perfect love which casteth out fear? (If the candidate shall answer no, then this question shall be asked, Will you diligently seek until you obtain it?)

3. Is it your purpose to devote yourself the remainder of your life wholly to the service of God, doing good to your fellow men, and working out your own salvation with fear and trembling?

4. Will you forever lay aside all superfluous ornaments, and adorn yourself in modest apparel, not with gold, nor pearls nor costly array, but, which becometh those professing godliness, with good works?

5. Will you abstain from connection with all secret societies, keeping yourself free to follow the will of the Lord in all things?

6. Do you subscribe to our articles of religion, our general rules, and our Discipline, and are you willing to be governed by the same?

7. Have you Christian fellowship and love for the members of this society, and will you assist them, as God shall give you ability, in carrying on the work of the Lord?

The person giving affirmative answers to the above questions shall, with the consent of three-fourths of the members present be admitted to all the privileges of a member. Any person in good standing in any evangelical church may be received into full membership upon his meeting the other requirements of this chapter, without having been on probation in our church. (6) All members in full connection under sixteen years of age shall be known as Junior Members.

As noted in the above rules there are three classes of members, probationers, full members and junior members, but when membership figures are given they will refer to the total of all classes of members.

Appendix III. Untitled column by Jim Ferguson, *Oklahoma Conference Heritage*, circa 1979.

This editorial occupies the left column of the front page of a one-sheet periodical.

"This is an exciting time to be a Christian and to be a part of the Free Methodist Church. We are looking ahead to annual conference and general conference with the confidence that the Lord is leading us into greater and greater adventures as we trust and follow Him. Our thoughts are turned constantly toward the future.

As we look at the past, we see a somewhat dim picture of numerous small and unsuccessful churches which are now closed. If that is all we see, it is no wonder we look only to the future and dream and plan as if we had no past.

I have never been able to withstand the temptation to take a quick look over my shoulder as I try to go forward. When I began to look back at the history of the Oklahoma Conference, I was pleasantly surprised. I found that our heritage is not centered in a multitude of tiny churches that failed. Our heritage is centered in men and women who dared to accept the challenge of God to take the word of God into a newly opened territory and to build the church in a new state. It is a history of the love of God reflected through the lives of very human men who attempted to surrender their hearts to God. It is a story that I have only heard in bits and pieces and that most of my generation has not heard at all.

The purpose of this page in the conference paper is to try to tell that story. It is urgent that we do so now, or it will be lost forever. Most of our heritage is locked away in the hearts and minds of our older members. If we are to preserve those memories, we must encourage those who hold them in trust to communicate them to those of us who would like to know how we came to be what we are today.

This section of the paper will be published about every three months, depending on your response. If you have a tale to tell, send it to me at the address below. If your eyesight makes it difficult for you to write, I will be glad to visit you with my tape recorder and preserve what you have to say. Stories of the founding of the churches, the lives of early ministers and laymen, and significant works of the Holly Spirit are all needed. Your interest in this project will provide us with a heritage that can inspire us to move forward into the future with the confidence that the Gospel works."

"Jim Ferguson
Route 1, Box 63
Carmen, Oklahoma 73726"

Appendix IV. The Evangelical Church

Although widely used, "evangelical" is difficult to define. Dictionary definitions emphasize the authority of scripture and zeal, and a connection to Protestants, but these are too generic to fit the use of the word by detractors and proponents. John Dyer, in "The New Gutenburg" (*Christianity Today*, December 2022) quotes Bruce Shelley in 1960 that "Evangelical Christianity is not a religious organization. It is not primarily a theological system. It is more of a mood, a perspective, and an experience" (p.53). He adds that evangelicals believe in and strive for "spiritual change" (change in experience) (ibid) and "The Bible is not just a religious text for evangelicals, but a deep source of spiritual life and connection to God" (p.54). I add "perseverance" to their definition. Evangelicals *work* to spread spiritual change, they expect difficulties in the work, and they persevere in doing it.

Various records of the Kansas and Oklahoma Conferences of the Free Methodist Church show that leadership and regular membership of the Church considered "evangelical" to be an essential part of their identity. This may be seen in the frequent use of the word "evangelical" in various records, such as the *History of the Oklahoma Conference*. Associated with that is the word "missionary." The missionary fields typically referenced in the records are both "home" and "world."

Evangelicals evangelize. They engage in missions. They have zeal, which is energy and commitment. A zeal which is sustained over millennia can only be Spirit-driven. Evangelicalism originates in Pentecostalism. The original evangelists were formed on the Day of Pentecost, which Jesus told his followers to wait on because then they would "receive power when the Holy Spirit has come upon you; and you will be my witnesses in Jerusalem ... and to the ends of the earth" (Acts 1:8). The Spirit animated them, and they immediately went out and evangelized, notwithstanding the very real threats and oppositions of the ruling powers in those days.

Seminal to modern American evangelism is the Pentecostal movement in the mid to late nineteenth century. This movement was mostly a mid- to lower socio-class phenomenon, as was true of the original Pentecost. It also cut across denominations. The nineteenth and early twentieth century Pentecostals, to use the term generically, often expressed their zeal in camp meetings and brush arbors, and by circuit-riding evangelists, the great majority of whom were lay men and women. Some were later ordained, but few underwent the highly structured, ecclesiastically controlled processes of ordination (seminaries, higher education degrees, and ceremonies of pomp and circumstance). Indeed, the Pentecostal movement was largely opposed by the ecclesiastical authorities.

The Methodist movement of courses originates in the eighteenth century. Its practice included reaching outside the traditional church, especially but not limited to the working classes, who mostly could not afford to rent pews, a common requirement for attending church in those days. A core belief was that the Spirit was essential to salvation, witnessing, and preaching. These practices and beliefs caused John Wesley to be threatened with expulsion from the Church of England. When the nineteenth century Pentecostal movement began, Methodists were naturally in the middle of it. John Wesley was an evangelical.

Liberty FMC was formed in 1935 by a lay evangelical couple who "preached the good old fashioned gospel." Liberty was and is a small, rural church in the mid-west U.S. In its eight-six-year-old history it has usually been financially challenged. Yet the record shows that from year one the congregants were vigilant in funding and supporting what they called "world missions" as well as ministries to local needy persons. Missions was, and is, as important for the Liberty members as having an ordained pastor or an elegant, well-appointed church. There are thousands and thousands of churches like Liberty across north America – small, poor, constantly challenged, yet committed through thick and thin to sending and supporting missions around the world and at home, even if it's just a few hundred dollars a year.

The great majority of Christian churches around the world are small and poor. They typically consist of a few families and friends. Often a few key persons, women as much as men, keep these churches together and going. In other words, the great majority of Christian churches in the world are like evangelical churches in America, or vice versa. And all these churches are like the first churches formed after the original day of Pentecost about two thousand years ago.

These small churches have evangelized most of the world. Individually their resources are small, but as a whole their resources are great. Large, wealthy churches, which typically eventually associate themselves with reigning cultural, economic, and political powers, sometimes have had bursts of missionary activity, but their tendency is to become associated with the status quo. I am generalizing. There have been and are some amazing Spirit-driven large churches. But large, wealthy churches tend to be human-driven rather than spirit-driven. Again, this is not always true. Often such large, worldly-powerful churches/institutions, do not depend as exclusively on faith for their continued existence as small churches. And the missionaries they do send are not much like the persons that they are ministering to.

There are of course other religions today that seek to make converts. A typical method is to go to a foreign country (which might be the U.S.), and build an imposing, architecturally elegant, expensive "church" (it might be called something else), in a strategic part of town, well supplied with leaders and staff, and with the funds to operate a variety of programs to appeal to potential converts. And this type of institution is attractive to certain people.

On the other side is the evangelist-missionary, who lives month-to-month, if not hand-to-mouth, usually with his (or her) spouse and children, in similar circumstances as the people they are trying to spread the gospel to. The foundation of their whole enterprise is faith, not money. Probably their "church" is someone's home. Possibly they are opposed by local or regional rulers. And one of the efforts of such missionaries is to recruit other persons of faith from the local culture, and to support such locals in further expanding the gospel. Such "recruits" are not from the elites of the culture in question. They may well be from the lower classes or from disadvantaged populations. Not only that, when such locals become converted, it is often expensive for them. It may cost them prestige with the local elites, it may cause prejudice against them, it may cause open oppression, or loss of employment, and it is not unheard that they would pay with their life.

How different are these two methods of proselytizing, and their "converts"! One is materially prosperous, culturally prestigious, and exerts overt political and worldly influence. One seems precarious but has lasted two thousand years and created the largest faith group in the history of the world. This faith group, "the body of Christ," is not socially stratified – not only not within their own culture (that is, among the Christians in their own culture), but also not within the "kingdom" of Christians around the world. *Never in the history of the world has there been such a long-living, non-stratified, faith-tested, body of astonishingly diverse people.*

This body has not been recruited according to any human plan, or by any human group or organization. The thousands of small "evangelical" churches are incapable of being humanly organized on any large scale. What I call "evangelical" churches, are extremely diverse, both at any point in time as well as across history. They often are not in theological agreement with each other, to put it mildly. They often are not in political agreement with each other. They differ in styles of worship. And so on. A guiding hand must be involved, and that is the hand of the Spirit of Jesus Christ.

I believe the key to the success of such churches, is the faith-commitment of at least a few people. In Liberty's history is the story I relate in the section "Summary of the 1950's." This story was told by Lillie Johnson, probably in the 1970's, to several of the members still attending in 2022. Attendance had dropped, there was no pastor, finances were thin, there seemed to be no future, and the decision was made to close the church. Lillie and Minnie Heginbotham went to church and began to roll up the carpet. One looked up and asked the other, "do you really want to close the church?" The other said "no." So, they left the carpet, continued to have services with just a few, and probably without an official pastor. The church continues to this day some sixty years later. Liberty FMC is an evangelical church. My guess is that, as long as it remains evangelical, it will survive.

Appendix V. Why Lynda Grimes Decided to Attend Liberty FMC.

The following was written by Lynda Grimes in late 1978 or early 1979.

"My story begins as the scriptures read in Matthew 25:26.

I was hungry and ye gave me meat: I was thirsty and ye gave me drink: I was a stranger and ye took me in.

That is how I felt in April of 1974.

My father-in-law became very sick we were all lost because of his illness. He was the backbone of our family which is very large, four sons, four daughters, their husbands and wives and at times 32 grandchildren.

The most unbelievable part of all is; not one of us attended any church, study the scriptures, or worshiped God in anyway in our homes. Not even my father or mother-in-law. Religion just wasn't discussed.

Then sickness hit! As so many people do we panicked.

Those of us who had attended church when we were younger tried to pray.

We were frightened as the days passed and we learned that Dad had a brain tumor that had to be removed. It was at this time that God sent us one of His disciples.

Charlie was the ministry (sic) from the Free Methodist Church that was about a mile from Mom and Dad's house. Someone we knew, but hadn't learned to trust or listen too (sic).

From the first time Charlie came to the hospital it seemed that things were a little better because he represented someone stronger than the doctors.

Over the next few months we went threw (sic) a very difficult time for any family. Dads tumor was malignant and there wasn't much that could be done for him, but during his illness he did something for his family that I will never forget.

With Charlie as his guide he gave what was left of his life to God. This was the last thing he did before he became to (sic) ill to do anything on his own.

Dad passed away in August of that year and during this time Charlie had been there when we needed him. Never asking for anything and never preaching at us about the way we were living.

I know now that he must of been praying for all of us as I feel the church was doing.

At times we weren't very kind or polite to Charlie, but I know he has forgiven us for these wrong doings.

Eleven days after Dad passed away my youngest daughter was born. Strong and healthy, I was very thankful. I wanted to thank God for my baby.

I decided to go to the church on the hill where Charlie was the ministry.

The first Sunday I went to church there was eight other people there, but I never felt more welcome at any place in my whole life. I enjoyed myself very much and I felt good about taking my children to God's house.

The next Sunday I returned and God touched my heart and I felt the need to learn all I could about God. I wanted my husband to go with me, I wanted the whole family to go. I was excited.

The people at Liberty were wonderful to us as we very gradually and skeptically started attending church.

Charlies was very kind, gentle and loving as he told us of God's love for us and His Son that had died for us.

That was four and a half years ago. In that time several in our family has found this wonderful love.

In this time Charlie has been our ministry, our teacher, our brother, and become someone we all love very much.

God sent us one of His disciples at a time when we were hungry. He had a difficult task and I feel he's done a wonderful job.

Now Charlie is retiring as ministry at Liberty, but he will never be forgotten by all of us he has lead (sic) to God with his love and prayers.

As far as the Liberty Free Methodist Church goes my family has found a home. May we grow strong with God's help and thank Him for giving us a new beginning.

And as we pray our Thanksgiving let us remember to thank Him for His wonderful Son and His loyal disciple Charlie and his wonderful wife Beulah. May God be with them and protect both of them always."

Appendix VI. Lynda Grimes' Prepared Statement for the 30th Re-Union of the Sandyland Community

"A Look at the Sandyland

Today is Sept. 3, 1979 and my family and I spent this Labor Day at the FM campground with former students or members of the community of Sandyland. Today was their 30th year reunion.

There was several people there that I did not know and some there that I love dearly, but from attending this reunion I feel that Sandyland must have been quit a place and from listening to little bits and pieces of information and hearing a few conversations I formed my own opinion of Sandyland.

From seeing people talk to each other and from the happy greetings this is how I feel Sandyland School must have been. Thought I could be entirely wrong pupils that attended Sandyland were a rare breed of country kids that knew what life was all about. They wore patches on their knees or big brother or sister's hand me down clothes. They carried the lunches to school in little pails instead of a Superman thermos lunch box. And in that lunch bucket they had cold meat on a biscuit or peanut butter, apple butter, or sometimes just plain mustard there wasn't any hostess twinkes (sic) or Fritos or a Snicker candy bar.

They went off to school walking not riding a big yellow bus. They froze when it was cold, drowned when it rained and played hooky when it was pretty and the fish were biting.

They worked hard at home to help their parents, played hard at school and did their homework so there'd be no trips to the smokehouse with a hickory switch when report card time came.

They not only learned their 3' rs at Sandyland they learned to love one another to care for their friends and learn what a friend really is, and about sharing and giving. Things I wish my children could learn today in their school.

And for the parents of the children that went to Sandyland they were the ones that made all of these things possible. It would have been easier for them to keep their kids home to chop cotton or help with the farming or wood cutting but they knew that the day would come when a (sic) education would be very important. So to school their kids would go and the school became the gathering place of the community.

So today I've learned a little about what its like to be a real friend and a loving neighbor thru (sic) watching the people from Sandyland hugging, shaking hands, telling stories and some weeping for those who have gone home to be with their Lord.

I'm glad I attended this reunion and have these memories to hold. I pray that their reunions can be held forever and that someday when the time comes for our reunion in Heaven their parting will be never.

God bless each of you.

Lynda Grimes

Appendix VII. Liberty FMC Elected Positions 2017-2022.

The Greater and Local Church's Mission:	"To love God and people, and to make disciples" (*2015 Book of Discipline*, p. 125).			
The FMC Vision:	"To bring wholeness to the world through healthy biblical communities of holy people multiplying disciples, leaders, groups and churches" (*2015 Book of Discipline*, p. 125).			
Liberty Free Methodist Church Elected Positions 2017, 2019, 2021, 2023				
Pastor Ron Faulk; Deacon Sondra Ford; Assistant Pastor Eddie Ware; co-pastor Jeff Johnson.				
Position	2016-17	2018-19	2020-21 as of 12-20-20; same as 19-20	2022-23 as of 10-16-22; same as 21-22
Board of Administration Officers				
Chair is the Pastor (does not vote)	Rev. Ron Faulk	Rev. Ron Faulk	Rev. Ron Faulk	Rev. Ron Faulk
Secretary (Board and Society)	Carolyn Grimes	Lisa Baker	Lisa Baker	Lisa Baker
Finance Comm Chair (Treasurer)	Sam Savory	Sam Savory	Sam Savory	Sam Savory
Finance Committee members	Gene Grimes, John Huff, Sam Savory	Eddie Ford, Gene Grimes, Sam Savory	Eddie Ford, Sam Savory, Eddie Ware	Eddie Ford, Sam Savory, Eddie Ware
Sunday School Superintendent		Almeda Sumpter	Almeda Sumpter	Anita Grimes
Delegate		Jeff Grimes	Jeff Grimes	Eddie Ware
Membership Care Committee same as Board of Administration				
Sunday School				
Sunday School Superintendent	Almeda Sumpter	Almeda Sumpter	Almeda Sumpter	Anita Grimes

Sunday School Assistant Super	unfilled	Dustin Ford	Dustin Ford	Dustin Ford
Sunday School Secretary	Danita Savory	Danita Savory	Danita Savory	Danita Savory
Sunday School Adult Teacher	Anita Grimes	Eddie Ware	Eddie Ware	Eddie Ware
Sunday School Adult Asst Teacher	John Huff	Jeff Grimes	Jeff Grimes	not filled
Sunday School Junior High Teacher	Lynda Grimes	Lynda Grimes	Lynda Grimes	Lynda Grimes
Sunday School Pre-School Teachers	Mary Huff	Sondra Ford, Mary Huff, Almeda Sumpter	Sondra Ford, Mary Huff, Almeda Sumpter	Sondra Ford, Linda Grimes, Stephanie Lehew
Children's Church Teacher	Lynda Grimes	Lynda Grimes	Lynda Grimes	Lynda Grimes
Children's Church Asst Teacher				Lisa Baker
Worship				
Song Leader	Lisa Baker	Lisa Baker	Lisa Baker	Lisa Baker
Asst Song Leader	Danita Savory	Carol Holman	Danita Savory	Danita Savory
Musician	Teresa Ware	Teresa Ware	Teresa Ware	Teresa Ware
Other Ministries				
Missions	Amanda Grimes	Anita Grimes	Anita Grimes	Anita Grimes

Appendix VIII. Liberty Balance Sheet 2019-2021

2019-2021 Liberty FMC Balance Sheet			2019	2020	2021
Expenses:					
Chairs & gen church repairs			5221.00		
Mid American Conference apportionment			2000.00	1770.00	1820
Dr. Johnson & family Christmas			300.00		
Bishop Kendall			200.00		
Church insurance			3700.00	3914.00	4788
Dime-a-day			189.00	188.00	166
Church literature, Sunday School			1322.00	1460.00	1197
cleaning supplies			120.00		
propane			270.00	405.00	784
electric			663.00	618.00	709
miscellaneous				376.00	100
Pastor's salary			8400.00	7800.00	8200
Pastor fill-in			200.00	600.00	600
Conf covid relief paid out					500
ministry				1389.00	1930
website					
		total:	$22,585.00	$18,520.00	$20,794.00
Income:					
offerings			13961.00	16105.00	17776
interest					
Conf covid relief					500
pews sold				1600.00	
		total:	$13,961.00	$17,705.00	$18,276.00
Balance:			-$8624.00	-$815.00	-$2,518.00
Assets:					
checking:				$5,800.00	$8,341.00
Reserves:			$65,407.00	$67,000.00	$65,019.00
Total:				$72,800.00	$73,360.00

Historical Income:					
2015	$19,320.00				
2016	$23,327.00				
2017	$16,900.00				
2018	$15,780.00				
2019	$13,961.00				
2020	$17,705.00				
2021	$18,276.00				

Notes:

1. In 2019 about $800 was raised for food for local families. This was not counted as revenue, but it will be next year.

2. $1,600 was received for the old pews, which we replaced with chairs. This will go to 2020.

3. For 2020, the $5,800 is about what was carried over the previous year. Also, there is a positive difference of $778 (-$815 plus the difference of reserves), which is probably mostly from interest, of which we do not have a statement.

4. In 2021, the $500 from the conference in Covid relief was pass-thru for one person who applied for it. Ministry expenses included $1200 at Thanksgiving and Christmas for Wallmart cards for indigents, and also $560 sent to Heiffer International.

Appendix IX. Tryon Ministerial Alliance Balance Sheet 2020-2022

Tryon Ministerial Alliance Revenue and Expenses 2020--10/2022								
	2020		2021		2022		Totals 2020-2022*	
	debits	credits	debits	credits	debits	credits	debits	credits
31-Jan	733.2	0	0	0	0	0	733.2	0
28-Feb	150	175	150	900	300	60	600	1135
31-Mar	0	0	125	271	150	0	275	271
30-Apr	0	0	0	0	300	0	300	0
31-May	91.76	0	0	0	350	0	441.76	0
30-Jun	0	0	0	0	151.37	266	151.37	266
31-Jul	0	0	380	0	0	0	380	0
31-Aug	0	0	0	0	150	157	150	157
30-Sep	499.51	0	150	0	0	0	649.51	0
31-Oct	0.09	300	150	710			150.09	1010
30-Nov	0	0	0	270			0	270
31-Dec	100	0	0	500			100	500
totals:	1,574.56	475.00	955.00	2,651.00	1,401.37	483.00	3,930.93	3,609.00
ending balance	$144.92		$1,840.92		$915.55			
* 2022 data is for 9 months only								

Annotated Bibliography

Account Book/S308-15-J. undated. 12 ¾ x 8 inches, olive green cover with the upper right and lower left corners bound in red, sold by Shaws, on the spine is S308/J/150.

The *Account Book* is essentially a book of minutes for the Board, and Society, of Liberty Free Methodist Church, located a few miles NW of Tryon, Oklahoma, in the north central of the state. It primarily covers 1935 to 1975, with some omissions and a few later entries. On the first page (unnumbered) is inscribed in pencil "Property of Liberty Free Methodist Church." The page opposite the first numbered page is titled "Roll Call of Liberty F.M. Church 1948" and records various names with commentary, mostly about roll status (e.g., "given letter," "dropped," etc.). The *Account Book* has 152 numbered pages, with one unnumbered page (front and back) at the beginning and one at the back. On page 105 is a record dated 1975. Pages 106 to 109 are blank. Pages 110 records "Liberty F.M. Proposed Assignments/ 2009-2010," and page 111 is titled "August 30, 2009" and contains a record for that date. Pages 112 through 151 are blank. Page 152 has written at the top "Official Board Roll 1950-51" and has records for "1951-52" and "52-53." On the next page, unnumbered, is attached (with a sewing pin) a page titled "Roll for 53-54." On the inside of the last page (unnumbered) are records for "1966 May 22," and other years. The various entries are handwritten in ink or pencil, normally by the secretary of the Board and Society, often but not always are signed at the end, and occasionally are difficult to decipher. Spelling varies considerably. The *Account Book* is in fairly good physical condition and is kept at Liberty Free Methodist Church.

Ferguson, Jim ed. (1979). *Oklahoma Conference Heritage.* Vol.1, No.1. Self-published.

Found in the records of Liberty Free Methodist Church, this is a two-page periodical (single sheet, front and back, two columns per page). It is titled "Oklahoma Conference Heritage," with "Heritage" in three-quarter inch capitals, and to its immediate right an outline of the state of Oklahoma, approximately 1 1/8 inch wide and ¾ inch deep, with a two-pointed flame emerging from its center and extending a half-inch above the state's norther border. The editor, Jim Ferguson, calls it a "conference paper." It is undated, but internal evidence suggests it is from 1979 (on the second page, following the title "Fifty Years Ago in WMS," is a list titled "1929 Conference WMS Officers").

Gilmore, J. Marcus (Ed.) *Yearbook 1989/ Official Personnel, Organization and Statistics of the Free Methodist Church Around the World.* Winona Lake, Indiana: The Office of the General Administrator Free Methodist Church of North America. 637 pp. On the top of the title page in black pen is written "C.N. Thompson," who is the longest serving Liberty pastor.

Huff, John, Delegate Liberty FMC. "Claiming The New Millennium For Jesus!" 101st Annual Session of the Mid-America Conference Free Methodist Church of North America.

This is a blue, three-ring binder (1-inch rings), with a label on the front stating "John Huff Delegate Liberty FMC." It contains materials from the 101st Annual Session of the Mid America Conference (1999), plus some additional materials John no doubt took with him to the conference, such as Liberty's church directory and a list of church elected positions. Also in this binder are the February, April, and June 1999 editions of *In Touch*, the conference periodical.

Ledger Book. Undated. Approximately seven and one-half inches wide, and twelve and 3/16 inches long. It is a dark tan with dark red trim. On the front is "D.E. Ledger/ No. 1120". On the spine is "D.E. Ledger".

This is primarily a financial record, with entries from 1968 to 1979. It has twenty-four leaves, or forty-eight pages. The pages are lined and have two columns. The pages are not numbered but the first six pages (front and back being one page) have alphabetical tabs on the right side. The entries are dated. Handwritten in the upper right-hand corner of the front cover is "69". On the inside of the front cover is written "July-1968/ Liberty Free Methodist Church./ Virginia

Thompson. Trea." This is written in ink, in Virginia Thompson's usually neat hand. She was one of the charter members of Liberty FMC and served the church about fifty years. The *Ledger Book* is in fairly good physical shape and is in possession of Liberty Church.

Nelson, Walter O. (1949). *History of the Oklahoma Conference Of the Free Methodist Church Of North America.* Siloam Springs, Arkansas: THE SILENT MINISTER BOOKLET PRESS.

This booklet has 36 pages. It is about 5 x 7 3/4 inches, with a medium-blue cover. The pages are held together with two staples in the spine. It is full of information on the early church and contains appendices on "General Rules," "Membership," "Finances," "Property," "District Superintendents of the Oklahoma Conf.," "Brief History of the Home of Redeeming Love," and a "Postscript." Liberty Church is discussed on p.20.

Sheads, Kelly (Ed.) *Yearbook 2007/ Personnel, Organization and Statistics of the Free Methodist Church.* Indianapolis, In.: Gerald Coates. 632 pp.

Wayman, Hugh. (1970). *Past and Present/ Oklahoma In Action/ The Free Methodist Church.*

This is an 8 ½ x 11-inch booklet with a black plastic spiral cover, presumably printed by the Oklahoma Conference. At the bottom right on the cover is "Hugh Waymon, Sup't/ 4312 N.W. 44 St./ Oklahoma City, Okla. 73112/ 942-6723." It is an annual report on the conference churches. The churches are listed alphabetically, with Liberty FMC between Guthrie and Midwest City. Each church is covered in two pages. On the first page is one or more photos of the church and information about when the church was built, pastors, etc. On the second page are various data concerning finance, membership, Sunday School, etc., from 1955 to 1970. The booklet is not paginated, but contains twenty-four leaves, i.e., forty-eight pages, not included the front and back covers. The Introduction reads as follows.

"The purposes of this book is to give a picture of the Oklahoma Conference of the Free Methodist Church.

It is hoped that in looking back at our history ….. seeing areas of success and failure; and seeing our potential at the present time, that we can better determine the approach for the years ahead.

The material for this book was gathered during December 1969; and January, 1970; in meetings by the conference Superintendent with the Official Boards of the local churches.

Other material came from the book, *History of the Oklahoma Conference*, by Walter O. Nelson.

The population figures in the book are taken from the 1960 census. The potential giving of each local church was determined by estimates given by members of each local Official Board.

The conference totals were determined by combining the totals of each local church, and by the YEARBOOK for the various years. The average church is shown in comparison with the national average church of the denomination."

A grey metal box, 12.5 x 5.5 wide x 10 inches deep, with "Liberty Free Methodist Church" across the top, is mostly full of disorganized loose-leaf material primarily financial in nature – a few bank statements, insurance documents, receipts, etc. It is in the possession of Liberty Church.

A manilla envelope, 13 x 10 inches, contains a few dozen loose leaf notes mostly handwritten, scraps of paper, several insurance documents, two copies of the "Oklahoma Conference Heritage" periodical, a few bank statements, and so on. Many of these are not datable. It is in the possession of Liberty Church.

About the Author

Ron Faulk is a chaplain, pastor, scholar, and naturalist who lives in the Cross-Timbers region of Oklahoma. His first interest is in the work of the Spirit. He is also interested in language (perhaps the definitive human behavior) and analytical psychology, or, the influence of the unconscious in individual and corporate human life. A retired professor with a specialty in language, he and his wife enjoy travelling and exploring the Colorado Plateau, visiting ruins of the Hohokam, Ancestral Pueblo, and Mogollon cultures, and attempting to decipher the rock art produced by these ancient peoples.

Ron is a husband, father, and grandfather. He has careers in community mental health and as a university professor. He was saved at the age of twenty-one, born-again at 25, trained in spiritual discernment, called as a jail chaplain, ordained by the Church of the Nazarene, and has pastored Liberty Free Methodist Church of Tryon, OK, since 2016. He has graduate degrees from Northwestern University, IL, and the University of Oklahoma Health Sciences Center. However, he affirms that true knowledge only comes from actual experience, and the greatest truth from the day-to-day experience of following Jesus Christ. As Jesus said repeatedly, "those who want to save their life will lose it, and those who lose their life for my sake, and for the sake of the gospel, will save it."

www.ingramcontent.com/pod-product-compliance
Lightning Source LLC
Chambersburg PA
CBHW071216090426
42736CB00014B/2847